VALENTIA BAY.

MAP OF THE HARBOR OF VALENCIA SHOWING THE ATLANTIC TELEGRAPH STATION IN EUROPE

ATLANTIC TELEGRAPH STATION IN EUROPE

THE QUEEN'S MESSAGE.

TO THE HONORABLE
THE PRESIDENT OF THE UNITED STATES:

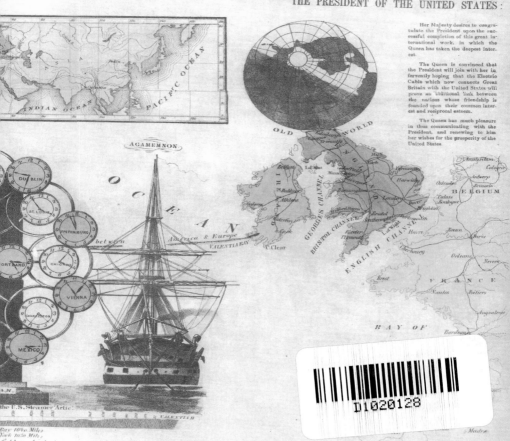

Her Majesty desires to congratulate the President upon the successful completion of this great international work, in which the Queen has taken the deepest interest.

The Queen is convinced that the President will join with her in fervently hoping that the Electric Cable which now connects Great Britain with the United States will prove an additional link between the nations whose friendship is founded upon their common interest and reciprocal esteem.

The Queen has much pleasure in thus communicating with the President, and renewing to him her wishes for the prosperity of the United States.

OLD WORLD

AGAMEMNON

OCEAN between America & Europe VALENTIA BAY

U.S. Steamer "Artic"

Bay 1040 Miles
York 1650 Miles

of the district Court of the United States of the Southern district of New York

TELEGRAM!

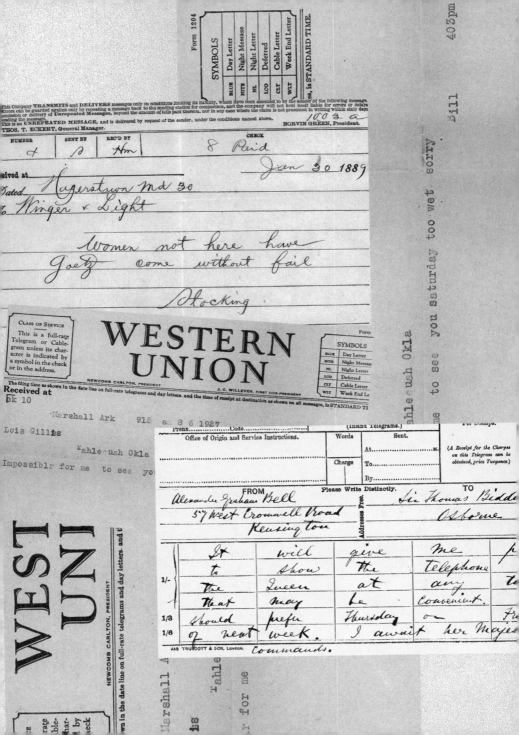

Form 1204

SYMBOLS

	STANDARD TIME.
BLUE	Day Letter
NITE	Night Message
NL	Night Letter
LCO	Deferred
CLT	Cable Letter
WLT	Week End Letter

403pm

Bill

This Company TRANSMITS and DELIVERS messages only on conditions limiting its liability, which have been assented to by the sender of the following message.
Errors can be guarded against only by repeating a message back to the sending station for comparison, and the company will not hold itself liable for errors or delays in transmission or delivery of Unrepeated Messages, beyond the amount of tolls paid thereon, nor in any case where the claim is not presented in writing within sixty days after sending the message.
This is an UNREPEATED MESSAGE, and is delivered by request of the sender, under the conditions named above.

THOS. T. ECKERT, General Manager.   NORVIN GREEN, President.

1003 a

NUMBER	SENT BY	REC'D BY	CHECK
4	P	Hm	8 Paid

Jan 30 1889

Received at

Dated Hagerstown Md 30

To Winger & Light

Women not here have
Goetz come without fail

Stocking

sorry too wet saturday you to see

Tahlequah Okla

to see you

CLASS OF SERVICE

This is a full-rate Telegram or Cablegram unless its character is indicated by a symbol in the check or in the address.

WESTERN UNION

NEWCOMB CARLTON, PRESIDENT   J. C. WILLEVER, FIRST VICE-PRESIDENT

Form

SYMBOLS

BLUE	Day Letter
NITE	Night Message
NL	Night Letter
LCO	Deferred
CLT	Cable Letter
WLT	Week End Le

The filing time as shown in the date line on full-rate telegrams and day letters and the time of receipt at destination as shown on all messages, is STANDARD TI

Received at
Bk 10

Marshall Ark   915 a 8 6 1927

Lois Gillis

Tahlequah Okla

Impossible for me to see yo

WEST
UNI

NEWCOMB CARLTON, PRESIDENT

wn in the date line on full-rate telegrams and day letters. and t

rate
ble-
har-
by
eck

Marshall A

Tahle

r for me

is

the conditions

			(Inland Telegrams.)		For Stamps.
Office of Origin and Service Instructions.		Words	Sent.		
	Prefix.......... Code..........		At..............M.		(A Receipt for the Charges on this Telegram can be obtained, price Twopence.)
		Charge	To..............		
			By..............		

FROM   Please Write Distinctly.   TO

Alexander Graham Bell   Sir Thomas Biddu
57 West Cromwell Road   Osborne
Kensington

	It	will	give	me	p
	to	show	the	Telephone	
1/-	the	Queen	at	any	t
	that	may	be	convenient.	
1/3	should	prefer	Thursday	on	Fr
1/6	of	next	week.	I await	her Majes
		Commands.			

JAS TRUSCOTT & SON, LONDON.

Addressee Free.

TELEGRAM!

MODERN HISTORY AS TOLD
THROUGH MORE THAN 400
WITTY, POIGNANT, AND
REVEALING TELEGRAMS

LINDA ROSENKRANTZ

HENRY HOLT AND COMPANY
NEW YORK

Henry Holt and Company, LLC
Publishers since 1866
115 West 18th Street
New York, New York 10011

Henry Holt® is a registered trademark of Henry Holt and Company, LLC.

Library of Congress Cataloging-in-Publication Data

Rosenkrantz, Linda.
    Telegram! : modern history as told through more than 400 witty, poignant, and revealing
telegrams / Linda Rosenkrantz.—1st ed.
    p.   cm.
    Includes index.
    ISBN 0-8050-7101-6
    1. Telegraph—History.   2. History, Modern—19th century—Sources.   3. History,
Modern—20th century—Sources.   4. Technological innovations—Social aspects.
5. Information technology—Social aspects.   I. Title.
D351.R57 2003
973.9—dc21   2003049913

First Edition 2003

Designed by Oksana Kushnir

Printed in the United States of America
10   9   8   7   6   5   4   3   2   1

In loving memory of
Susan Brockman

CONTENTS

INTRODUCTION

FROM THE JAZZ AGE through the years following World War II, there was scarcely a Hollywood melodrama or screwball comedy whose story didn't turn on the sudden arrival of a telegram. The scene might vary from film to film, but it usually went something like this: Doorbell rings. Enter polite, smartly dressed Western Union messenger who hands over an envelope, gets a coin or two in return, and exits. Envelope is torn open by recipient, whose face is transformed by extreme emotion as he or she reads it. Finally, a close-up of the telegram itself lets the audience in on the news that provoked the smile, shriek, or sob—or sometimes even a full-blown swoon.

In real life, too, the sight of the Western Union messenger coming up the walk made hearts flutter and pulses quicken, because for the average American, telegrams were usually bearers of momentous news, all too often unpleasant, particularly in times of war. But for many others—those active in commerce and the arts, politics and the military—telegrams, from their invention in the mid-nineteenth century through the post–World War II period, when they began to be made redundant by cheap long-distance phone rates, the fax, and eventually e-mail, were common currency. There were people, such as movie moguls Jack Warner and David O. Selznick, who virtually ran their businesses via Western Union. Broadway impresario Florenz Ziegfeld was famous for routinely sending telegrams to people within shouting distance. For nine years, from 1926 to 1935, Will Rogers wrote a "Daily Telegram" feature in the *New York Times,* in which he cabled from wherever he was in the world a sample of his homespun political humor. And, though we think of telegrams now—if at all—in terms of wiring congratulations and trans-ferring funds, there were some, such as the Zimmermann Telegram, that altered the course of history, in that case by contributing to America entering World War I.

It is not precisely true that the telegraph was invented single-handedly by Samuel Finley Breese Morse. The famous 1844 WHAT HATH GOD WROUGHT wire that Morse sent the forty miles from Washington to

Samuel Morse.

Baltimore was preceded by a complex network of earlier discoveries and experiments in Great Britain, France, Switzerland, and elsewhere, some of them involving such Rube Goldbergian elements as silk thread, clocks, mechanical arms, pith balls, and bells. But it was Morse—discovering the first practical use for electricity, before the lightbulb and the telephone were invented—who grasped the concept that a systematic interruption of electric current flashing along a wire could be structured into a code enabling a message to be sent over that wire, and his tireless persistence in promoting his ideas turned the key. His system was relatively simple. An operator opened and closed a switch to send electricity from a battery along the telegraph wire. At the receiving end, the pulses of current operated a pen, which marked a strip of paper whenever the current was active. (Later, skilled telegraphers were able to spell out the message just by listening to the sound the pen made.) To represent the letters of the alphabet, Morse used a code of short and long pulses (dots and dashes), assigning shorter symbols to the most common letters: "e," the most used letter of the alphabet, was represented by a single dot. Morse code would remain in universal use even after Guglielmo Marconi developed wireless telegraphy.

The value of the telegraph was demonstrated during the Civil War, when strands of wire strung on makeshift poles throughout the fields of the countryside allowed for the instantaneous communication of military intelligence. It was also a key factor in the development of both commercial and social life in the United States in the succeeding decades. Among its many accomplishments were standardizing time, revolutionizing the dispatching of trains (making them more efficient and safe), and allowing the instant transmission of news via press wire services and of stock market price fluctuations, both regulating and speeding up the very pace of daily life. In short, particularly in the second half of the nineteenth century, the impact of the telegraph was as great as that of the printing press some 400 years before. It was the technological revolution that was essentially the first stop on the information superhighway.

The name Western Union, despite the existence of competitors, became synonymous with the word telegram. Originally known as the New York and Mississippi Valley Printing Telegraph Company, the firm built the nation's first transcontinental telegraph line in 1861—the first cross-country wire was sent to President Lincoln, assuring him that California would stand by the Union. In 1866, it was Western Union that introduced stock tickers to speed New York Stock Exchange quotes to brokerage firms across the country. By the end of the century, the company was transmitting 58 million messages per year and required a complete wardrobe department to outfit its 14,000 uniformed messengers. In an effort to combat the anxiety produced by the sight of a uniformed delivery boy approaching on foot or on his bicycle, a Western Union

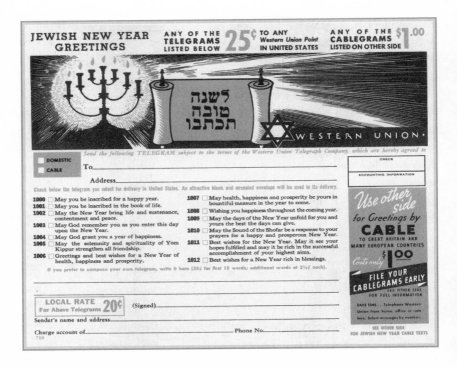

A template from Western Union for Jewish New Year telegrams.
Similar ready-made forms were produced for most holidays.

public relations executive conceived the idea of the singing telegram, the first one being sung to popular crooner Rudy Vallee in 1933. Western Union put out brochure after brochure instructing the public on the protocol of telegramming ("Naturally, there is a right way and a wrong way of wording telegrams"), how to eliminate and save words (for example, writing "1,000,000" would count as nine words including commas, while spelling out "one million" would be charged as two), the precise rules of address writing and punctuation ("stop" to indicate a period), and the differences between full-rate services and Day Letters,

Night Letters, and Night Messages. A new language termed telegramese developed—precise, concise, each word weighed and measured and the unnecessary pronouns and connectives whittled away.

Telegraphy permitted individuals—friends, rivals, lovers—to transmit words in a new way, speeding declarations of eternal devotion, desperate pleas for a few dollars to tide them over, news of life's passages from the remotest rural areas to urban centers thousands of miles away. Telegrams followed people into their ocean liner staterooms and streamlined train compartments. The urgency of the telegram made it far more insistent than the handwritten, days-old letter, something impossible to ignore or set aside or—as in our day—dump into an electronic trash bin.

If the historic importance of the telegram as a tool of communication has previously been acknowledged, the unique character of these electrically transmitted messages has never really been explored. When looked at as a whole, there emerges a discrete body of fascinating literature—sometimes witty, sometimes poignant, sometimes even ecstatic—that constitutes an undeservedly overlooked literary genre. Until now the odd few have been folded into biographies and epistolatory compendia, while thousands of others are stored away in the boxes and files of various libraries and other scholarly institutions. It is the aim of this book to illuminate some of those dark corners and reveal something of the scope of this unexplored genre.

What has surprised me most in unearthing this material has been both the emotional and the stylistic richness found in what I would have expected to be straightforward dispatches. They range from the poetic (such as Abraham Lincoln's dramatic eyewitness reports from the battlefields of the Civil War) to the prosaic (Lotte Lenya wiring transcontinentally her husband, Kurt Weill, that his blue slacks are still at the cleaners). To be sure, there are the predictable epigrammatic witticisms of Oscar Wilde, George Bernard Shaw, Noël Coward, and Dorothy Parker and her fellow knights of the Algonquin Round Table, but there are also effusive outpourings of love from Eugene O'Neill, Winston and Clementine Churchill, and Elvis Presley, rashly randy wires from the young John

Kennedy, desperate pleadings for money by some of the twentieth century's most renowned authors, sycophantic dispatches to gossip doyenne Hedda Hopper from stars like Gary Cooper and John Wayne, vituperative outbursts from Jack London and Ernest Hemingway, Alexander Graham Bell's affectionate dispatches to his daughters, Hannah Nixon's loyal defense of her boy Richard, and a request from George Bush Sr. for the delivery of 700 hot dog rolls to China in time for the Fourth of July, 1975.

In the two parts of this book, I have attempted to present a pointillistic view of modern history and the vagaries of human experience and endeavor as recorded via the dots and dashes of the telegram, looking at both earthshaking events and mundane moments from a new and immediate perspective—as they were transmitted by the telegraph, the technology that inaugurated the telecommunications revolution.

PART ONE

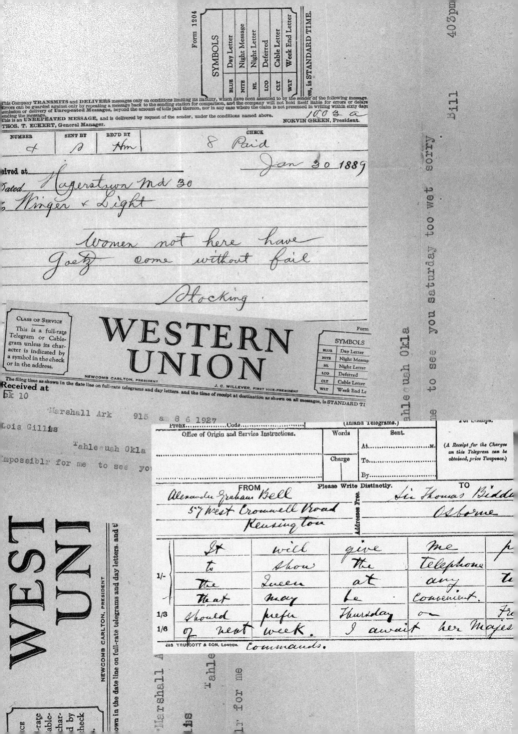

NUMBER	SENT BY	REC'D BY	CHECK
4	S	Hm	8 Paid

Jan 30 1889

Received at Hagerstown Md 30

To Winger & Light

Women not here have
Goetz come without fail

Stocking

403pm

Bill

sorry

too wet

you saturday

see

to

me

ahlequah Okla

WESTERN UNION

NEWCOMB CARLTON, PRESIDENT
J. C. WILLEVER, FIRST VICE-PRESIDENT

SYMBOLS	Form
BLUE	Day Letter
NITE	Night Message
NL	Night Letter
LCO	Deferred
CLT	Cable Letter
WLT	Week End Le

The filing time as shown in the date line on full-rate telegrams and day letters, and the time of receipt at destination as shown on all messages, is STANDARD TI

Received at
Bk 10

Marshall Ark   915   a   8 6 1927

Lois Gillis

Tahlequah Okla

Impossible for me to see you

Prefix.	Code.		(Inland Telegrams.)	For Stamps.
Office of Origin and Service Instructions.		Words	Sent.	(A Receipt for the Charges
			At........M.	on this Telegram can be
		Charge	To........	obtained, price Twopence.)
			By........	

FROM   Please Write Distinctly.   TO

Alexander Graham Bell   Sir Thomas Bidda
57 West Cromwell Road   Osborne
Kensington

	It	will	give	me	p
	to	show	the	Telephone	t
1/-	the	Queen	at	any	t
	that	may	be	convenient.	
1/3	should	prefer	Thursday	on	Fri
1/6	of next	week.	I await	her Majes	
		commands.			

JAS. TRUSCOTT & SON, LONDON.

CONCISE. COMPRESSED. CONDENSED. This was the character of most telegrams, but there were occasions when these qualities were taken to an extreme, and the fact that you could send first up to ten, then fifteen, words for the same price as one was totally ignored.

The two shortest wires on record concerned a rather long novel. Wondering how the sales of *Les Misérables* were going, Victor Hugo, in exile on the island of Guernsey, telegraphed his publisher:

?

To which the reply came back:

!

Rudyard Kipling was at one time the most popular—and best paid— writer in England. Upon reading that he earned fifty pence per word, some Cambridge University students sent that sum to the writer, along with the request for one of his very best words. Kipling replied with a single-word telegram:

THANKS.

In 1865, William Booth established the Salvation Army and would do almost anything to win over converts. On one occasion, two Salvation Army officers who had set out to found a new rescue mission met with such strong opposition that they appealed to General Booth to cancel the effort. Unswerving, he wired back:

TRY TEARS.

Word has it that it worked.

When New York Governor Al Smith was nominated for the presidency in 1928, his being a Catholic caused a great deal more controversy than the nomination of John F. Kennedy would three decades later. Rumors were that the Pope had his bags packed, ready to come and take over the United States government. On Election Day, however, Smith was

Sigmund Freud to his wife, Martha, following the commencement of his U.S.
lecture series at Clark University in Worcester, Massachusetts, in 1909.

trounced by Herbert Hoover and jestingly told a news conference that
he had sent a one-word telegram to the Vatican:

UNPACK!

And when underdog Harry S. Truman ran for the presidency against
Thomas E. Dewey in 1948, and the *Chicago Daily Tribune* prematurely
printed the inaccurate headline DEWEY DEFEATS TRUMAN, Bob Hope
immediately sent Truman the same single-word wire.

In the late 1920s, the Walt Disney Studios had already gained a reputation as the producer of the popular Mickey Mouse shorts. In 1929, Disney decided to inaugurate a second series to be known as "Silly Symphonies," meant to give a dominant role to music. The initial offering was titled "The Skeleton Dance" and featured imaginative animation by the great Ub Iwerks. However, when it was viewed by the distributor of the Mickey shorts, his opinion was expressed in a two-word telegram:

MORE MICE.

Newspaper mogul William Randolph Hearst wielded considerable political power and often wired his editors to promote or blackball various public figures. He took an interest in an obscure young preacher named Billy Graham, who shared many of his ultraconservative, anticommunist views. After Hearst sent the following brief wire to all his editors, it wasn't long before the Reverend Graham was preaching to audiences of 350,000 people:

PUFF GRAHAM

When a movie starring Humphrey Bogart and Lauren Bacall and directed by Howard Hawks was being made from Raymond Chandler's convoluted novel *The Big Sleep,* Hawks became a little lost in the plot and cabled the author to ask who was supposed to have killed General Sternwood's chauffeur in the original story. Chandler wired back:

NO IDEA.

When twenty-five-year-old James Thurber was informed by his ex-girlfriend Minnette Fritts that she had "unexpectedly married" in 1919, his shock was obvious in the telegram he sent:

WHAT THE HELL!

"A man never feels more important than when he receives a telegram containing more than ten words."
——George Ade

Theoretical physicist Richard Feynman made his greatest contribution to quantum mechanics in 1948, but it wasn't until 1965 that he became one of three winners of the Nobel Prize in physics. On the day the prize was announced, Robert Oppenheimer, former head of the Manhattan Project, fired off a one-word telegram to Feynman, who had worked under him:

ENFIN!

When British actor Derek Jacobi undertook to revive a set piece that Laurence Olivier had made famous—a double bill of Oedipus and Mr. Puff from Sheridan's *The Critic*—Olivier sent off this succinct wire:

YOU CHEEKY BUGGER.

In December of 1964, Raymond Walters Jr. of the *New York Times Book Review* wrote to Vladimir Nabokov, asking for a 150-word statement on what paperbacks had done for him. The novelist found that that was 147 more words than he needed; he sent this cable from Montreaux, Switzerland, which was published in the *Book Review* on January 10, 1965:

NEAT LITTLE THINGS

BIRTH AND DEATH

THE MOST ANTICIPATED and dreaded of telegrams are those that announce the beginning or the end of life.

When the fourth of legendary editor Maxwell Perkins's five daughters was born, he sent this rather ho-hum wire to his mother:

GIRL.

Photo only Copyright 1910.
By J. Baumann.

710-18

IT'S A GIRL.

Similarly, the prolix author of *Ulysses* and *Finnegans Wake* could be quite the opposite when he was sending a telegram for which he had to pay by the word. On July 7, 1905, James Joyce dispatched the following to his brother Stanislaus:

SON BORN JIM

> We can only hope that the father of psychoanalysis was jesting when Sigmund Freud wrote to his close friend and colleague Wilhelm Fliess in 1895, upon the birth of his daughter Anna: "If it had been a son I should have sent you the news by telegram, but as it is a little girl . . . you get the news later."

In 1927, when George Bernard Shaw was asked to be the godfather to the son of Kenneth Barnes, head of what became the Royal Academy of Dramatic Art, he declined with his characteristic sly wit:

AFTER CONSCIENTIOUS STUDY OF PRAYERBOOK FIND CANNOT COMPLY WITHOUT GROSS PERJURY BESIDE[s] WHY TAR HELPLESS INFANT WITH MY BRUSH NEUTRAL TINTED SPONSOR SAFER.

Algonquin Round Table wit Dorothy Parker sent the following wire to her friend Mary Anderson, wife of the playwright Robert Anderson, on the birth of their baby:

DEAR MARY, WE ALL KNEW YOU HAD IT IN YOU.

When his daughter Jane was born on December 21, 1937, Henry Fonda sent a wire to director William Wyler, ostensibly in the newborn's own voice, describing herself and saying she would like to work for him. Wyler (who shared an ex-wife, Margaret Sullavan, with Fonda) replied the same day:

```
MY DEAR MANY THANKS FOR YOUR KIND WIRE HEARTY
CONGRATULATIONS ON YOUR ARRIVAL AND HEARTFELT CONDOLENCE ON
YOUR CHOICE OF FATHER HOWEVER WE FEEL IT IS OUR DUTY TO
CORRECT ANY ILLUSION YOU MAY HAVE BEEN UNDER IN THE PAST AS
WE FEEL YOU ARE OLD ENOUGH NOW TO BE TOLD THE HAPPY NEWS
YOUR FATHER NEVER WAS AN ACTOR STOP WE ARE SMOKING TO YOUR
HEALTH WYLER WANTS TO MAKE A TEST OF YOU AS SOON AS
POSSIBLE UNDER CERTAIN PROVISIONS [TO] YOUR CONTRACT AND
HEREWITH REQUESTS YOU CALL HIM UNCLE BECAUSE HE FEELS THERE
IS AN UNDEFINABLE BUT NONETHELESS DEFINITE RELATIONSHIP
SOMEWHERE SOMEHOW. . . .
```

Elvis Presley and his factotum, Colonel Parker, sent this congratulatory wire to Ringo Starr on the birth of his son Zak in 1965:

```
CONGRATULATIONS TO YOU AND THE MRS. ON THE NEW MEMBER OF
YOUR FAMILY. IF COL. EPSTEIN IS NOT INTERESTED IN SIGNING
THIS NEW ARTIST, SHIP TAPE WITH VOICE TRACK.
```

A very different kind of birth announcement was sent by physicist Edward Teller after he watched the successful detonation of the first hydrogen bomb on a seismograph in his laboratory in Berkeley, California. Claiming paternity for this powerful force, Teller fired off this rather chilling telegram to his colleagues at Los Alamos:

```
IT'S A BOY.
```

In fact, birth imagery had surrounded the nuclear bomb from its inception. When President Truman was at the Potsdam conference shortly before dropping the bomb on Japan, General Leslie Groves cabled to report that its second test was successful:

```
DOCTOR . . . MOST ENTHUSIASTIC AND CONFIDENT THAT THE LITTLE
BOY IS AS HUSKY AS HIS BIG BROTHER . . . I COULD HAVE HEARD
HIS SCREAMS FROM HERE. . . .
```

And when the bomb was dropped on Hiroshima, Groves wired Truman:

THE BABY WAS BORN.

Sometimes there is a tragic convergence of life and death: shortly after Theodore Roosevelt sent the following telegram on February 13, 1884, his adored young wife, Alice Lee, died, and on the very same night, he lost his mother. The little daughter grew up to be the colorful Alice Roosevelt Longworth.

WE HAVE A LITTLE DAUGHTER. THE MOTHER ONLY FAIRLY WELL.

Charlie Parker, the celebrated jazz saxophone player, was devastated by the news of the death of his child. When he learned that his young daughter Pree had succumbed to pneumonia, he sent a series of four distraught telegrams within the space of twenty-four hours across the country to his common-law wife, Chan:

MY DARLING. MY DAUGHTER'S DEATH SURPRISED ME MORE THAN IT DID YOU. DON'T FULFILL FUNERAL PROCEEDINGS UNTIL I GET THERE. I SHALL BE THE FIRST ONE TO WALK INTO OUR CHAPEL. FORGIVE ME FOR NOT BEING THERE WITH YOU WHILE YOU ARE AT THE HOSPITAL. YOURS MOST SINCERELY, YOUR HUSBAND, CHARLIE PARKER.

MY DARLING. FOR GOD'S SAKE HOLD ON TO YOURSELF. CHAS. PARKER

CHAN, HELP. CHARLIE PARKER

And the somewhat confused, perhaps heroin-affected, final one:

MY DAUGHTER IS DEAD. I KNOW IT. I WILL BE THERE AS QUICK AS I CAN. MY NAME IS BIRD. IT IS VERY NICE TO BE OUT HERE. PEOPLE HAVE BEEN VERY NICE TO ME OUT HERE. I AM COMING IN RIGHT AWAY. TAKE IT EASY. LET ME BE THE FIRST ONE TO APPROACH YOU. I AM YOUR HUSBAND. SINCERELY, CHARLIE PARKER

Shortly before his death, the great Russian novelist Leo Tolstoy sent the following telegram from the Astapovo train station:

```
FELL ILL YESTERDAY STOP SEEN BY PASSENGERS STOP LEFT TRAIN
FEELING WEAK STOP FEAR PUBLICITY STOP FEELING BETTER NOW
STOP TRAVELING ON STOP . . .
```

While in Europe, Mark Twain, startled to read his own obituary, shot off this oft-quoted (and misquoted) cable to the Associated Press on June 2, 1897:

```
THE REPORT OF MY DEATH WAS AN EXAGGERATION
```

Twain was not the only notable whose demise was reported prematurely. In 1899, when famed portrait painter John Singer Sargent was forty-three years old and living abroad, his death also was erroneously reported in American newspapers. He hastened to send a telegram to Isabella Stewart Gardner, his patron and friend:

```
ALIVE AND KICKING. SARGENT
```

The fact that it took two weeks for Samuel Morse to receive the news of the death of his twenty-five-year-old wife almost certainly sparked his interest in improving the speed of communications.

Swedish-born Joe Hill (né Joel Emmanuel Hagglund) was a labor organizer for the IWW—Industrial Workers of the World or "Wobblies"—as well as the composer of such union songs as "Casey Jones." He was convicted of murder on circumstantial evidence in Salt Lake City, Utah, in 1914, and, despite calls from President Woodrow Wilson and the Swedish government and wires from such notables as Helen Keller demanding a retrial, he was executed in 1915, becoming a martyr for the labor movement. The night before his execution, he sent a telegram to fellow union organizer Bill Haywood:

```
I WILL DIE LIKE A TRUE-BLUE REBEL. DON'T WASTE ANY TIME
MOURNING. ORGANIZE.
```

FAMOUS ONETIME WESTERN UNION MESSENGERS

ANDREW CARNEGIE

DAVID SARNOFF

AL CAPONE'S OLDEST BROTHER

EDWARD STEICHEN

HENRY MILLER (at the age
of twenty-nine)

BUCK OWENS

MANFRED B. LEE (aka Ellery Queen)

WILLIAM SAROYAN

GARSON KANIN

JOSEPH HELLER

EDWARD DAHLBERG

ROBERT INDIANA

EDWARD ALBEE

AND IN IRELAND

FRANK MCCOURT

SINGING TELEGRAM DELIVERERS

NATHAN LANE

SINEAD O'CONNOR

TELEGRAPH OPERATORS

THOMAS EDISON (at the age of
seventeen an itinerant Morse
telegrapher)

ANDREW CARNEGIE (for twelve
years)

DAVID SARNOFF

RICHARD W. SEARS, founder
of Sears Roebuck & Co.

GENE AUTRY (at work strumming
his guitar, he was discovered by
Will Rogers, who came in to send
a telegram)

CHET HUNTLEY

When John Barrymore was on his deathbed in 1942, his dear friend
W. C. Fields wired him:

YOU CAN'T DO THIS TO ME.

Immediately after being notified by a telegram from Harry Hopkins of
the death of Franklin D. Roosevelt, Joseph Stalin, who had met with the
president and Winston Churchill just two months before at Yalta in the
Crimea, responded with this cable on April 15, 1945:

... I HEARTILY AGREE WITH YOU IN YOUR ESTIMATION OF THE
ROLE AND SIGNIFICANCE OF ROOSEVELT FOR THE SOVIET UNION. I
AM PERSONALLY DEEPLY SADDENED BY THE LOSS OF A TESTED
FRIEND, A MAN OF GREAT SPIRIT.
J. STALIN

Robert Kennedy and Lyndon Johnson did not always have the best relationship, but after the assassination of John Kennedy and Johnson's
ascendance to the presidency, LBJ sent Bobby Kennedy this benevolent
telegram on the following New Year's Day:

I KNOW HOW HARD THE PAST SIX WEEKS HAVE BEEN FOR YOU. UNDER
THE MOST TRYING CIRCUMSTANCES YOUR FIRST THOUGHTS HAVE BEEN
FOR YOUR COUNTRY. YOUR BROTHER WOULD HAVE BEEN VERY PROUD
OF THE STRENGTH YOU HAVE SHOWN. AS THE NEW YEAR BEGINS, I
RESOLVE TO DO MY BEST TO FULFILL HIS TRUST IN ME. I WILL
NEED YOUR COUNSEL AND SUPPORT.

PARENTS AND CHILDREN

TELEGRAMS WERE USED by parents to scold and support their progeny and
by children to express both reverence and rebellion. Most interestingly,

they often reveal a tender and playful side of some public figures who were more usually seen as tough and severe.

During the Civil War, Confederate cavalry commander James Ewell Brown (Jeb) Stuart received a telegram that is every father's worst nightmare, informing him that his beloved daughter Flora was dying. He made the decision to put his cause first, however, when he replied:

> I SHALL HAVE TO LEAVE MY CHILD IN THE HAND OF GOD, MY DUTY TO MY COUNTRY REQUIRES ME HERE.

The long-reigning (1837 to 1901) Queen Victoria had convoluted relationships with her nine children, her sons- and daughters-in-law, grandchildren, and great-grandchildren, that linked her to the royal families of Russia, Germany, Greece, Denmark, and Romania. In March of 1888, when her dearly loved son-in-law Emperor Frederick III of Germany was critically ill (and his son, the future Kaiser Wilhelm II, was inappropriately eager to succeed him), Victoria was determined to visit Frederick, despite all warnings against it, and wired her daughter:

> I SHALL BRING MY OWN MATRASS—LEAVE IT TO YOU TO SAY WHO I MUST SEE OR *NOT*, BESIDES MY GRANDCHILDREN AND GREAT GRANDCHILDREN, BUT BEG NOT MANY.

At the precocious age of six, Franklin Delano Roosevelt wrote out this telegraph, dated November 20, 1888, in pencil, on a Poughkeepsie, New York, Western Union form, to his adored mother:

> MY DEAR MAMA
> I WENT TO MY LESSONS THIS MORNING. THIS AFTERNOON I PLAYED WITH MARY NEWBOLD. HER MAMA SAYS MARY CAN COME TO MORROW, BUT I DONT KNOW IF THE RODGERS CAN COME. THEIR MAMA WENT THIS MORNING TO NEW YORK. I SEND LOVE TO MAMA AND PAPA AND UNCLE FRED ADRIAN PARTICULAR AND HIS INTENDED WESTERN WIFE. I HOPE DEAR GRANDPAPA IS WELL AND GRANDMAMA WITH LOVE TO YOU AND PAPA. YOUR OWN LOVING LITTLE
>   FRANKLIN

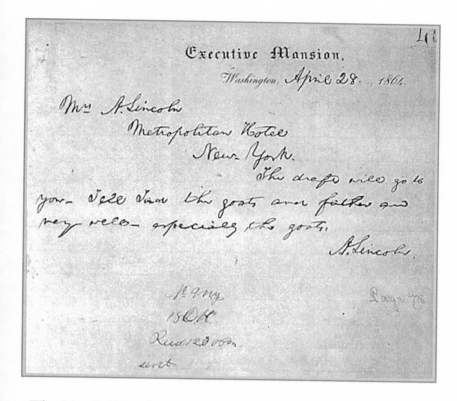

When Mary Todd Lincoln telegraphed her husband to request a $50 draft and news of their son's pet goats, Lincoln replied with his typically wry humor, "The draft will go to you. Tell Tad the goats and father are very well—especially the goats." The handwritten draft above is dated April 28, 1864.

⚜

When his father, the eighth Marquis of Queensberry, threatened to disinherit Lord Alfred Douglas if he didn't stop seeing Oscar Wilde in a homosexual relationship that the marquis described as "most loathsome and disgusting," Douglas responded with the following mocking telegram on April 2, 1894:

WHAT A FUNNY LITTLE MAN YOU ARE.

Wilde later referred to this message as "a telegram of which the commonest street-boy would be ashamed" and Queensberry's furious reply to his son was "If you send me any more such telegrams . . . I will give you the thrashing you deserve. Your only excuse is that you must be crazy. . . ."

On November 5, 1903, inventor Alexander Graham Bell sent this endearing wire to his daughter Marian, on the train taking her to Augusta, Maine:

GOOD MORNING MERRY SUNSHINE. THERE'S NOBODY HERE. MISS YOU MUCH.

In the heyday of the telegram, Western Union offered other options in addition to the regular wire. A night letter of fifty words could be sent for the cost of a ten-word telegram, i.e., from 20¢ to $1.20, depending on the distance. A day letter of fifty words would cost from 30¢ to $1.80, or one and a half times the night letter rate. A twenty-five-word weekend cable letter could be sent from New York to London for 75¢, or 3¢ a word.

To facilitate communication, early telegraphers developed a system whereby numbers would represent phrases, such as 1 = "Wait a minute" and 2 = "Get answer immediately."

Five years later, on May 9, 1908, Bell sent this birthday wire to his other daughter, Elsie:

MANY HAPPY RETURNS OF THE DAY I REMEMBER SO WELL MAY YOUR CHILDREN BRING AS MUCH HAPPINESS INTO YOUR LIFE AS YOU HAVE BROUGHT INTO MINE, IS THE FINEST WISH OF YOUR LOVING FATHER
ALEXANDER GRAHAM BELL

These sentiments were echoed by hard-boiled writer Dashiell Hammett on his daughter Mary's birthday in 1943, in a telegram alluding to her postpartum jaundice:

```
TWENTY TWO YEARS AGO I WAS WORKING A HORSE SHOW WHILE YOU
WERE BEING BORN AND A STRANGE REDDISH ORANGE CREATURE YOU
WERE. . . .MOSTLY EYE LASHES AND MOUTH BUT YOU SOON IMPROVED
STOP HAPPY BIRTHDAY LOVE PAPA
```

In 1915, when he was fifty-two years old, newspaper publisher William Randolph Hearst became the father of a pair of twin boys, the fourth and fifth of his sons. The following year, while en route to see them, he sent the following playful telegram from the train:

```
GET UP EARLY AND EAT YOUR BACON AND EGGS WITH YOUR LONESOME
FRONT TEETH AND MEET US AT OAKLAND FRIDAY MORNING. THIS IS
THANKSGIVING DAY AND YOU OUGHT TO BE THANKFUL YOU HAVE SUCH
A DEAR DEVOTED GRANDMA, SUCH KIND NURSES, SUCH NICE NOISY
BROTHERS, SUCH A HANDSOME FATHER AND SUCH A LOVING
MOTHER. . . . NOW RISE UP ON YOUR HIND LEGS, DRINK A BUMPER
OF IMPERIAL GRANUM, LOOK EMBARRASSED AND MAKE A PROPER
SPEECH IN REPLY. SAY, AS TINY TIM SAID, GOD BLESS US EVERY
ONE
```

In 1917, when Ernest Hemingway was eighteen years old, he wrote to his parents that he was engaged to be married. Shocked, his physician father, Clarence, sent him a cautionary cable, to which his son replied capriciously:

```
CHEER UP YE OLD POP FOR NOBODY GETS MY INSURANCE SAVE
YOURSELF. ALSO THE MATRIMONIAL STATUS IS NEGATIVE AND WILL
BE FOR SOME YEARS.
```

Far from the most altruistic of sons, Charlie Chaplin wrote to his brother Sydney about bringing their ailing mother (who had had a long history of mental illness) over to America in 1919:

```
SECOND THOUGHTS CONSIDER BE BEST MOTHER REMAIN IN ENGLAND
SOME GOOD SEASIDE RESORT. AFRAID PRESENCE HERE MIGHT
DEPRESS AND AFFECT MY WORK.
```

Playwright Eugene O'Neill had a similar response to the illness of his own long-disturbed mother. When she suffered a massive stroke in 1922, O'Neill sent this defensive telegram to his brother, James:

```
NO QUESTION OF TEMPERAMENT. BE FAIR. SPECIALIST SAYS MEANS
COMPLETE NERVOUS COLLAPSE IF UNDERTAKE TRIP PRESENT
CONDITION. WOULD NOT HELP MOTHER OR YOU. ALSO YOU WIRE SHE
IS UNCONSCIOUS, WILL NOT KNOW ME. WANT TO HELP ANY POSSIBLE
WAY. EVERYTHING I HAVE IS AT YOUR COMMAND. WIRE ME WHAT AND
HOW . . . WOULD LEAVE IMMEDIATELY IF ABLE. YOU MUST ACCEPT
TRUTH. I AM IN TERRIBLE SHAPE.
```

When, at the age of eighteen, Ethel Barrymore informed her father that she was engaged to be married, he cabled:

```
CONGRATULATIONS LOVE FATHER
```

Soon after, when she let her father know that she had broken the engagement, he once again wired:

```
CONGRATULATIONS LOVE FATHER
```

Ethel's niece Diana Barrymore was the youngest generation of the illustrious Barrymore-Drew acting dynasty when she made her Broadway debut. Her mixed feelings are reflected in the wire she sent her father, John Barrymore:

```
DEAREST DADDY, THANK YOU FOR THE APPLE FLOWERS AND
WIRES . . . SO DADDY DARLING I AM DOING MY BEST TO CARRY ON
THIS STINKING TRADITION.
```

F. Scott Fitzgerald, no matter how severe his own work, financial, emotional, and medical problems, was an extremely loving but strict and demanding father (especially when it came to education) to his only daughter, Scottie (Frances Scott Fitzgerald). This was particularly true in

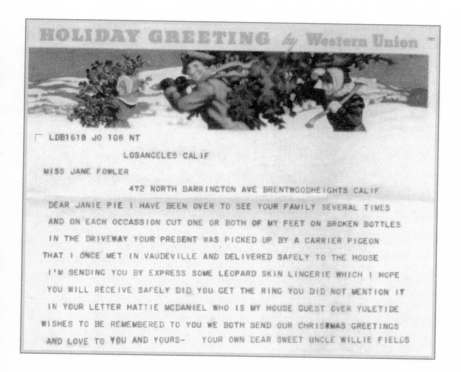

HOLIDAY GREETING *by* Western Union

```
 LDB1618 JO 108 NT
                LOSANGELES CALIF
MISS JANE FOWLER
               472 NORTH BARRINGTON AVE BRENTWOODHEIGHTS CALIF
DEAR JANIE PIE I HAVE BEEN OVER TO SEE YOUR FAMILY SEVERAL TIMES
AND ON EACH OCCASSION CUT ONE OR BOTH OF MY FEET ON BROKEN BOTTLES
IN THE DRIVEWAY YOUR PRESENT WAS PICKED UP BY A CARRIER PIGEON
THAT I ONCE MET IN VAUDEVILLE AND DELIVERED SAFELY TO THE HOUSE
I'M SENDING YOU BY EXPRESS SOME LEOPARD SKIN LINGERIE WHICH I HOPE
YOU WILL RECEIVE SAFELY DID YOU GET THE RING YOU DID NOT MENTION IT
IN YOUR LETTER HATTIE MCDANIEL WHO IS MY HOUSE GUEST OVER YULETIDE
WISHES TO BE REMEMBERED TO YOU WE BOTH SEND OUR CHRISTMAS GREETINGS
AND LOVE TO YOU AND YOURS-   YOUR OWN DEAR SWEET UNCLE WILLIE FIELDS
```

W. C. Fields to the daughter of his close friend Gene Fowler.

the years when his wife, Zelda, was institutionalized, as evidenced in these wires to his agent, Harold Ober, who often opened his home to the girl:

On September 12, 1937:

> NOTE YOUR LETTER ASKS ABOUT UNCHAPERONED PARTIES IN NEW YORK AT NIGHT STOP AFRAID IM ABSOLUTELY OPPOSED TO THAT AT FIFTEEN. . . .

And on December 31, 1931:

> . . . PLEASE TELL SCOTTY THAT HER FUTURE PLANS DEPEND ON HOW MUCH LATIN GROUNDWORK SHE CAN DO IN EIGHT DAYS . . .

Though he could be cold and ruthless in his striving for power, Joseph Kennedy had extremely strong bonds with his children, and not just in terms of the exalted ambitions he had for his four sons. When his wife, Rose, was away on a trip, as she frequently was, he often dropped his other engagements to oversee the daily activities of their brood of nine, wiring her frequent reports:

April 8, 1923:

ROSA DEAR I STILL MAINTAIN A REPUTATION AS THE GREATEST MANAGER IN THE WORLD THE CHILDREN ARE FINE JACK IS SLEEPING EVERY NOON AND IS GREATLY IMPROVED. . . .

April 23, 1923:

. . . TODAY IS HOLIDAY AND FATHER TOOK BOYS TO MARATHON. . . . JOE JACK AND ROSE WENT OVER TO BUNKER HILL YESTERDAY AND THE BOYS WENT TO THE TOP. . . .

October 6, 1934:

I HAVE TAKEN THE CHILDREN TO LUNCH AT THE PLAZA AND MOVIES AND THEY ARE ALL IN FINE SHAPE EUNICE HAS GAINED ONE AND A HALF POUNDS AND THE REST CORRESPONDINGLY JACKS BLOOD COUNT WAS CHECKED YESTERDAY AND IT IS BACK TO NORMAL. . . .

Kennedy also closely monitored the progress of his sons when they were away at school, as exemplified by this telegram to his son Jack, on his sixteenth birthday, at Choate:

. . . I AM REALLY VERY MUCH PLEASED WITH THE WAY YOU HAVE TAKEN HOLD OF THINGS THIS YEAR AND IT IS A GREAT SATISFACTION TO BOTH OF US TO FEEL THAT YOU REALLY ARE DOING THE JOB WE KNEW YOU WERE CAPABLE OF. . . . ALL KINDS OF GOOD LUCK ON THE EXAMS TRY AND CLEAN THEM UP SO WE CAN HAVE A NICE PEACEFUL SUMMER LOVE DAD

When the senior Kennedy was serving as the American ambassador to the Court of St. James in London, he created a media sensation when he hit

a hole in one during his first golf game there. He received a teasing cable from his two sons at Harvard, Joe, Jr., and Jack, to which he replied:

> I AM MUCH HAPPIER BEING THE FATHER OF NINE CHILDREN AND MAKING A HOLE IN ONE THAN I WOULD BE AS THE FATHER OF ONE CHILD MAKING A HOLE IN NINE.

Later in life, when Senator John F. Kennedy was campaigning for the presidency in 1960, he liked to insert an imaginary telegram into his speeches, attempting to deflect with humor all the accusations that his father was trying to buy him the election. "I got a telegram from my father," he would begin, "it reads:

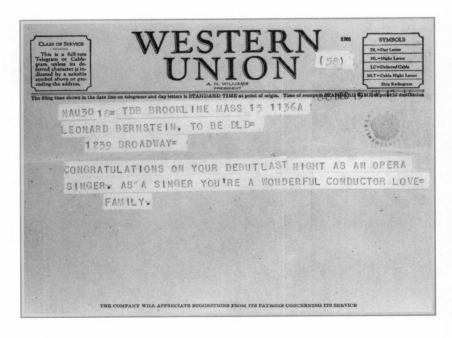

Sam and Jennie Bernstein to their son Leonard after his first attempt
at singing opera in public on December 15, 1945.

ornament

DEAR JACK: DON'T BUY ONE MORE VOTE THAN NECESSARY. I'LL BE
DAMNED IF I PAY FOR A LANDSLIDE."

Some parents were vehemently defensive. When the *Washington Post*
music critic Paul Hume wrote a scathing review of First Daughter Margaret Truman's vocal recital, her father, President Harry Truman, wrote
him an equally scathing letter, which drew a wave of mostly hostile
response from the public, among which was this telegram:

HOW CAN YOU PUT YOUR TRIVIAL PERSONAL AFFAIRS BEFORE THOSE
OF ONE HUNDRED AND SIXTY MILLION PEOPLE. OUR BOYS DIED
WHILE YOUR INFANTILE MIND WAS ON YOUR DAUGHTER'S REVIEW.
INADVERTENTLY YOU SHOWED THE WHOLE WORLD WHAT YOU ARE.
NOTHING BUT A LITTLE SELFISH PIPSQUEAK.

Other parents defended their offspring despite whatever negative evidence there was to the contrary. For example, Richard Nixon's staunch-
est supporter was his mother, Hannah Milhous Nixon, so when he was
being investigated about an alleged secret fund, she sent off the following telegram to her son's running mate, Republican presidential candidate Dwight D. Eisenhower, which was read to the audience of his
speech in Wheeling, West Virginia, in 1950:

DEAR GENERAL: I AM TRUSTING THAT THE ABSOLUTE TRUTH MAY
COME OUT CONCERNING THIS ATTACK ON RICHARD, AND WHEN IT
DOES I AM SURE YOU WILL BE GUIDED RIGHT IN YOUR DECISION,
TO PLACE IMPLICIT FAITH IN HIS INTEGRITY AND HONESTY. BEST
WISHES FROM ONE WHO HAS KNOWN RICHARD LONGER THAN ANYONE
ELSE. HIS MOTHER.

Elvis Presley had extremely close ties to his parents, as seen in this wire
he sent on November 26, 1954:

HI BABIES, HERE'S THE MONEY TO PAY THE BILLS. DON'T TELL NO
ONE HOW MUCH I SENT. I WILL SEND MORE NEXT WEEK. THERE'S A
CARD IN THE MAIL. LOVE, ELVIS

SIBLINGS

TELEGRAMS BETWEEN BROTHERS and sisters often display the expected sibling rivalries but also sometimes reveal deep wells of emotion.

The great Jazz Singer, Al Jolson, had the reputation of being among the most egotistical characters in show business history. In this 1933 wire to his brother Harry, ostensibly congratulating him on becoming an agent/manager, the subtext of who's on top is clearly in evidence:

> HOPE YOU ARE BIG SUCCESS AS AN AGENT YOU CAN'T MISS BECAUSE
> I'M YOUR FIRST CLIENT AND YOU'RE MY FIRST MANAGER HURRAH
> FOR US STOP WITH THE SALARY I GET IF I WORK FOR ONE WEEK
> YOU'LL LIVE A YEAR.

Jack Warner ran his movie studio with an iron hand—or so it seemed. Always metaphorically standing over him and looking down was his older brother Harry who ran the business side of the enterprise from New York and frequently sent him reproachful telegrams concerning Jack's rash, ill-considered decisions. The example below deals with the age-old debate about actors getting involved in politics. In September of 1944, Jack Warner tried to prevent Bette Davis from appearing at a political rally but, as usual, big brother Harry slapped him down:

> IF BETTE DAVIS OR ANYONE ELSE WANTS TO APPEAR AT ANY RALLY,
> WHETHER REPUBLICAN OR DEMOCRATIC, THAT IS THEIR BUSINESS.
> PEOPLE ARE NOT GOING INTO THEATRES BECAUSE DAVIS IS
> REPUBLICAN OR DEMOCRATIC. . . . I ADMIRE PERFORMERS OR ANYONE
> ELSE WHO FIGHT FOR WHAT THEY THINK IS RIGHT. ARE WE THE
> SAME PEOPLE WHO MADE "CONFESSIONS OF A NAZI SPY," "MISSION
> TO MOSCOW" AND MANY OTHER MOVIES WHICH EVERYONE CONDEMNED
> US FOR MAKING? . . . HEREAFTER WHEN IT COMES TO MATTERS OF
> THIS KIND PLEASE DO NOT MAKE ANY DECISIONS UNLESS YOU HAVE
> DISCUSSED THE MATTERS WITH ME. . . .

Read the telegram Eddie and Debbie are sending for Mother's Day

A Western Union advertisement for Mother's Day telegrams.

The bantering and teasing—as well as the confiding—that went on among the Kennedy siblings was legendary. In the telegram below, we see why John F. Kennedy definitely gets the award for President Most Likely to Be Excessively Descriptive over the Public Telegraph Wires (particularly in his younger years). This was sent on June 3, 1943, when he was serving in the navy in the Pacific, to his sister Kathleen, known to the family as Kick:

```
. . . THAT BUBBLE I HAD ABOUT LYING ON A COOL PACIFIC ISLAND
WITH A WARM PACIFIC MAIDEN HUNTING BANANAS FOR ME IS
DEFINITELY A BUBBLE THAT HAS BURST. YOU CAN'T EVEN SWIM—
THERE'S SOME SORT OF FUNGUS IN THE WATER THAT GROWS OUT OF
YOUR EARS—WHICH WILL BE ALL I NEED. WITH PIMPLES ON MY
BACK—HAIR ON MY CHEST AND FUNGUS IN MY EARS I OUGHT TO BE A
NATURAL FOR THE OLD SOLDIERS HOME IN CHELSEA, MASS.
```

LOVE AND MARRIAGE

FOR MUCH OF ITS HISTORY, the telegram was a public medium, with an operator translating the sender's words into Morse code. But that didn't seem to inhibit those who proceeded to transmit their most intimate feelings across the wires—endearments, passions, pet names, even the occasional obscenity slipped through. Others dealt with the mundane day-to-day routine of married life.

During the Civil War, Mary Todd Lincoln spent a lot of her time traveling, but she and her husband kept in close touch via telegraph. Their exchanges ranged from the trivial to the discreetly affectionate, as seen in these two examples.

Form No. 1.

THE WESTERN UNION TELEGRAPH COMPANY.

This Company TRANSMITS and DELIVERS messages only on conditions limiting its liability, which have been assented to by the sender of the following message.
Errors can be guarded against only by repeating a message back to the sending station for comparison, and the company will not hold itself liable for errors or delays in transmission or delivery of Unrepeated Messages, beyond the amount of tolls paid thereon, nor in any case where the claim is not presented in writing within sixty days after sending the message.
This is an UNREPEATED MESSAGE, and is delivered by request of the sender, under the conditions named above.
THOS. T. ECKERT, General Manager.   NORVIN GREEN, President.

NUMBER	SENT BY	REC'D BY		CHECK
4	B	Hm	8	Paid

Received at
Dated *Hagerstown Md 30*   Jan 30 1889
To *Winger & Light*

Women not here have
Goetz come without fail

Hocking .

On June 15, 1863, to Mrs. Lincoln:

TOLERABLY WELL. HAVE NOT RODE OUT MUCH YET, BUT AT LEAST
GOT NEW TIRES ON THE CARRIAGE WHEELS AND PERHAPS SHALL RIDE
OUT SOON.

September 21, 1863, to Mrs. Lincoln at the Fifth Avenue Hotel, New York:

THE AIR IS SO CLEAR AND COOL AND APPARENTLY HEALTHY THAT I
WOULD BE GLAD FOR YOU TO COME. NOTHING VERY PARTICULAR BUT
I WOULD BE GLAD TO SEE YOU AND TAD.

George Bernard Shaw had some trepidation about committing to his future wife, Charlotte Payne-Townshend, but when at last he did, in October of 1896, it was via telegram:

ALL CLEAR NOW YES A THOUSAND TIMES

After an eight-year courtship, Will Rogers finally proposed to and was accepted by his sweetheart, Betty Blake, in 1908. However, instead of going with her to break the news to her folks, they faced their families separately, as he wired her from the Oologah, Indian Territory, train station:

BACK TO THE SCENES OF OUR CHILDHOOD. WISH YOU WAS AT THE
OLD DEPOT. LOVE, BILLY.

In April of 1916, during World War I, just a year before the Bolshevik revolution would erupt and destroy him, Czar Nicholas II was overseeing his troops in Stavka. As often as several times a day, he sent letters and telegrams—all of them signed Nicky—to his wife, Czarina Alexandra, who was falling more and more under the influence of the enigmatic mystic Rasputin. Typical of his loving telegrams:

HAVE ARRIVED SAFELY. EVERYTHING IS COVERED WITH DELICIOUS
VERDURE, IT SMELLS SO GOOD. I HAVE FINISHED A DELIGHTFUL
BOOK WITH TEARS IN MY EYES. I LONG FOR YOU GREATLY. I KISS
YOU TENDERLY.

Meantime, back at the Imperial Palace . . . If there was any doubt that Alexandra became romantically involved with Rasputin, the illiterate Eastern Orthodox mystic sometimes known as the "Mad Monk," strong evidence has been found in a recently discovered secret file on him compiled by the Bolsheviks soon after his murder in 1916. Included was this telegram from Alexandra to Rasputin dated December 7, 1914:

TODAY I SHALL BE BACK IN EIGHT DAYS. I SACRIFICE MY HUSBAND
AND MY HEART TO YOU. PRAY AND BLESS. LOVE AND KISSES—DARLING.

During World War I, doughboy Harry Truman sent a wire to his beloved Bess on April 21, 1919:

ARRIVED IN CAMP MILLS THIS AFTERNOON. HAVE BEEN EATING PIE
AND ICE CREAM EVER SINCE . . . NEW YORK GAVE US A GRAND
WELCOME. GOD'S COUNTRY SURE LOOKS GOOD.

This buoyant telegram was sent by F. Scott Fitzgerald to his future wife, Zelda Sayre, before they were married, on February 22, 1919, when the future seemed filled with promise:

DARLING HEART AMBITION ENTHUSIASM AND CONFIDENCE I DECLARE
EVERYTHING GLORIOUS THIS WORLD IS A GAME AND WHITE [SIC] I
FEEL SURE OF YOU [SIC] LOVE EVERYTHING IS POSSIBLE I AM IN
THE LAND OF AMBITION AND SUCCESS AND MY ONLY HOPE AND FAITH
IS THAT MY DARLING HEART WILL BE WITH YOU SOON.

Twelve years later, when their lives had shattered and Zelda, now his
wife, was suffering from severe mental problems, Fitzgerald wired journalist H. L. Mencken in Baltimore for a referral:

WILL YOU KINDLY WIRE ME THE NAME OF THE BIGGEST
PSYCHIATRIST AT JOHNS HOPKINS FOR NONORGANIC NERVOUS
TROUBLES. . . .

Mencken himself was one of the many who couldn't resist sending wires
and cables to their loved ones during interminably long train trips and
ocean voyages. Here are two he sent on the same day to his future wife
Sara Haardt as she traveled east aboard the Santa Fe Sunset Limited:

DON'T DALLY TOO LONG IN MONTGOMERY THE DAYS SEEM ENDLESS

IT IS CHARMING TO THINK THAT YOU ARE A THOUSAND MILES NEARER

Playwright Eugene O'Neill was passionately in love with his second
wife, Carlotta Monterey, and while he was sailing on the SS *Coblenz* in
early January 1929, he cabled her sometimes several times a day.

January 6:

. . . NEED YOUR HELP MORE THAN EVER BEFORE BECAUSE I AM HALF
MAD WITH UTTER LONELINESS WITHOUT FRIENDS PLANS OR
HOPES . . . IT WOULD BE A TREMENDOUS HELP IF YOU CABLE ME
EVERY DAY. . . .

January 7:

I KNOW DEAREST THE BEST MEDICINE IS THOU. . . .

January 7:

GOOD NIGHT DEAREST ONE MORE DAY GONE

January 7:

> . . . MISS YOUR HELP LOVE TREMENDOUSLY HAVE HORRIBLE
> DESERTED FEELING DARLING AND THESE DAYS ARE LONGEST
> EMPTIEST IN MY LIFE

January 11:

> ITS HIDEOUS THIS LAST STRETCH OF HADES I MISS YOU SO GOOD
> NIGHT DEAR ONE

In the case of producer David O. Selznick and his fiancée, Irene Mayer, daughter of Louis B., the wires came fast and furious in February 1930 as she crossed the country by rail, coming closer and closer to California.

DS, February 1:

> I'LL SEE YOU AGAIN. DEVOTEDLY. LUCKY FOOL

IM, February 1:

> MORPHEUS HAS BEGUN TO EVADE ME. OH PLEASE HURRY TO SAVE ME.
> LOVE AND MMMMM.

DS, February 3:

> MY ARMS ARE FRANTIC MY MIND SINGLE TRACKED AND MY HEART IN
> PASADENA

IM, February 3:

> I WISH THAT ENGINEER HAVE MERCY ON THE PIT OF MY
> STOMACH. . . . CANNOT DECIDE IF IT IS BETTER TO GO TO SLEEP
> AND SHORTEN THE HOURS OR STAY AWAKE AND THINK OF HOW VERY
> SOON MY LITTLE ONE WILL BE IN THE ARMS OF IRENE.

Dashiell Hammett and Lillian Hellman met in 1930 and had a long, often tempestuous relationship, documented in letters and telegrams. After the success of the film *The Thin Man,* Hammett was invited to come to Hollywood to work on a sequel. The following two telegrams

> "My life as a telegraph messenger was in every respect a happy one. . . . A messenger boy in those days had many pleasures. There were whole-sale fruit stores, where a pocketful of apples was sometimes to be had for the prompt delivery of a message; bakers' and confectioners' shops, where sweet cakes were sometimes given to him . . . One great excitement of this life was the extra charge of ten cents we were permitted to collect for messages delivered beyond a certain limit. . . ."
>
> —*The Autobiography of Andrew Carnegie*

were both written on October 27, 1934, and wired from the transcontinental train. The first was signed in the name of the book's hero, Nick Charles, and sent from Kansas City; the second was dashed off when the train stopped at Albuquerque.

```
SO FAR SO GOOD ONLY AM MISSING YOU PLENTY LOVE
    NICKY

HAVE NOT GOT USED TO BEING WITHOUT YOU YET WHAT SHALL I DO
    LOVE
    DASH
```

When the Disney brothers first left Kansas City to set up shop in Los Angeles, they lived together in a one-room apartment. It was Roy who

cooked the evening meal, which never—to put it mildly—met with Walt's approval. One night in 1925, Roy couldn't take the disparaging remarks any longer and poured a plate of stew over his brother's head. The very next day, Roy Disney sent this telegram to his longtime sweetheart, Edna Francis:

WHAT ARE WE WAITING FOR STOP WHY DON'T YOU COME OUT HERE
AND TIE THE KNOT STOP

An unlikely couple: reserved, literary, *New Yorker* editor Harold Ross was quite taken with brassy movie star Ginger Rogers, and they were to remain lifelong friends. He sent her this telegram on April 18, 1931:

OH DEAR, OH DEAR, BUT YOU ARE FORGIVEN IF YOU REALLY WOULD
RATHER BE WITH ME AND I WILL CALL YOU SUNDAY AND SAY SO
PERSONALLY. I TRIED TO CALL YOU THIS MORNING FOR SOLID HOUR
BUT YOUR PHONE WAS BUSY. PRINCETON BOYS, I GUESS, AND IF
THEY GO TOO FAR THEY WILL FIND THE CITY ISN'T BIG ENOUGH TO
HOLD BOTH THEM AND ME.
    VERY BESTEST,
    NON PRINCETON BOY

The Franklin/Eleanor Roosevelt marriage was a good deal more complex, and their lives more separate, than the public suspected, both of them traveling extensively and sometimes not even quite knowing where the other was. This peevish telegram was sent by Eleanor to her husband in September of 1932:

ALMOST IMPOSSIBLE TO GET ANY INFORMATION AS TO YOUR PLANS
OR WHEREABOUTS FROM STEVE. APPARENTLY HE IS AS MUCH IN THE
DARK AS THE REST OF US. WHAT HAS HAPPENED TO MAC AND YOU?
IS IT UNCOMMUNICATIVENESS ON HIS PART OR LACK OF DECISION
ON YOURS? OUR LOVE TO YOU. E.R.

When Joseph Kennedy had his affair with screen star Gloria Swanson, their relationship had a lightness and levity that his marriage lacked, as evidenced in this telegram the glamorous star wrote when she arrived back in California from the east coast in February of 1928:

EVERYTHING ALL RIGHT NOW YOU DON'T HAVE TO HAVE CAMPBELLS
[THE FUNERAL HOME] MEET BODY. I HAD TWELVE HOURS SLEEP.

Despite Joe Kennedy's philandering, however, he retained strong ties to his wife, Rose, sending her this telegram on their twentieth anniversary in 1934:

> . . . I CANNOT TELL YOU HOW HAPPY THESE YEARS HAVE BEEN FOR ME AND WHAT A MARVELOUS PERSON YOU HAVE BEEN THROUGH IT ALL. THE THING THAT MAKES THIS SO TRUE IS THAT I LOVE YOU NOW MORE THAN EVER. I HAVE TAKEN THE CHILDREN TO LUNCH AT THE PLAZA AND MOVIES. . . . I WISH I WERE WITH YOU IN PARIS TODAY TO CELEBRATE OUR ANNIVERSARY.

Marlene Dietrich's real life was as filled with passion as her screen persona suggested, with her list of paramours comprising a veritable *Who's Who* of Hollywood, London, and countless other places. Several of her affairs can be corroborated via Western Union: this telegram from the director sometimes referred to as her "Svengali," Josef von Sternberg (she herself once telegraphed him, "Without you I am nothing"), was addressed to:

> MARLENE SIEBER [HER MARRIED NAME], SANTAFE CHIEF DRAWING ROOM B CAR 202 =DUE KANSASCITY 945 PM:
> BELOVED GODDESS
> EVERYTHING IS EMPTY AGAIN AND I BURN BECAUSE OF LONGING FOR YOU AND LOVE. PLEASE EXCUSE MY STUPIDITIES. MY THOUGHTS ARE WITH YOU.

And she to him:

> TAKE FOR YOURSELF FROM MY IMMENSE LOVING AS MUCH AS YOU NEED STOP NOT SO MUCH THAT IT WOULD DISTURB YOU AND NOT TOO LITTLE EITHER THAT IT WOULD GIVE YOU TROUBLE . . .

From one of her costars, Brian Aherne:

> . . . I ADORE YOU CRAZY DIETRICH

And another, Maurice Chevalier:

> YOU WERE RIGHT MARINOU OUR MEETING WAS GRAND YESTERDAY. . . .

Martha Gellhorn, a successful journalist and novelist, was the third and most accomplished of Ernest Hemingway's four wives. This Hemingway marriage, like those preceding it, started out on a high note, then became precarious at best. On December 9, 1940, shortly after the wedding, she telegraphed her friends Tillie and Lloyd Arnold:

```
. . . EVERYTHING FINE HERE CLOSELY RESEMBLING LIFE IN
RUNAWAY ELEVATOR STOP AM OFF TO BURMA ROADS SOON AS
POSSIBLE STOP ALL THIS AND HEAVEN TOO . . .
```

But by early 1944, Hemingway had grown frustrated by his wife's adventurous journalistic globe-trotting and wired her angrily:

```
ARE YOU A WAR CORRESPONDENT OR WIFE IN MY BED?
```

Singer Lotte Lenya on one occasion allowed Western Union to express her emotions by sending their standard Valentine's Day greeting in 1942 to husband Kurt Weill:

```
I KNOW I'M LUCKY BECAUSE YOU'RE MINE; YOU'LL ALWAYS BE MY
VALENTINE=LINNERL
```

Through the fifty-seven years of their life together, Winston and Clementine Churchill wrote to each other almost daily when they were apart, often communicating by telegram, as in this playful exchange dated January 1935. Clementine, away on a trip, wired:

```
CAUGHT SEVEN LOVELY BUTTERFLIES ON DESERT ISLAND. SUMATRA
TOMORROW. LOVE CLEMMIE
```

To which Winston replied:

```
CAUGHT THREE LOVELY FILMS HERE. DELIGHTED ABOUT
BUTTERFLIES. ALL WELL HERE. FILM PROSPERING . . . FONDEST
LOVE       WINSTON
```

The Churchill correspondence is rife with pet and code names, some assigned by the Ministry of War. The sixty-nine-year-old prime minis-

Every so often over the years, Western Union would put out a pamphlet of "Suggested Sentiments for Many Occasions for Use in Telegrams" for their patrons who just couldn't figure out for themselves what to say. From a late 1920s edition:

(Valentine) To tell you what I think of You, the mail is far too slow. My message must fly swift and true, as the arrow from the bow.

(Christmas) The success of our business is largely due to the fidelity and zeal of our representatives. We appreciate your efforts and wish you a Merry Christmas.

(Speech) Your address last night I have read with pride. You voice what we all would say had we your gift of expression. I congratulate you on your courage and eloquence.

A few more from a 1947 publication:

(Birthday) Love and best wishes for a happy birthday.

(Anniversary) Our heartiest congratulations on your wedding anniversary.

(Engagement) Cheer up. The worst is yet to come.

(Election) It has been a rousing campaign and we are proud of the way you put it over.

(On opening a new store) Good luck on the opening of your new store.

(Bon Voyage) May each white-capped crest on the ocean's blue bear out my wish—happy voyage to you.

ter received this seductive message from his wife while he was meeting with the other Allied leaders in the Mideast on February 2, 1943.

MRS FRANKLAND TO AIR COMMODORE FRANKLAND.
I AM FOLLOWING YOUR MOVEMENTS WITH INTENSE INTEREST. THE
CAGE IS SWEPT AND GARNISHED WITH FRESH WATER AND HEMP SEED

ARE TEMPTINGLY DISPLAYED. THE DOOR IS OPEN AND IT IS HOPED
THAT SOON MR. BULL FINCH WILL FLY HOME.

To which he replied on the following day:
KEEP CAGE OPEN FOR SATURDAY OR SUNDAY. MUCH LOVE.

and again on the fifth:
THE BULLFINCH HOPES TO MAKE A LONG HOP HOME TONIGHT.

In the midst of war, the personal and the trivial coexist with the universal and momentous. Following a short leave, General Dwight Eisenhower cabled his wife, Mamie, on January 16, 1944:
TRIP FINALLY COMPLETED WITH ONLY UNFORTUNATE INCIDENT THE
THEFT OF MY BAG OF PECANS AND CHOCOLATE. I AM TRULY
DISAPPOINTED BECAUSE I WANTED TO TRY THE VITAMIN
CHOCOLATES. . . . WHILE OUR VISIT TOGETHER WAS OFTEN
INTERRUPTED AND THE PAIN OF PARTING WAS AS BAD AS EVER, I
AM STILL GLAD I MADE THE TRIP. I FEEL MUCH BETTER AFTER
HAVING THOSE TEN DAYS WITH YOU. . . .

On July 23, 1941, the callow and cocky twenty-four-year-old John F. Kennedy sent a telegraph to his friend Cam Newberry, seeking temporary digs:
DEAR PRIVATE NEWBERRY AS THE COLUMBIA TRUST CO OF EAST BOSTON
HAS HAD THE RATHER UNUSUAL GOOD FORTUNE OF ADDING ME TO THEIR
STAFF FOR THE NEXT THREE WEEKS I WAS WONDERING WHETHER I
MIGHT USE YOUR APARTMENT TO LAY MY HAT AND A FEW FRIENDS
PENDING RENTAL WILL BRING MY OWN MATTRESS REGARDS MOE.

A dozen years later, Long Island socialite Jacqueline Lee Bouvier was in England covering the coronation of Queen Elizabeth II for the *Washington Times Herald,* when her beau, John F. Kennedy, sent her a telegram:
ARTICLES EXCELLENT. BUT YOU ARE MISSED.

The day after she returned, they became engaged.

Then, three days after John Kennedy and Jacqueline Bouvier were married, the bridegroom wired his parents from his Acapulco honeymoon, on September 15, 1953:

AT LAST I KNOW THE TRUE MEANING OF RAPTURE JACKIE IS
ENSHRINED FOREVER IN MY HEART THANKS MOM AND DAD FOR MAKING
ME WORTHY OF HER YOUR LOVING SON JACK

Jazz great Charlie Parker would frequently call and wire his common-law wife, Chan, keeping her up to date on events while he was on the road. This telegram was sent from Seattle on February 24, 1954:

. . . HAVE PRESENT FOR YOU WHEN I ARRIVE. FINALLY REACHED
SEATTLE LANTHEIE BROKE HIS OLD LADIES NECK LAST NIGHT AFTER
WE SPOKE ON THE PHONE. GETZ OUT ON SUSPENDED SENTENCE
LOOKING FOR HIM TO KILL HIM IN A CERTAIN TOWN. DARLING HAVE
HUNDRED DOLLARS SENDING YOU RIGHT AWAY CALL ME IMMEDIATELY
OLYMPIC HOTEL BY THE WAY HAVING A WONDERFUL TIME. THANK YOU
FOR MAKING A MAN OF ME I WILL ALWAYS LOVE YOU
    GUESS WHO

Beginning in 1950, shortly after they met, Ronald Reagan wrote frequent, doting letters to Nancy Davis, later Nancy Davis Reagan, which she gathered into the book *I Love You, Ronnie.* Among them were some equally loving telegrams, including this one dated May 18, 1958:

ONLY TILL TOMORROW MORNING BUT IF IT WERE ONLY A MINUTE IT
WOULD BE TOO LONG I LOVE YOU
    POPPA

WHAT AM I DOING HERE WHEN I WANT TO BE THERE. I MISS YOU &
LOVE YOU. WHY IS IT I DON'T GET AROUND TO SPEAKING MY MIND
MORE OFTEN LIKE HOW MUCH I LOVE YOU AND HOW LOST I'D BE
WITHOUT YOU.

In August of 1956, the twenty-one-year-old Elvis Presley wired his eternal love to his Memphis girlfriend June Juanico:

```
HI WIOOLE BITTY I MISS YOU BABY. HAVENT HAD YOU OUT OF MY
MIND FOR A SECOND. ILL ALWAYS BE YOURS AND YOURS ALONE TO
LOVE. DREAMED ABOUT YOU LAST NIGHT. LOVE YA YEA UH-HUH EP
```

FRIENDSHIP

THE MORE PLATONIC SIDE of love, too, was often tapped out over the telegraph wires.

Sara and Gerald Murphy were parental figures and generous friends to a whole generation of expatriate American writers in France. When the second of their sons died tragically in 1935, they received this sympathetic telegram from four of their closest chums, Ernest Hemingway and his wife, Pauline, and John Dos Passos and his wife, Katy, sent from Key West, Florida, on March 26:

```
DEAR SARA AND GERALD WE WISH WE WERE THERE WITH YOU OR YOU
WERE HERE WITH US WE MUST ALL HOLD TOGETHER WE ARE YOUR
FAITHFUL FRIENDS AND YOU ARE PART OF OUR LIVES YOUR WAY IS
OUR WAY WE SEND LOVE AND ARE WRITING SOON
    DOS KATY ERNEST PAULINE
```

And again three days later:

```
WE WILL COME SINGLE OR IN SWARM AT ANYTIME TO LAKE PLACID
OR WHEREVER YOU GO HOW ABOUT COMING DOWN HERE FIRST OR TO
BIMINI ANYTIME DURING APRIL MUCH LOVE
    KATY DOS PAULINE ERNEST
```

Two of America's most significant twentieth-century novelists, F. Scott Fitzgerald and Ernest Hemingway, had a highly intense and complex relationship that was at times competitive, at times supportive. The mid-1930s were a dark time for Fitzgerald. His wife, Zelda, was in a mental hospital and he himself was ill, in debt and despair, struggling with alcoholism, his writing career at a low ebb. Not having seen Hemingway for a while, he sent him this telegram on May 13, 1935, in an attempt at arranging a reunion:

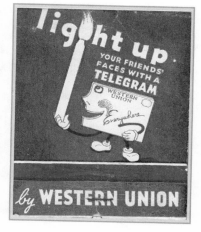

WANT TO SEE YOU AS AM GOING
TO CAROLINA FOR SUMMER COULD
MAKE THREE DAY STAY KEYWEST ARRIVING THIS THURSDAY . . . NOT
UP TO ANYTHING STRENUOUS PROBABLY RESULT OF TEATOTALING
SINCE JANUARY . . .

In a rare display of show business loyalty, star Leslie Howard sent this wire to studio head Jack Warner about casting the little-known Humphrey Bogart in the movie version of *The Petrified Forest* as Duke Mantee, the part Bogart had played with Howard on the stage:

INSIST BOGART PLAY MANTEE NO BOGART NO DEAL

Over their many meetings during the World War II period, Winston Churchill and Franklin D. Roosevelt developed a strong bond that grew into a warm friendship. This is evident in a wire from the British prime minister to future Labour Party Prime Minister Clement Attlee, dated late December 1941:

WE LIVE HERE AS A BIG FAMILY IN THE GREATEST INTIMACY AND
INFORMALITY, AND I HAVE FORMED THE VERY HIGHEST REGARD AND
ADMIRATION FOR THE PRESIDENT. HIS BREADTH OF VIEW,
RESOLUTION AND HIS LOYALTY TO THE COMMON CAUSE ARE BEYOND
ALL PRAISE.

And also in the teasing tone of this 1942 telegram from Roosevelt to Churchill:

```
. . . INCIDENTALLY WHILE YOUR FRENCH GRAMMAR IS BETTER THAN
MINE, MY ACCENT IS MORE ALLURING.
```

MUNDANITIES

IN THE HEYDAY of the telegram, it was not unheard of to send a wire to someone nearby telling him you might be arriving late to dinner that evening, as in this one sent from novelist Joseph Conrad to his host Warrington Dawson, on May 28, 1914:

```
JESSIE [CONRAD'S WIFE] WENT OUT THIS MORNING AND NOT BACK
YET TO DRESS. AFRAID IMPOSSIBLE ARRIVE IN TIME. REPLY
CONRAD NORFOLK HOTEL SURREY ST STRAND
```

Sometimes a message that seems mundane can become momentous when placed in context. This one from renowned adventurer T. E. Lawrence—better known as Lawrence of Arabia—was sent minutes before he met his death, not riding a camel across the desert but astride a Brough motorcycle in a British village on May 13, 1935. He had come to town to send the following telegram to Henry Williamson:

```
LUNCH TUESDAY WET FINE COTTAGE ONE MILE NORTH BOVINGTON
CAMP.
```

The use of the telegram could be carried to an absurd extreme. Impresario Florenz Ziegfeld was famous for habitually wiring people who were sitting in the same room. According to his wife, Billie (Glinda the Good Witch) Burke, Ziegfeld would, if he saw something that displeased him during a rehearsal or performance, dash back to his office and dictate a telegram to the company manager, such as:

ANY GIRL WHO CHANGES OR TWISTS HER HAT WILL BE FIRED.

> "[Florenz Ziegfeld] had two gold telephones on his desk, and he enriched the telegraph companies considerably by his fondness for sending 500-word telegrams."
> —Ziegfeld obituary, *The New York Times*, July 23, 1932

And he wasn't the only one. One afternoon, Peter Sellers was busy in the study of his London flat while his wife, Anne, was working in the kitchen. When she went to answer the doorbell, she was startled to be presented with a telegram that read:

BRING ME A CUP OF COFFEE. PETER

Then there was the time that comedian Henny Youngman was having lunch in a hotel dining room with the far more popular Jerry Lewis when a mob of Lewis's fans disrupted their conversation. Youngman got up and slipped away unnoticed, going to the lobby and ordering a telegram to be sent to Mr. Lewis. When it arrived a short time later, Lewis read:

JERRY. PLEASE PASS THE SALT. HENNY.

Telegrams also were employed to convey the most prosaic of messages over longer distances. When he was living in the United States, German *Threepenny Opera* composer Kurt Weill often carried on a bicoastal correspondence with his singer wife and muse, Lotte Lenya. On one occasion in 1944, Lenya wired Weill from New City, New York, to Beverly Hills:

DARLING I HOPE YOU HAD A NICE TRIP. . . . BLUE SLACKS STILL AT CLEANERS.

Slacks made another appearance in a lighthearted exchange between Harry Truman and an old friend of Scandinavian descent with whom he had gone on a fishing trip to Puget Sound in 1955. When the former president discovered that some of his clothing was missing on his return, he wired:

WE ARE SHORT ONE SUIT TAN PAJAMAS BEARING INITIALS HST WHEN LAST SEEN THEY WERE BEING WORN BY A FAT SWEDE. HST

And the reply came back:

SWEDE IN CUSTODY PAJAMAS BEING HELD FOR SCREENING WILL SHIP SHORTLY FURTHER SURVEY WILL REVEAL PLAID SLACKS MISSING . . .

In May of 1948, Graham Greene sent this apparently trivial telegram to his paramour Catherine Walston (he also had a wife and another long-term mistress) from Agadir, Morocco. Recent research has revealed that "onion sandwiches" had a coded sexual significance for the pair.

DO YOU LIKE ONION SANDWICHES GREENE

In May of 1954, Greene's tone had changed from matter-of-fact to dramatic:

DO FORGIVE STUPIDITY DUE DRINK DESPAIR I'M SORRY GOODBYE LOTS OF LOVE G.

Here, a somewhat cryptic wire from Harold Ross to Noël Coward, January 26, 1931:

I REALIZED IN THE MIDDLE OF THE NIGHT I DIDN'T PAY THAT SIXTEEN DOLLARS BUT I GOT TO SLEEP ALMOST AT ONCE AND HAVE NOW SUCCEEDED IN DISMISSING THE MATTER FROM MY MIND. DON'T GIVE IT A SECOND THOUGHT.

SHOPPING

Ordering, buying, and selling of various kinds were the subject of a number of diverse telegrams.

First Lady Mary Todd Lincoln was known for her extravagance and compulsive shopping (not always disclosed to her husband), evidenced by two telegrams sent by her, via the War Department, to New York merchants.

On January 11, 1864:

> MY NARROW WIDTH WHITE FRINGE, HAS NOT YET REACHED ME—I NEED
> IT VERY MUCH.

And on February 25:

> PLEASE SEND IMMEDIATELY 1 BASKET CHAMPAGNE, THE WIDOW
> CLIQUOT BRAND.

The very next day she requested a second basket of champagne, "of the choicest quality you have in store."

On April 16, 1862, the president himself sent this telegram on behalf of his wife to a Hiram Barney in New York:

> MRS. L. HAS $1,000 FOR THE BENEFIT OF THE HOSPITALS, AND
> SHE WILL BE OBLIGED, AND SEND THE PAY IF YOU WOULD BE SO
> GOOD AS TO SELECT AND SEND HER $200 WORTH OF GOOD LEMONS
> AND $100 WORTH OF GOOD ORANGES.

During the Spanish-American War, when Theodore Roosevelt was commanding the volunteer force known as the Rough Riders, he sent this telegram, dated May 2, 1898, to no less a gentleman's purveyor than Brooks Brothers:

> ORDINARY CAVALRY LIEUTENANT COLONEL'S UNIFORM IN BLUE
> CRAVENETTE.

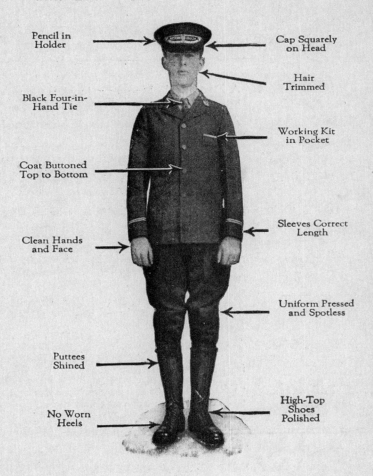

TAKE PRIDE IN YOUR JOB
and IN YOUR APPEARANCE

Pencil in Holder

Cap Squarely on Head

Hair Trimmed

Black Four-in-Hand Tie

Working Kit in Pocket

Coat Buttoned Top to Bottom

Sleeves Correct Length

Clean Hands and Face

Uniform Pressed and Spotless

Puttees Shined

High-Top Shoes Polished

No Worn Heels

CORRECTLY UNIFORMED WESTERN UNION MESSENGER

Producer David O. Selznick was always on the lookout for properties that could be optioned and made into movies. One of his more outlandish ideas is seen in this telegram sent to his New York rep, Kay Brown, on December 11, 1941, just four days after Pearl Harbor:

> . . . DROP EVERYTHING AND RUSH OVER TO THE HAYS OFFICE TO REGISTER "MEIN KAMPF" AS WELL AS ANYTHING ELSE NECESSARY TO PROTECT IT, SUCH AS "LIFE OF ADOLPH HITLER" AND "MY LIFE" BY ADOLPH HITLER. . . . KEEP IT UTTERLY SECRET. . . . TO POINT OUT IMPORTANCE OF TREATMENT I PLAN FOR SUBJECT, I AM THINKING ABOUT HECHT FOR SCRIPT AND HITCHCOCK FOR DIRECTION. . . .

On the fifth wedding anniversary of playwright George S. Kaufman and his wife, Beatrice, they received a wire from the caustic theater critic Alexander Woollcott saying that he had found them the perfect wooden gift—"Elsie Ferguseon's performance in her new play."

BREAKTHROUGHS

SIMON LAKE, the distinguished marine engineer who played a key role in making the submarine a practical device, had been inspired by Jules Verne's novel *Twenty Thousand Leagues Under the Sea*. In 1898, his New Jersey company built the first submarine to operate successfully in the open sea, at which point he received a telegram from Verne himself, sent from Amiens, France:

> WHILE MY BOOK 'TWENTY THOUSAND LEAGUES UNDER THE SEA' IS ENTIRELY A WORK OF IMAGINATION, MY CONVICTION IS THAT ALL I SAID IN IT WILL COME TO PASS. A THOUSAND MILE VOYAGE IN THE BALTIMORE SUBMARINE BOAT IS EVIDENCE OF THIS. THE

CONSPICUOUS SUCCESS OF SUBMARINE NAVIGATION IN THE UNITED STATES WILL PUSH ON UNDER-WATER NAVIGATION ALL OVER THE WORLD. . . . THE NEXT GREAT WAR MAY BE LARGELY A CONTEST BETWEEN SUBMARINE BOATS. . . . I THINK THAT ELECTRICITY RATHER THAN COMPRESSED AIR WILL BE THE MOTIVE POWER IN SUCH VESSELS. . . . SUBMARINE NAVIGATION IS NOW AHEAD OF AERIAL NAVIGATION AND WILL ADVANCE MUCH FASTER FROM NOW ON. BEFORE THE UNITED STATES GAINS HER FULL DEVELOPMENT SHE IS LIKELY TO HAVE MIGHTY NAVIES NOT ONLY ON THE BOSOM OF THE ATLANTIC AND PACIFIC, BUT IN THE UPPER AIR AND BENEATH THE WATER'S SURFACE.

The first wireless telegraph between America and Europe was sent on January 18, 1903, from President Theodore Roosevelt at the South

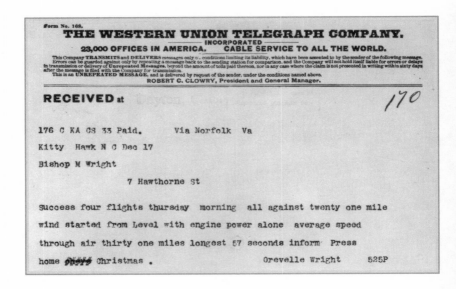

Orville Wright to his father, Bishop Milton Wright, on December 17, 1903, after his first successful powered flight in Kitty Hawk, North Carolina.

Wellfleet Station on Cape Cod to King Edward VII in Cornwall, England. The message was:

IN TAKING ADVANTAGE OF THE WONDERFUL TRIUMPH OF SCIENTIFIC RESEARCH AND INGENUITY WHICH HAS BEEN ACHIEVED IN PERFECTING A SYSTEM OF WIRELESS TELEGRAPHY, I EXTEND ON BEHALF OF THE AMERICAN PEOPLE MOST CORDIAL GREETINGS AND GOOD WISHES TO YOU AND TO ALL THE PEOPLE OF THE BRITISH EMPIRE.

After eight failed efforts, Admiral Robert E. Peary reached the North Pole on April 6, 1909. The following cable was released to the public five months later:

STARS AND STRIPES NAILED TO THE NORTH POLE.
—PEARY.

In 1910, wireless telegraphy from ship to shore led to the apprehension of a criminal for the first time. In a notorious case, Dr. Hawley Crippen was attempting to flee to Canada with his paramour by ship after poisoning his wife, then dismembering and burying her in the cellar of their London home. On July 22, the telegrapher aboard the Atlantic liner *Montrose* sent the wire that would lead to Crippen's hanging:

HAVE STRONG SUSPICION THAT CRIPPEN LONDON CELLAR MURDERER AND ACCOMPLICE ARE AMONGST SALOON PASSENGERS MOUSTACHE TAKEN OFF GROWING BEARD ACCOMPLICE DRESSED AS BOY VOICE MANNER AND BUILD UNDOUBTEDLY A GIRL BOTH TRAVELING AS MR AND MASTER ROBINSON

Inventor Thomas Edison sent this telegram after the Associated Press transmitted a play-by-play of the World Series directly from the ballpark for the first time, using a special 26,000-mile circuit:

THE ASSOCIATED PRESS MUST BE WONDERFULLY ORGANIZED TO BE ABLE TO ACCOMPLISH WHAT WAS DONE IN THE BALL GAMES. UNCLE SAM HAS NOW A REAL ARTERIAL SYSTEM AND IT IS NEVER GOING TO HARDEN.

Philo T. Farnsworth is credited with the invention of television, having succeeded in demonstrating the principle and process in San Francisco on September 7, 1927. After this first successful transmission, Farnsworth's backer, George Everson, sent a wire to his partner, Les Gorrell, in Los Angeles:

THE DAMNED THING WORKS!

When primatologist Jane Goodall discovered a wild chimpanzee named David Greybeard making twigs into tools and using them to perform various functions, she wrote and described her discovery to famed anthropologist Louis Leakey in 1960, and he replied:

NOW WE MUST REDEFINE TOOL, REDEFINE MAN, OR ACCEPT
CHIMPANZEES AS HUMAN.

At the time of the U.S.-USSR space wars, there was an exchange of polite telegrams between President Kennedy and Premier Nikita Khrushchev when either country made an advance. This one was sent by President Kennedy to Khrushchev on February 13, 1961:

I WISH TO EXTEND MY CONGRATULATIONS AND THOSE OF THE
AMERICAN PEOPLE FOR THE IMPRESSIVE SCIENTIFIC ACHIEVEMENT
REPRESENTED BY THE LAUNCHING OF YOUR SPACE VEHICLE TO
VENUS. WE SHALL WATCH ITS PROGRESS WITH INTEREST AND WISH
YOU SUCCESS IN ANOTHER CHAPTER OF MAN'S EXPLORATION OF THE
UNIVERSE.

Eight years later, upon the successful completion of the Apollo 9 mission, President Richard Nixon sent the following telegram to the crew, leavened with a touch of Nixonian wit, on March 13, 1969:

THE EPIC FLIGHT OF APOLLO NINE WILL BE RECORDED IN HISTORY
AS TEN DAYS THAT THRILLED THE WORLD. YOU HAVE BY YOUR
COURAGE AND YOUR SKILL HELPED TO SHAPE THE FUTURE OF MAN IN
SPACE. . . . KNOWING THAT THE DINING IN APOLLO NINE, WHILE
NOURISHING, LACKED SOME OF THE AMENITIES OF EARTH-BOUND

DINING, MRS. NIXON AND I INVITE YOU AND YOUR WIVES TO HAVE
DINNER WITH US AT THE WHITE HOUSE AT 8:00 THURSDAY EVENING,
THE TWENTY-SEVENTH OF MARCH.

FELICITATIONS

ONE OF THE MOST common reasons for telegraphing has always been to send congratulations on the occasion of a birth, a birthday, an engagement, a marriage, an anniversary, a promotion, a graduation, an opening night, a nomination, or an election.

When Theodore Roosevelt was reelected by a landslide in 1904, one of his oldest and closest friends, Owen Wister—author of the best-selling novel *The Virginian*—sent him a congratulatory telegram:

RICHARD THIRD ACT ONE SCENE ONE LINES ONE AND TWO.

The highly literate Roosevelt undoubtedly recognized at once that these lines are: "Now is the winter of our discontent made glorious summer by this sun of York."

Four years later, when his term was ending, and Congress was doing little that Roosevelt recommended, Wister sent another wire:

ROMEO AND JULIET ACT THREE SCENE ONE LINE THREE PRECEDING
MERCUTIO'S EXIT

This line is, "A plague o' both your houses!"

When Charles Lindbergh made his record-breaking transatlantic solo flight in 1927, the whole world hailed him as a hero, but he was also a

Suggested Telegrams
Welcoming Captain Lindbergh
On His Home-Coming
Your choice for 30 CENTS

**Check the one you want to send and write your name. That's all; we do the rest.
Your message will be delivered on a blank especially decorated for the occasion.**

1 America's heart goes out to you. Welcome home.

2 Glad you're back, Captain. When you fly out this way drop in and see us.

3 A marvelous flight, a royal reception, a perfect attitude on your part—truly it's a gorgeous record, Captain. Welcome home.

4 You've done as much for the good relations of the United States with Europe as for the progress of aviation. America greets you.

5 We're for you a hundred million strong. Welcome home.

6 Back seats for George and Albert. We're prouder than kings. Welcome home.

7 Here's to Lindbergh—master pilot, superb diplomat, idol of a dozen nations! America welcomes you home.

8 For superb courage, high intensity of purpose and profound common-sense, you are unsurpassed. America greets you.

9 You're now a citizen of the world, but you'll always be our own particular pride. Welcome home.

10 There is not one American who doesn't feel an individual, personal pride in your glorious achievement. Welcome home.

11 The flight was wonderful, the reception marvelous, but we are proudest of your modesty and eternal sense of the fitness of things. Welcome home.

12 Time will not dim the splendor of your achievement. Welcome home.

13 The whole nation takes pride in your achievement. Welcome home.

14 It's the most glorious individual achievement in the history of the human race. Welcome home.

15 The............Club of.........sends greetings. In the good old American way you put it over and now we're glad to have you home again.

16 Lindbergh's fame is America's glory. Welcome home, Captain.

17 It's true you belong to history but you also belong to us. Welcome home.

18 ....Chamber of Commerce extends you an invitation to visit our town.

19 Gangway, Kings and Potentates! The American people want to greet their own. Welcome home.

20 With welling heart America greets her knight of the air and ambassador of good-will.

(Sign here)...

Other expressions at regular rates
THE WESTERN UNION TELEGRAPH CO.

twenty-five-year-old whose parents worried about him. So it's not surprising that the American ambassador to France sent the following reassuring cable to Lindbergh's parents in Detroit from Paris:

WARMEST CONGRATULATIONS STOP YOUR INCOMPARABLE SON HAS
HONORED ME BY BEING MY GUEST STOP HE IS IN FINE CONDITION
AND SLEEPING SWEETLY UNDER UNCLE SAMS ROOF.

Even to his future wife, Sara Haardt, cynical curmudgeon, journalist, and editor H. L. Mencken would sometimes show his misanthropic side, as he did in this 1926 holiday greeting:

ALL THE USUAL INSINCERE FELICITATIONS ON THE WORST OF ALL
CHRISTIAN HOLIDAYS. THIS IS A SWELL TOWN. HAVING A SWELL
TIME. EVERYBODY IS TREATING ME SWELL

It's hard to imagine a more unlikely pairing than the shuffling cowboy and commentator Will Rogers and the ultrasophisticated Noël Coward, but the former sent the following to the latter in 1928:

YOU GAVE ME SUCH A GRAND EVENING IN THE TEATRE LAST WEEK I
FEEL I MUST WIRE AND TELL YOU.

On December 19, 1939, after *Gone With the Wind* had its wildly successful premiere in Atlanta, playwright Moss Hart sent this facetious telegram to producer David O. Selznick:

OH, ALL RIGHT. GO AHEAD AND HAVE A VULGAR COMMERCIAL
SUCCESS!

When former actress Helen Gahagan Douglas (whose biggest hit on Broadway had been in a play called *Tonight or Never*) was running against Richard Nixon for a Senate seat in 1950, she received the following telegram from Greta Garbo on the day of the race:

HELEN—TONIGHT OR NEVER, GOD BLESS YOU.

The outrageously flamboyant—and bisexual—actress Tallulah Bankhead is reputed to have sent a deliberately ambiguous telegram to Bette Davis on the premiere performance of her stage act wishing her "kisses on her opening." This was not unlike Noël Coward's first-night telegram to his dear childhood chum, Gertrude Lawrence:

A WARM HAND ON YOUR OPENING.

Then, when Gertie married Richard Aldrich, Coward wired her this facetious congratulatory verse:

DEAR MRS A. HOORAY HOORAY

AT LAST YOU ARE DEFLOWERED

ON THIS AS EVERY OTHER DAY

I LOVE YOU, NOEL COWARD

And on the premiere performance of his play *A Streetcar Named Desire*, Tennessee Williams sent the following jazzy, if not particularly politically correct, wire to its star, Marlon Brando, who played Stanley Kowalski:

RIDE OUT BOY AND SEND IT SOLID. FROM THE GREASY POLACK YOU
WILL SOMEDAY ARRIVE AT THE GLOOMY DANE.

```
CLASS OF SERVICE
This is a fast message
unless its deferred char-
acter is indicated by the
proper symbol.                                                    SYMBOLS
                  WESTERN UNION                    DL=Day Letter
                          TELEGRAM                      NL=Night Letter
                         W. P. MARSHALL, PRESIDENT    1201  LT=International
                                                              Letter Telegram
The filing time shown in the date line on domestic telegrams is STANDARD TIME at point of origin. Time of receipt is STANDARD TIME at point of destination

LLE272 0C391

0 NRA067 PD=NEWPORT BEACH CALIF 14 1216P PDT=

SENATOR JOHN F KENNEDY=

     SPORTS ARENA LOSA=
                                    1960 JUL 14 PM 12 45
FIRST=CONGRATULATIONS. SECOND=DO YOU NEED A HARP

PLAYER IN YOUR CABINET. THIRD=MY BEST TO YOUR MA AND PA=

     HARPO MARX=...

THE COMPANY WILL APPRECIATE SUGGESTIONS FROM ITS PATRONS CONCERNING ITS SERVICE
```

Harpo Marx to Senator John F. Kennedy, after Kennedy received
the Democratic nomination for president.

⌘∼⌘

On the occasion of Groucho Marx's seventy-first birthday in 1961,
songwriter Irving Berlin sent him this lyrical wire:

THE WORLD WOULD NOT BE IN SUCH A SNARL, HAD MARX BEEN
GROUCHO INSTEAD OF KARL.

In 1906, at the age of fourteen, Groucho Marx appeared with seven
other boys in the vaudeville act *Gus Edwards' Postal Telegraph Boys,*
singing and telling jokes, dressed in a telegram messenger uniform in a
telegraph office.

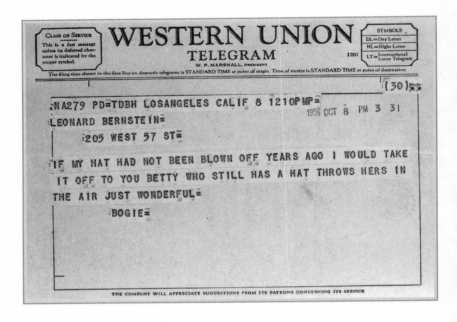

Humphrey Bogart to his friend Leonard Bernstein
after watching one of his *Omnibus* television shows.

And on October 25, 1962, upon hearing that John Steinbeck had just
won the Nobel Prize for literature, fellow novelist John O'Hara sent him
the following wire:

> CONGRATULATIONS. I CAN THINK OF ONLY ONE OTHER AUTHOR I'D
> RATHER SEE GET IT.

On the occasion of the Dean Martin Friar's Club roast on November 8,
1959, Elvis Presley and Colonel Tom Parker sent this telegram, which is
not shy about promoting the titles of Elvis's hit songs:

> CONGRATULATIONS AND GOOD ROCKING TONIGHT—WITH SO MANY
> FRIENDS LOVING YOU—AND FEELING LIKE A TEDDY BEAR—WE KNOW
> THAT YOU MUST BE ALL SHOOK UP—SO DON'T, I BEG OF YOU, DON'T

When Samuel Beckett won the 1969 Nobel Prize for literature, among the numerous telegrams he received was one from a Parisian named Georges Godot, who apologized for having kept him waiting.

BE CRUEL, I'M COUNTING ON YOU NOT TO GET ON JAILHOUSE ROCK, TREAT ME NICE OR YOU'RE NOTHING BUT A HOUND DOG.

Comedians were perpetually sending humorous telegrams to each other. Here's a birthday greeting from George Burns to Bob Hope, sent in 1991:

I HEARD ON THE RADIO THAT YOU'RE 88, SO I'M SENDING YOU THIS WIRE. IF YOU'RE NOT 88 SEND IT BACK AND I'LL SEND IT TO YOU WHEN YOU ARE.

ACCEPTANCE AND REGRETS

THE DOORBELL WOULD RING and the uniformed messenger would hand you your invitation to this or that, and you would either accept or decline on the spot or wire back later.

A typical—and oft-quoted—example of droll British wit: a telegram from Charles Beresford, the first Baron Bedford, to Edward, Prince of Wales, replying to a dinner invitation at short notice:

VERY SORRY CAN'T COME. LIE FOLLOWS BY POST.

George Bernard Shaw was known for his bitingly caustic repartee; in this case, referring to the initial performance of *Pygmalion,* he meets his match in the redoubtable Winston Churchill.

Alexander Graham Bell to Sir Thomas Biddulph on January 2, 1878, in response to a request from Queen Victoria to demonstrate his newly invented telephone.

❦

From Shaw:

AM RESERVING TWO TICKETS FOR YOU FOR MY PREMIERE. COME AND BRING A FRIEND—IF YOU HAVE ONE.

And Churchill's retort:

IMPOSSIBLE TO BE PRESENT FOR THE FIRST PERFORMANCE. WILL ATTEND THE SECOND—IF THERE IS ONE.

This is *New Yorker* founding editor Harold Ross's irreverent response to an invitation from Bennett Cerf and Donald Klopfer of Random House to a reception for Gertrude Stein and Alice B. Toklas, sent October 31, 1934:

NUTS TO GERTRUDE STEIN. IF YOU WANT TO PLAY BACKGAMMON TONIGHT TELEPHONE ME.

When Jack Benny wanted to do a parody of one of Eugene O'Neill's plays—possibly *Ah, Wilderness!*—on his weekly radio show in January of 1935, O'Neill demonstrated in this telegram that he was willing to go along with the gag:

```
GIVE BENNY MY CONSENT TO GO AHEAD WITHOUT CHARGE. . . . THINK
BENNY VERY AMUSING GUY AND BELIEVE KIDDING MY STUFF EVERY
ONCE IN A WHILE HAS VERY HEALTHY EFFECT AND KEEPS ME OUT OF
DEAD SOLEMN ILLUSTRIOUS STUFFED SHIRT ACADEMICIAN CLASS.
```

Informed that the play based on his novel *Of Mice and Men* had been given the Critics' Circle award, John Steinbeck responded to the Critics' Circle on April 23, 1938:

```
GENTLEMEN: I HAVE ALWAYS CONSIDERED CRITICS AS AUTHORS
NATURAL ENEMIES SO I FEEL VERY MILLENIAL BUT A LITTLE TIMID
TO BE LYING DOWN WITH THE LION THIS DISTURBANCE OF THE
NATURAL BALANCE MIGHT CAUSE A PLAGUE OF PLAYWRIGHTS I AM
HIGHLY HONORED BY YOUR GOOD OPINION BUT MY EGOTISTICAL
GRATIFICATION IS RUINED BY A SNEAKING SUSPICION THAT GEORGE
KAUFMAN AND THE CAST DESERVE THEM MORE THAN I. I DO HOWEVER
TAKE THE RESPONSIBILITY OF THANKING YOU.
```

When Russian novelist and poet Boris Pasternak was awarded the Nobel Prize in 1958, he telegraphed his acceptance on October 26 of that year:

```
IMMENSELY GRATEFUL, TOUCHED, PROUD, ASTONISHED, ABASHED.
```

His tone changed four days later, however, when, after criticism by the Soviets, he reversed his position and rejected the prize in light of its significance "in the community to which I belong," hoping that his "voluntary" decision would not be met with ill will.

As the curtain was about to rise on Camelot in early 1961, President-elect John Kennedy invited eighty-six-year-old poet Robert Frost to participate in his inauguration. Frost accepted the invitation by telegram:

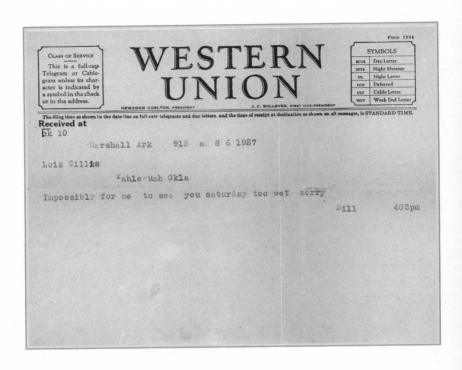

WESTERN UNION

CLASS OF SERVICE

This is a full-rate Telegram or Cablegram unless its character is indicated by a symbol in the check or in the address.

NEWCOMB CARLTON, PRESIDENT   J. C. WILLEVER, FIRST VICE-PRESIDENT

SYMBOLS

BLUE	Day Letter
NITE	Night Message
NL	Night Letter
LCO	Deferred
CLT	Cable Letter
WLT	Week End Letter

The filing time as shown in the date line on full-rate telegrams and day letters, and the time of receipt at destination as shown on all messages, is STANDARD TIME.

Received at

bk 10

Marshall Ark   915 a 8 6 1927

Lois Gillis

        Tahlequah Okla

Impossible for me to see you saturday too wet sorry

                                        Bill   403pm

IF YOU CAN BEAR AT YOUR AGE THE HONOR OF BEING MADE
PRESIDENT OF THE UNITED STATES, I OUGHT TO BE ABLE AT MY
AGE TO BEAR THE HONOR OF TAKING SOME PART IN YOUR
INAUGURATION. I MAY NOT BE EQUAL TO IT BUT I CAN ACCEPT IT
FOR MY CAUSE—THE ARTS, POETRY—NOW FOR THE FIRST TIME TAKEN
INTO THE AFFAIRS OF STATESMEN. . . .

When John Lennon was awarded his MBE—Membership in the Order
of the British Empire—he at first accepted it, but later sent it back, taking advantage of the occasion to make a political statement in the telegram he sent to Queen Elizabeth:

YOUR MAJESTY, I AM RETURNING THIS MBE IN PROTEST AGAINST
BRITAIN'S INVOLVEMENT IN THE NIGERIA-BIAFRA SCENE, AGAINST

OUR SUPPORT OF AMERICA IN VIETNAM AND AGAINST COLD TURKEY
SLIPPING DOWN THE CHARTS. WITH LOVE, JOHN LENNON

SEND MONEY STOP

AMONG THE MOST moving telegrams on record are those in which some of our greatest authors literally plead with their friends, agents, and publishers for enough money to keep them going.

The august author of such classics as *Lord Jim* and *Heart of Darkness,* Joseph Conrad, was not above wiring his agent, J. B. Pinker, when he was in dire straits, as he did from the Palace Hotel in Milan on October 20, 1914:

> . . . PLEASE SEND MONEY THROUGH COOK TELEGRAPHICALLY TO SAVE TIME AND EXPENSE HERE IN AMOUNTS OF FORTY POUNDS ON THREE SUCCESSIVE DAYS TOGETHER HUNDRED AND TWENTY IS ABSOLUTELY NECESSARY OWING PECULIAR CIRCUMSTANCES . . .

Sometimes, when the money did show signs of coming in, a writer's excitement would buzz over the telegraph wires, as in this example from poet Carl Sandburg to his wife, Paula, sent April 4, 1925:

> HARCOURT WIRES BOOK SERIAL RIGHTS SOLD TO PICTORIAL REVIEW FOR $20,000. FIX THE FLIVVER AND BUY A WILD EASTER HAT.

When Harold Ober, a young literary agent with the Paul R. Reynolds agency, took on the twenty-three-year-old F. Scott Fitzgerald as a client in 1919, it was the beginning of an association that would last through most of Fitzgerald's career. Much of their telegraphed correspondence was based on the writer's desperate need for money.

March 6, 1922:

> . . . THANKS FOR TWO HUNDRED AWFUL MESS IN CHECK BOOK CAN
> YOU DEPOSIT FOUR HUNDRED MORE IMMEDIATELY. . . .

May 3, 1922:

> IF WARNER CANNOT DEPOSIT TWELVE HUNDRED BY THURSDAY NIGHT
> WIRE ME

March 18, 1928:

> MY INCOME TAX CHECK IS DUE IN NEWYORK TOMORROW MONDAY CAN
> YOU POSSIBLY DEPOSIT THREE HUNDRED FIFTY DOLLARS TO KEEP ME
> OUT OF JAIL STOP

December 9, 1928:

> I HAVE ACCIDENTALLY OVERDRAWN MY ACCOUNT DOWN HERE I HATE
> TO BOTHER YOU BUT CAN YOU WIRE FIVE HUNDRED. . . .

February 21, 1934:

> WANT TO DECIDE NOW HOW TO RAISE MONEY TO TIDE ME OVER THE
> MONTH BEFORE FINISHING FINAL BOOK REVISION . . . LUNCHING
> WITH CLARK GABLE TOMORROW AND WANT TO KNOW PRESENT STATUS
> OF GATSDY [sic] AS HE WOULD LIKE TO PLAY IT . . .

December 28, 1935:

> HAVE TRIED LIFE ON SUBSISTANCE LEVEL AND IT DOESN'T WORK
> STOP I THOUGHT IF I COULD HAVE THIS MONEY I COULD HOLD MY
> HEAD UP AND GO ON STOP . . .

May 11, 1937:

> TO REMAIN HERE AND EAT MUST HAVE ONE HUNDRED AND THIRTY
> TODAY . . .

October 4, 1939:

> PLEASE ANSWER ABOUT TUITION MONEY STOP YOU HAVE NO IDEA HOW
> MUCH A HUNDRED DOLLARS MEANS NOW

THE COMPANY WILL APPRECIATE SUGGESTIONS FROM ITS PATRONS CONCERNING ITS SERVICE

1201-S

WESTERN UNION

CLASS OF SERVICE		SYMBOLS
This is a full-rate Telegram or Cablegram unless its deferred character is indicated by a suitable symbol above or preceding the address.	R. B. WHITE PRESIDENT — NEWCOMB CARLTON CHAIRMAN OF THE BOARD — J. C. WILLEVER FIRST VICE-PRESIDENT	DL = Day Letter NM = Night Message NL = Night Letter LC = Deferred Cable NLT = Cable Night Letter Ship Radiogram

The filing time shown in the date line on telegrams and day letters is STANDARD TIME at point of origin. Time of receipt is STANDARD TIME at point of destination.

Received at 59 Elm St., New Canaan, Conn.

NAC47 71 NL=TDS ENCINO CALIF JUL 3

MAXWELL PERKINS=

NEW CANAAN, CONN.

=HAVE BEEN WRITING IN BED WITH TUBERCULOSIS UNDER DOCTORS
NURSES CARE SIS ARRIVING WEST. OBER HAS DECIDED NOT TO
BACK ME THOUGH I PAID BACK EVERY PENNY AND EIGHT THOUSAND
COMMISSION. AM GOING TO WORK THURSDAY IN STUDIO AT FIFTEEN
HUNDRED CAN YOU LEND ME SIX HUNDRED FOR ONE WEEK BY WIRE
TO BANK AMERICA CULVERCITY. SCOTTIE HOSPITAL WITH
APPENDIX AND AM ABSOLUTELY WITHOUT FUNDS. PLEASE DO NOT
ASK OBERS COOPERATION=

SCOTT.

JUL 4 730A.

WESTERN UNION MESSENGERS ARE AVAILABLE FOR THE DELIVERY OF NOTES AND PACKAGES

F. Scott Fitzgerald to Maxwell Perkins in 1938,
one of his frequent pleas for financial aid.

And on October 6, 1936, when Fitzgerald was experiencing delays in accessing his inheritance from his mother, he wired his editor, Maxwell Perkins, to tide him over.

... WHAT DO YOU DO WHEN YOU CANT PAY TYPIST OR BUY
MEDICINES OR CIGARETTS STOP. ...

Fitzgerald also turned to his friend Gerald Murphy for money on September 21, 1939:

WAS TAKEN ILL OUT HERE LAST APRIL AND CONFINED TO BED FIVE
MONTHS AND NOW UP AND WORKING BUT COMPLETELY CLEANED OUT

FINANCIALLY WANT DESPERATELY TO CONTINUE DAUGHTER AT VASSAR
CAN YOU LEND 360 DOLLARS FOR ONE MONTH

To which came the reply the following day:

DISTRESSED YOU HAD BEEN ILL WE HAD BEEN WONDERING ABOUT YOU
MONEY READY WHERE SHALL I SEND IT PLEASE TAKE CARE OF
YOURSELF NOW. . . .

And Fitzgerald's on the same day:

THANK YOU STOP THIS WAS THE FIRST EXPERIENCE OF PERSONAL
LOAN YOUR WIRE TOOK THE CUTTING EDGE OFF IT WOULD IT BE
POSSIBLE TO TELEGRAPH THE SUM TO BANK OF AMERICA CULVER
CITY CALIFORNIA TODAY OR TOMORROW LOVE TO ALL AM WRITING=

In 1928, a few years after Ernest Hemingway began what would be his long-lasting relationship with Scribner's, Hemingway, too, turned to editor Maxwell Perkins in a moment of crisis:

PLEASE WIRE $100 IMMEDIATELY WESTERNUNION NORTH
PHILADELPHIA STATION MY FATHER DEAD MUST GET FIRST TRAIN
CHICAGO

This was followed by a second telegram three hours later: Hemingway had been bailed out by his friend F. Scott Fitzgerald, who was for once on the other side of the money-lending game:

DISREGARD WIRE GOT MONEY FROM SCOTT=

From Hollywood where he was working on screenplays, novelist Dashiell Hammett wrote to his publisher, Alfred A. Knopf, on April 29, 1931:

IN DESPERATE NEED OF ALL THE MONEY I CAN FIND STOP CAN YOU
DEPOSIT THOUSAND DOLLARS IN MY ACCOUNT IRVING TRUST COMPANY
FIFTY NINTH STREET BRANCH AND DEDUCT FROM MONTHLY PAYMENTS
STOP IF CONVENIENT PLEASE WIRE ME AS SOON AS POSSIBLE
STOP. . . .

WESTERN UNION

CLASS OF SERVICE

This is a full-rate Telegram or Cable-gram unless its de-ferred character is in-dicated by a suitable sign above or preced-ing the address.

SIGNS

DL = Day Letter
NM = Night Message
NL = Night Letter
LCO = Deferred Cable
NLT = Cable Letter
WLT = Week-End Letter

NEWCOMB CARLTON, PRESIDENT   J. C. WILLEVER, FIRST VICE-PRESIDENT

The filing time as shown in the date line on full-rate telegrams and day letters, and the time of receipt at destination as shown on all messages, is STANDARD TIME.

Received at Main Office, 608-610 South Spring St., Los Angeles, Calif. ALWAYS OPEN

NB31 50 NL=NEWYORK NY 20   928 SEP 21 AM 12 39

WALT DISNEY STUDIO=

2719 HYPERION AVE HOLLYWOOD CALIF=

KNOW OF NO OTHER IMMEDIATE EXPENSES ADVISE YOU IMMEDIATELY

GET AS LARGE A LOAN AS POSSIBLE MUST HAVE SUFFICIENT CASH TO

CARRY THINGS THROUGH PROPERLY DONT THINK THIRTY FIVE HUNDRED

ENOUGH TRY FOR MORE OUR FUTURE DEPENDS ON FIRST PICTURE

THEREFORE AM NOT SPARING EXPENSE TO MAKE IT GOOD REGARDS=

=WALT.

THE QUICKEST, SUREST AND SAFEST WAY TO SEND MONEY IS BY TELEGRAPH OR CABLE

Walt Disney to his brother Roy in 1928, about raising money to record
Steamboat Willie, his first cartoon with synchronized sound.

❦

and again on August 6, 1931:

WANT TO RETURN TO NEWYORK NEXT WEEK BUT AM IN TERRIBLE
FINANCIAL DIFFICULTY STOP CAN YOU DEPOSIT TWENTYFIVE
HUNDRED DOLLARS TO MY ACCOUNT. . . .

William Faulkner was another writer who often found himself in economic peril and would contact his agent, Harold Ober (the same belea-
guered Ober so frequently hounded by Fitzgerald), as he did on January
16, 1941:

```
WIRE ME COLLECT WHAT POSSIBILITY OF ANY SUM WHATEVER AND
WHEN FROM ANY MSS OF MINE YOU HAVE. URGENTLY NEED ONE
HUNDRED BY SATURDAY.
```

And then there was poet Dylan Thomas who, despite his literary success and popular renown, struggled all his life to eke out enough money to support his family, a struggle reflected in this telegram written to arts patron Ellen Borden Stevenson, former wife of Adlai Stevenson, just two weeks before Thomas died in 1953:

```
DEAR ELLEN OSCAR WILLIAMS HAS TOLD ME THAT YOU WOULD LIKE
ME TO PRESENT MY PLAY ENTITLED 'UNDER MILKWOOD' IN CHICAGO
I SHALL BE DELIGHTED TO DO SO WITH OR WITHOUT CAST BUT NOT
WITHOUT CASH
```

But believe it or not, writers did have concerns other than monetary ones.

Two major American writers, Bret Harte and Mark Twain, got together in 1876 and collaborated on a play titled *Ah Sin,* a mystery-comedy centering on a Chinese laundryman. At the conclusion of the premiere performance, Charles T. Parsloe, who played the lead, stepped forward and read the following telegram from Mark Twain to the audience:

```
I AM ON THE SICK-LIST AND THEREFORE CANNOT COME TO
WASHINGTON; BUT I HAVE PREPARED TWO SPEECHES—ONE TO DELIVER
IN EVENT OF FAILURE OF THE PLAY, AND THE OTHER IF
SUCCESSFUL. PLEASE TELL ME WHICH I SHALL SEND. MAY BE
BETTER TO PUT IT TO VOTE.
```

The audience cheered the letter and, when it was put to a vote, decided unanimously that the play had been a success.

Twain, like many writers, felt that it was often easier to write at length than to keep a piece short and succinct. Thus, when he received a telegram from a publisher that read:

```
NEED 2-PAGE SHORT STORY TWO DAYS.
```

WESTERN UNION

CLASS OF SERVICE	SYMBOLS
This is a full-rate Telegram or Cablegram unless its deferred character is indicated by a suitable symbol above or preceding the address.	DL=Day Letter
	NT=Overnight Telegram
	LC=Deferred Cable
	NLT=Cable Night Letter

R. B. WHITE
PRESIDENT

NEWCOMB CARLTON
CHAIRMAN OF THE BOARD

J. C. WILLEVER
FIRST VICE-PRESIDENT

(56)

DEC 17

The filing time shown in the date line on telegrams and day letters is STANDARD TIME at point of origin. Time of receipt is STANDARD TIME at point of destination

SG101 64 DL VIA RCA=COYOACAN DELDISTRIOFEDERAL 16 1200

MISS EMMY LOU PACKARD, CARE STENDAHAL GALLERIES=

3006 WILSHIRE BLVD LOSA=

EMMY LUCHA LETTER LEFT THIS MORNING AFRAID ARRIVE LATE WOULD
LIKE ASK YOU ENORMOUS FAVOR TELL ARENSBERG PAINTING BIRTH
BELONGS KAUFMANN STOP WISH YOU COULD CONVINCE THEM TO BUY
INSTEAD "I WITH MY NURSE" SAME SIZE SAME PRICE 300 BECAUSE
NEED BUCKS VERY URGENTLY BEFORE FIRST JANUARY PLEASE MAKE ALL
EFFORTS AS POSSIBLE STOP SENDING PHOTO LET ME KNOW RESULTS
MILLION THANKS LOVE=

FRIDA KAHLO.

300 BUCKS. *THE COMPANY WILL APPRECIATE SUGGESTIONS FROM ITS PATRONS CONCERNING ITS SERVICE

Frida Kahlo to Emmy Lou Packard on December 17, 1941, urging Packard to sell
one of Kahlo's best-known works to Walter Arensberg for a much needed $300.

⚜

Twain wired back:

NO CAN DO 2 PAGES TWO DAYS. CAN DO 30 PAGES 2 DAYS. NEED 30
DAYS TO DO 2 PAGES.

In his frantic efforts to support his family, F. Scott Fitzgerald sometimes
came up with some pretty bizarre ideas for articles, such as this one that
he wired to Harold Ober on July 14, 1927:

WOULD [SATURDAY EVENING] POST BE INTERESTED IN ARTICLE
TITLE QUOTE SISSY AMERICA UNQUOTE EMBODYING IDEA OF TOO
MUCH WOMAN EDUCATION AND GENERAL INEFFECTUALITY OF MALE IN
ANY LINE EXCEPT BUSINESS STOP NOT PROPOSING ANY REMEDY NOT

PUTTING ANY BLAME ANYWHERE BUT ON THE MAN FOR LETTING
CONTROL SLIP FROM HIS HANDS . . .

Writers then and now have pored over classics and reference books to find the perfect titles for their own books and Hemingway was no exception, as seen in this April 22, 1940, wire from Havana, Cuba, to Maxwell Perkins:

PROVISIONAL TITLE IS QUOTES FOR WHOM THE BELL TOLLS UNQUOTE
FROM PASSAGE JOHN DONNE OXFORD BOOK OF ENGLISH PROSE BOTTOM
PAGE ONE SEVENTY ONE STARTING QUOTES NO MAN IS AN ISLAND
ETC STOP PLEASE REGISTER TITLE= IMMEDIATELY. . . .

Fitzgerald, too, agonized over the titles of his novels. He was ambivalent about *The Great Gatsby* almost until the moment it went to press. His first idea was *Trimalchio at West Egg;* then, at the very last minute, he cabled Perkins:

CRAZY ABOUT TITLE UNDER THE RED WHITE AND BLUE STOP WHAT
WOULD DELAY BE?

Fortunately, Perkins was able to dissuade him.

Fitzgerald was also deeply invested in the graphics and designs of the covers of his novels. On January 28, 1934, he wired Perkins about the jacket for *Tender Is the Night:*

DECIDED REGRETFULLY DON'T LIKE JACKET MUCH TOO ITALIANATE
TOO RED AND YELLOW SKY DOES NOT GIVE WHITE AND BLUE SPARKLE
OF FRENCH RIVIERA AM SENDING REAL RIVIERA POSTER SHOWING
MAXWELL PARISH COLORS IF IMPRACTICAL WOULD PREFER SHENTON
WOODCUT

When Vladimir Nabokov's massive family chronicle, *Ada,* was published in March of 1969, it's not surprising that this exacting novelist would find some causes for objection, as seen in these two telegrams, the first to McGraw-Hill editor Frank E. Taylor:

LOVELY FAT ADA BUT NOTHING
IS PERFECT IN LIFE BAD
MISPRINT IN PENULT LINE LAST
PAGE OF BOOK VIEW DESCRIBED
SHOULD BE VIEW DESCRIED.

And then to *Playboy* magazine, which had gained the rights to reprint an excerpt:

DEAR PLAYBOY ADA FRAGMENTS
BEAUTIFULLY PRINTED BUT
GOODNESS WHAT ILLUSTRATIONS
THAT IMPROBABLE YOUNG MAMMAL
AND TWO REVOLTING FROGS

PIQUE

Just as surprisingly tender messages were sent across the public telegraph lines, so were malevolent feelings, ranging from mild irritation to white hot rage.

In the 1920s, there was an explosion of public interest in the medium of radio, the content of which was entirely unregulated. When Secretary of Commerce Herbert Hoover took control of the "wireless telephone" out of the hands of the Bureau of Navigation and began setting some limits on radio licenses, he received this furious telegram from famed melodramatic radio evangelist Aimee Semple McPherson:

PLEASE ORDER YOUR MINIONS OF SATAN TO LEAVE MY STATION
ALONE. YOU CANNOT EXPECT THE ALMIGHTY TO ABIDE BY YOUR

WAVELENGTH NONSENSE. WHEN I OFFER MY PRAYERS TO HIM, I MUST
FIT IN WITH HIS WAVE RECEPTION.

Sister Aimee later eloped with the Commerce Department representative sent to explain the realities of federal regulation to her.

Long before the phrase "Angry Young Men" was applied to British playwrights of the 1950s, there were several angry young and not so young writers venting their rage, often with a strong component of paranoia, over the telegraph wires. Jack London had notoriously contentious relationships with people he dealt with. In May of 1913, feeling that he was being wrongfully treated, he wanted to sever his relationship with the Century publishing company and sent them several irate telegrams, one of which read in part:

> . . . BETWEEN YOU AND ME AND THE WORLD YOUR ATTITUDE IS
> PATENTLY MERCENARY. YOU WOULD EAT DIRT BEFORE YOU WOULD
> FOREGO THE POUND OF FLESH. YOU WOULD SELL YOURSELF AND YOUR
> COMPANY'S GOOD NAME FOR A HANDFUL OF SILVER. PLEASE
> REMEMBER THAT I AM THE LIVEST WIRE YOU EVER GOT YOUR HANDS
> ON THAT I AM NOT A MONEY SCAVENGER AND THAT THE MILLIONS
> WHO READ JOHN BARLEYCORN WILL LATER ON READ ABOUT YOU. . . .
> WHEN YOU ARE DUST IN YOUR GRAVES THE ECHOES IN THE BRAINS
> OF THOSE YET UNBORN WILL STIR YOUR DUST. . . . I WANT AN
> ANSWER TO THIS AND I WANT YOUR ANSWER TO BE THAT YOU WOULD
> RATHER BE MEN THAN MONEY GRUBBERS.

Later that year, London was still ranting about real and imagined slights and deceptions. This telegraphed vitriol was directed at Frank A. Garbutt, a Paramount Pictures executive, and was in reference to copyright questions:

> . . . I SHALL NEVER WHIMPER. THE POINT IS I WANT FIGHT.
> HAMMER. BANG. BETWEEN THE EYES. STRAIGHT FROM THE SHOULDER.
> RAP RAP RAP . . . THE JEW IS MAKING US LOOK LIKE THIRTY
> CENTS. . . .

Frank Mason was the Paris chief of Hearst's International News Service who hired Ernest Hemingway in 1922 to be its correspondent in Constantinople. When the journalist later filed for his expenses, Mason asked for his receipts and a complete accounting. Enraged, Hemingway wired back:

SUGGEST YOU UPSTICK BOOKS ASSWARDS.

"A man high in American business life has been quoted as remarking that elimination of the word 'please' from all telegrams would save the American public millions of dollars annually. Despite this apparent endorsement of such procedure, however, it is unlikely that the public will lightly relinquish the use of this really valuable word. 'Please' is to the language of social and business intercourse what art and music are to everyday, humdrum existence. Fortunes might be saved by discounting the manufacture of musical instruments and by closing the art galleries, but no one thinks of suggesting such a procedure. . . . By all means let us retain the word 'please' in our telegraphic correspondence."
—"How to Write Telegrams Properly," 1928

Almost twenty years later, in 1941, Hemingway was in the midst of a bitter contractual dispute with his long-term publisher, Charles Scribner, and sent a choleric telegram about it to his editor, Maxwell Perkins, part of which reads:

AM PERFECTLY WILLING COMMIT HARIKARI RATHER THAN SUBMIT TO FURTHER GYPPING . . . PLEASE TELL CHARLIE THAT IT IS NOT GOOD POLICY TO CUT STAKES OUT OF HIS RACE HORSES TO MAKE A DIME OR WHATEVER HORSE MEAT BRINGS A POUND. . . .

In this angry telegram sent to Richard Madden on October 18, 1937, Eugene O'Neill expresses his views on cross-racial casting, in particular concerning his play *The Hairy Ape:*

UNDER NO CIRCUMSTANCES WILL I PERMIT PRODUCTION NEGRO ADAPTION OF HAIRY APE STOP IT IS STUPID AND RIDICULOUS STOP. . . . PLAY MUST BE DONE AS WRITTEN AND ONLY JONES AND ALL GODS CHILLUN CAN BE GIVEN BY NEGROES IN FUTURE I AM NOT INTERESTED IN FREAK THEATRE WHERE WHITE PLAYS ARE FAKED INTO BLACK PLAYS STOP IF NEGROES CANNOT PLAY WHITE PARTS AS WHITES HAVE PLAYED NEGROES THEY SHOULD NOT BE IN THEATRE. . . .

John Steinbeck was aghast at the final version of the Hitchcock film *Lifeboat,* for which he had written the script, and wrote as much to his agent, Annie Laurie Williams, on February 19, 1944:

. . . IN VIEW OF THE FACT THAT MY SCRIPT FOR THE PICTURE LIFEBOAT WAS DISTORTED IN PRODUCTION SO THAT ITS LINE AND INTENTION HAS BEEN CHANGED AND BECAUSE THE PICTURE SEEMS TO ME TO BE DANGEROUS TO THE AMERICAN WAR EFFORT I REQUEST THAT MY NAME BE REMOVED FROM ANY CONNECTION WITH ANY SHOWING OF THIS FILM.

When acclaimed novelist William Faulkner submitted the manuscript of *Absalom, Absalom* to his publisher, it fell into the hands of a junior editor when his own editor was away. Faulkner received a missive from this

After robbing the men carrying the $9,000 payroll of the local coal company, Butch Cassidy and his accomplice Eliza fled to Robbers' Roost, first cutting telegraph wires to prevent the news of the robbery from spreading to lawmen along their escape route.

underling criticizing his syntax and the length of his sentences, and advising him to begin again. Understandably incensed, Faulkner fired off this telegram:

WHO THE HELL ARE YOU?

Faulkner's temper was roused again in June 1954. He was adamantly averse to having a photograph of himself appear on any of his books, as evidenced by the following two telegrams. The first was sent to Bennett Cerf, head of Random House, on June 24, 1954:

DEAR BENNETT. LET ME WRITE THE BOOKS. LET SOMEONE WHO WANTS IT HAVE THE PUBLICITY. I PROTEST WHOLE IDEA BUT WILL NEVER CONSENT TO MY PICTURE ON COVER. ESTIMATE WHAT REFUSAL WILL COST RANDOM HOUSE AND I WILL PAY IT.

And again, three years later, to Douglas Borgstedt:

STILL DON'T WANT TO BE PHOTOGRAPHED . . . BUT WILL SUBMIT FOR ONE THOUSAND DOLLARS IN ADVANCE.

In Hollywood, too, there was a constant cross fire of hostile salvos, much of it the result of bruised egos. Case in point: Jack Warner was the youngest in a family of twelve children and the one of the four Warner brothers chosen to run the day-to-day business of the studio bearing their name, although he was by no means independent of Harry, the business head, Sam, the chief executive, and Albert, the treasurer. Both supersensitive and highly insensitive, Jack often had run-ins with his producers, directors, writers, and stars, and not infrequently expressed his injured feelings in telegraph form. On November 30, 1943, he vented his feelings to publicity head Charles Einfeld:

WANT YOU INFORM ALL PRODUCERS DIPLOMATICALLY IN GIVING STORIES OR INTERVIEWS THAT I SHALL BE DEFINITELY ACCREDITED AS EXECUTIVE PRODUCER OR IN CHARGE PRODUCTION. SICK, TIRED EVERYONE TAKING ALL CREDIT AND I BECOME SMALL BOY AND DOING MOST OF WORK . . .

> "I at sixteen, after classes at high school, would be cutting a dashing figure in a khaki quasi-military uniform as a part-time messenger boy delivering telegrams for Western Union, in office buildings in Manhattan weekdays, on a bicycle weekends to residences in Brooklyn, and mostly exulting in my duties with a sense of adventure and attentive curiosity. . . . At long last I could sport my dashing Western Union messenger garb right in Coney Island as I rode my bicycle back and forth between home and office . . . but a hovering dread I forged in my imagination dealt with the risk that sooner or later I would have to deliver to a family I knew a yellow envelope stamped with two red stars. In the days of the telegram, before the facsimile machine and the ubiquitous telephone rendered such communications all but obsolete, the two-starred message brought news of tragedy."
> —Joseph Heller, *Now and Then: From Coney Island to Here*

In May of 1944, it was Humphrey Bogart who irritated Warner, as seen in this note he added to a wire to casting director Steve Trilling:

THIS IS REALLY A TOUGH WIRE AND I MEAN TOUGH BECAUSE I AM SICK AND TIRED OF THESE UNGRATEFUL PUPS ANNOYING MY INDIGESTION AND AM NOT GOING TO GIVE ANY MORE THAN ONE STOMACH I HAVE ALREADY GIVEN.

And Bogart's indignant reply, on May 26:

YOU SPEAK OF MY SUCCESS AS IF YOU ALONE WERE RESPONSIBLE FOR IT. I FEEL THAT I HAVE HAD SOMETHING TO DO WITH THAT SUCCESS. . . . YOU ARE USING THE BOX OFFICE VALUE I FORTUNATELY HAVE AT THE MOMENT TO BOLSTER A PICTURE BY FORCING ME INTO A MEDIOCRE PART. . . . YOU HAVE ASSIGNED A DIRECTOR IN WHOM I HAVE NO CONFIDENCE. . . . I HAVE WAITED ONE SOLID YEAR TO GET A FEW UNINTERRUPTED WEEKS TO GAIN

BACK MY HEALTH AND PREVENT A BREAKDOWN. . . . I AM SICK OF
THE STUDIO'S ATTITUDE THAT I AM A HALF-WITTED CHILD.

Of all the divas on the Warners lot, Bette Davis was considered one of the most demanding, especially when it came to getting top billing. In an April 1939 telegram to Jack Warner, this concern went to extreme lengths:

I HAVE BEEN TRYING . . . FOR SOME WEEKS TO GET AN ANSWER FROM
YOU CONCERNING THE TITLE OF MY NEXT PICTURE. I FELT
CONFIDENT THAT YOU WOULD OF YOUR OWN VOLITION CHANGE IT,
CONSIDERING THE FACT THAT THE PLAY FROM WHICH IT IS TAKEN
WAS BOUGHT FOR ME AND WAS CALLED "ELIZABETH THE QUEEN." I
HAVE FOUND OUT TODAY YOU ARE NOT CHANGING IT. YOU OF COURSE
MUST HAVE REALIZED MY INTEREST IN THE TITLE CHANGE CONCERNED
THE BILLING. . . . THE SCRIPT "THE KNIGHT AND THE LADY," LIKE
THE PLAY, IS STILL A WOMAN'S STORY. I THEREFORE FEEL
JUSTIFIED IN REQUESTING FIRST BILLING, WHICH WOULD
AUTOMATICALLY CHANGE THE TITLE, AS THE PRESENT TITLE IS
OBVIOUSLY ONE TO GIVE THE MAN FIRST BILLING. I FEEL SO
JUSTIFIED IN THIS FROM EVERY STANDPOINT THAT YOU FORCE ME TO
REFUSE TO MAKE THE PICTURE UNLESS THE BILLING IS MINE. . . .

Two months later, she was still on the case:

I WAS PROMISED [TITLE] WOULD NOT BE "THE KNIGHT AND THE
LADY." THE PRESENT TITLE "THE LADY AND THE KNIGHT" . . . I
CONSIDER THE SAME THING. . . . YOU HAVE THE CHOICE OF
"ELIZABETH AND ESSEX," "ELIZABETH THE QUEEN," OR "THE LOVE
OF ELIZABETH AND ESSEX." . . .

Needless to say, she won: the film was ultimately titled *The Private Lives of Elizabeth and Essex*.

In contrast to his bashful on-screen image, Gary Cooper was quite the Lothario in his personal life, much to the consternation of his wife. One of his longest liaisons was with the actress Patricia Neal, his costar in films like *The Fountainhead.* On one occasion, when Neal sent a telegram congratulating Cooper on a radio performance, his wife, Veronica (known as Rocky), sent off her own irate, somewhat threatening reply, which began:

I HAVE HAD JUST ABOUT ENOUGH OF YOU.

It was signed "Mrs. Gary Cooper."

JIBES AND JOUSTS

FOR SOME of the sharpest wits of their time—the Oscar Wildes, George Bernard Shaws, Noël Cowards, Alexander Woollcotts, and Dorothy Parkers—the telegram could be the ideal rapier-sharp implement, and there were often rivalries over who could pierce deeper with the least number of words and who could come up with the cleverest riposte.

In a famous 1883 exchange of telegrams between two supreme egotists, writer Oscar Wilde and artist James Abbott McNeill Whistler, they comment on an item in the humor magazine *Punch:*

From Wilde:

PUNCH TOO RIDICULOUS. WHEN YOU AND I ARE TOGETHER WE NEVER TALK ABOUT ANYTHING BUT OURSELVES.

And Whistler's rejoinder:

NO, NO OSCAR, YOU FORGET. WHEN YOU AND I ARE TOGETHER, WE NEVER TALK ABOUT ANYTHING EXCEPT ME.

Rather than being insulted, the pair, by mutual consent, republished their telegrams in the *World* on November 14, 1883.

Practical jokes played their part in the telegram repertoire as well. For instance, Sir Arthur Conan Doyle of Sherlock Holmes fame is reputed to have sent a telegram to twelve prominent men, reading:

ALL IS DISCOVERED. FLY AT ONCE.

Supposedly, they all left the country within twenty-four hours.

Mark Twain is alleged to have sent a dozen of his friends a similar telegram saying:

FLEE AT ONCE—ALL IS DISCOVERED!

And they, too, it is said, all left town immediately.

In May of 1971, the Federal Communications Commission sent telegrams to all radio stations, threatening their licenses if they played rock music that glorified drugs.

When he was governor of the Philippines, William Howard Taft—who at times tipped the scales at 350 pounds—made a trip into the mountains for his health. He cabled back to Secretary of War Elihu Root:

STOOD TRIP WELL. RODE HORSEBACK 25 MILES TO 5,000 FEET ELEVATION.

To which Root replied:

REFERRING TO YOUR TELEGRAM . . . HOW IS THE HORSE?

One of the premier wordsmiths of modern times, Noël Coward sent the following telegram from Florence after catching a cold:

HAVE MOVED HOTEL EXCELSIOR COUGHING MYSELF INTO A FIRENZE

Another missive he wired from foreign parts read:

AM BACK FROM ISTANBUL WHERE I WAS KNOWN AS ENGLISH
DELIGHT.

The struggling young writer George Bernard Shaw submitted the manuscript of one of his plays to a top London producer but was resound-
ingly rejected. When, a few years later, Shaw had attained success, this
producer wired the playwright that he was now interested in producing
the work in question. With characteristic cleverness, Shaw cabled back:
BETTER NEVER THAN LATE.

When Shaw received a telegram from the Akron Little Theatre in 1930
reading:
AKRON OHIO POLICE REFUSE TO CONSIDER KNOCKING OUT TWO TEETH
SUFFICIENT JUSTIFICATION FOR JAILING. HOW CAN WE ATTRACT
ATTENTION TO FANNY'S FIRST PLAY.

Shaw wired back:
ASCERTAIN HOW MANY TEETH WILL SUFFICE AND ALTER TEXT
ACCORDINGLY

Similarly, there was the quite justified reply he telegraphed to the American Theatre Guild in December 1923, in response to their outlandish
request to:
PLEASE ALTER FOURTH ACT OF "ST. JOAN" SO COMMUTERS CAN
CATCH LAST TRAIN TO SUBURBS.

The reply:
ALTER THE TRAINS.

Popular wag/writer/actor Robert Benchley made it a game to come up
with the most outlandish excuses for being late with his copy, and one of
the most frequently quoted telegrams of the twentieth century is this
example that he sent back to Harold Ross, his editor at the *New Yorker,*
upon arriving in Venice on assignment:
STREETS FULL OF WATER. PLEASE ADVISE.

Several years later, in the fall of 1969, writer Burton Bernstein, also on assignment for the *New Yorker,* riffed on Benchley's wire when he telegraphed his brother Leonard and wife, Felicia, from Tel Aviv:

EVERYONE HERE JEWISH. PLEASE ADVISE.

But Dorothy Parker far outdid them all with this scurrilous telegram she sent (or is reputed to have sent, by Oscar Levant and others—there is some doubt that Western Union would have accepted it) to an editor who was badgering her for overdue copy while she was on her honeymoon:

TOO FUCKING BUSY, AND VICE VERSA.

George S. Kaufman's Pulitzer Prize–winning Broadway show *Of Thee I Sing* had been running for quite some time when the writer attended a particularly lackluster performance, inspiring him to wire its star, William Gaxton:

WATCHING YOUR PERFORMANCE FROM THE LAST ROW. WISH YOU WERE HERE.

In the same vein, when Orson Welles performed his notorious radio version of H. G. Wells's *War of the Worlds,* causing many members of the listening audience to panic and think it was reporting an actual invasion from Mars, the broadcast was running against the Edgar Bergen–Charlie McCarthy show on another network. Immediately after the show aired, the quick-witted critic and journalist Alexander Woollcott sent Welles a wire saying that the panic proved that the smart listeners were tuned in to a dummy, and the dummies were listening to Welles.

When the question

HOW OLD CARY GRANT?

was wired to the star's agent, Grant himself suggested the following sly reply, using to his own advantage the constricts of the telegram form:

OLD CARY GRANT FINE. HOW YOU?

FOR THE FIRST half century of its existence, Hollywood's history was chronicled in telegrams—questions of casting and credit, awards and discredit, feuds and tantrums, promotion and the ever-churning publicity machine. . . .

In late 1913, a small group of fledgling East Coast moviemakers, led by Cecil B. DeMille and associated with the Jesse L. Lasky Feature Play Company, boarded a train to Flagstaff, Arizona, in search of a western location to film *The Squaw Man*. The New York office was surprised, therefore, to receive a wire from DeMille stating:

> FLAGSTAFF NO GOOD FOR OUR PURPOSE. HAVE PROCEEDED TO CALIFORNIA. WANT AUTHORITY TO RENT BARN IN PLACE CALLED HOLLYWOOD FOR $75 A MONTH. REGARDS TO SAM [GOLDFISH, LATER GOLDWYN].

The reception to this wire was less than enthusiastic, with Goldfish particularly wary:

> AUTHORIZE YOU TO RENT BARN BUT ON MONTH-TO-MONTH BASIS. DON'T MAKE ANY LONG COMMITMENT.

In 1925, when silent screen diva Gloria Swanson was returning to Hollywood after a sojourn in France with her husband, the Marquis de la Falaise, she, taking no chances, alerted the publicity drones:

> ARRIVING WITH THE MARQUIS TOMORROW MORNING. STOP. PLEASE ARRANGE OVATION.

In 1928, preparations were being made for the first mainstream all-black Hollywood musical, *Hallelujah,* to be directed by King Vidor under the aegis of Irving Thalberg. A highly publicized nationwide casting search ensued, and one of the primary candidates for the female lead was Honey Brown, "the hotsy-totsy darling of the Club Harlem." Her looks and sex appeal became the subject of an extensive telegraphic dialogue between Thalberg and Vidor, ending in her finally losing the part to

Nina Mae McKinney, probably because of what Thalberg wrote in this November 27, 1928, wire:

```
. . . MY CHIEF OBJECTION TO HONEY BROWN IS CERTAIN UGLINESS
PARTICULARLY AROUND HER MOUTH HER FLAT CHESTEDNESS AND HER
UPPER LIP HAS VERY OUTSTANDING HAIR LINE
```

With the opening of the film *The Blue Angel,* Marlene Dietrich became an international sensation. She was sailing on the SS *Bremen* in April of 1930 when the reviews appeared, and her faithful husband, Rudi Sieber, cabled them to her:

```
UNRESTRAINED RAVE FROM KRACAUER QUOTE DIETRICHS LOLA-LOLA
IS A NEW INCARNATION OF SEX THIS PETTY BOURGEOIS BERLIN
TART WITH HER PROVOCATIVE LEGS AND EASY MANNERS SHOWS AN
IMPASSIVITY WHICH INCITES ONE TO GROPE FOR THE SECRET
BEHIND HER CALLOUS EGOTISM AND COOL INSOLENCE END QUOTE
KISSES PAPI
```

In the heady days of Hollywood's Golden Age, good writers were in particularly great demand. Herman Mankiewicz, screenwriter of *Citizen Kane,* urged his friend Ben Hecht (who would later script such classics as

> "When an actor has money, he doesn't send letters, but telegrams."
> —Anton Chekhov

The Front Page and *Wuthering Heights*) to come out to California and get in on the action:

```
WILL YOU ACCEPT THREE HUNDRED PER WEEK TO WORK FOR
PARAMOUNT PICTURES? ALL EXPENSES PAID. THREE HUNDRED IS
PEANUTS. MILLIONS ARE TO BE GRABBED OUT HERE AND YOUR ONLY
COMPETITION IS IDIOTS. DON'T LET THIS GET AROUND.
```

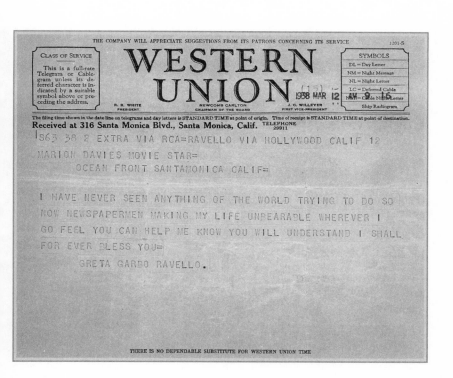

THE COMPANY WILL APPRECIATE SUGGESTIONS FROM ITS PATRONS CONCERNING ITS SERVICE

WESTERN UNION

R. B. WHITE
PRESIDENT

NEWCOMB CARLTON
CHAIRMAN OF THE BOARD

J. C. WILLEVER
FIRST VICE-PRESIDENT

1938 MAR 12

The filing time shown in the date line on telegrams and day letters is STANDARD TIME at point of origin. Time of receipt is STANDARD TIME at point of destination.

Received at 316 Santa Monica Blvd., Santa Monica, Calif. TELEPHONE 29911

S63 38 2 EXTRA VIA RCA=RAVELLO VIA HOLLYWOOD CALIF 12

MARION DAVIES MOVIE STAR=

OCEAN FRONT SANTAMONICA CALIF=

I HAVE NEVER SEEN ANYTHING OF THE WORLD TRYING TO DO SO NOW NEWSPAPERMEN MAKING MY LIFE UNBEARABLE WHEREVER I GO FEEL YOU CAN HELP ME KNOW YOU WILL UNDERSTAND I SHALL FOR EVER BLESS YOU=

GRETA GARBO RAVELLO.

THERE IS NO DEPENDABLE SUBSTITUTE FOR WESTERN UNION TIME

Greta Garbo to Marion Davies on March 12, 1938, when
Garbo was traveling in Italy.

A W. C. Fields telegram could be a veritable short story or comedy routine in itself. An example written to close friend Gene Fowler:

MY DEAREST AND MOST BELOVED NEPHEW A MILLION THANKS FOR THE
PAINTING WHICH THE BASSOON PLAYER RELUCTANTLY BROUGHT HERE
YESTERDAY WHEN I TOLD HIM THAT HORIZONTAL HOWARD WAS COMING
HE RUSHED THROUGH THE BRAMBLES PALMS AND THE THICKETS LIKE
A FRIGHTENED THING I WISH I HAD HAD TIME TO SAY IN MY
INIMITABLE WAY THANK YOU HE WILL NEVER AMOUNT TO A THING MY
LOVE TO AGNES I KNOW SHE PROMPTED THE IDEA WHEN YOUR READY

FOR . . . WHEN BARKUS IS WILLIN I VANT VE SHALL BE ALONE YOUR
LOVING AND APPRECIATIVE
    UNCLE CLAUDE

Gossip columnist Hedda Hopper was so powerful that some of the most important stars in Hollywood were known to grovel before her. This November 15, 1940, telegram was signed by a posse of well-known cowboy actors:

HEDDA YOU OLD HOPTOAD. FIRST YOU WENT TO TEXAS. NOW YOU'RE
IN ARIZONA. THAT'S COW COUNTRY AND THAT MEANS COWBOYS. AND
COWBOYS MEAN LOTS OF FUN FOR ALL AMERICA. SO HAVE A GOOD
TIME BUT FOR GOSH SAKES DON'T FORGET TO COME BACK TO US.

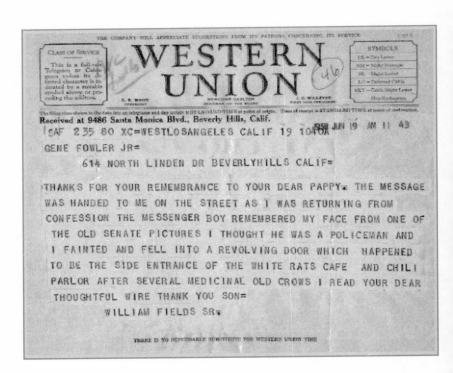

On March 30, 1942, studio head Jack Warner had written the U.S. Army asking for an extended thirty-day deferment for Ronald Reagan. On April 2, he received this reply:

REGRET TO INFORM YOU THAT ANOTHER DEFERMENT CANNOT BE GRANTED 2ND LT. RONALD WILSON REAGAN CAVALRY STOP SHORTAGE OF AVAILABLE OFFICERS PREVENTS FAVORABLE CONSIDERATION—

After Reagan had completed his military service, Warner wired his New York office:

. . . CAMPAIGN OF RONALD REAGAN WILL EMPHASIZE HIS QUICK RETURN TO FAME SINCE HIS RETURN FROM THE ARMY AND HIS QUALITY OF EVOKING WARM RESPONSE FROM ALL TYPES AND AGES OF MOVIE FANS AND WITH HIS PART AS BILL PAGE HE GAINS NEW STATURE . . .

CLASSIC FILMS

EVEN IN THE SILENT DAYS, producers and directors were concerned with the receipts earned by their films. When D. W. Griffith's silent master-piece *Intolerance* opened in London on April 7, 1917, the director was on hand to witness his triumph. The gross for the premiere was $500 more than any previous motion picture shown in England, and the following week, Griffith cabled home:

'INTOLERANCE' RECEPTION GREATEST IN DRURY LANE HISTORY. CHEERS AND APPLAUSE AFTER FIRST ACT LASTED SEVEN MINUTES. EVERYONE CERTAIN IT IS TREMENDOUS TRIUMPH. SPLENDID ADVANCE BOOKINGS AND SUNDAY NEWSPAPER REVIEWS PRAISE IT UNANIMOUSLY.

Hollywood history is strewn with what-ifs—what if Katharine Hepburn had gotten the part of Scarlett O'Hara, or George Raft had played Rick in *Casablanca*? This brief telegram shows that one of the iconic cinema images, that of Bela Lugosi as Count Dracula, almost didn't reach the screen because Universal Studios honcho Carl Laemmle Jr. had Lon Chaney Sr. in mind instead:

```
NOT INTERESTED BELA LUGOSI PRESENT TIME
```

In May of 1936, producer David O. Selznick was still undecided about acquiring the rights to Margaret Mitchell's soon-to-be-published novel *Gone With the Wind* (which would, of course, go on to become his greatest success), as he wrote to his New York rep, Kay Brown, on the twenty-fifth:

```
HAVE GONE OVER AND CAREFULLY THOUGHT ABOUT "GONE WITH THE
WIND." THINK IT IS FINE STORY AND I UNDERSTAND YOUR FEELING
ABOUT IT. IF WE HAD UNDER CONTRACT A WOMAN IDEALLY SUITED
TO THE LEAD, I WOULD PROBABLY BE MORE INCLINED TO BUY IT
THAN I AM TODAY. . . . THEREFORE MOST SORRY TO HAVE TO SAY NO
IN FACE OF YOUR ENTHUSIASM FOR THIS STORY.
```

By the next day he had changed his mind:

```
. . . I HAVE THOUGHT FURTHER ABOUT "GONE WITH THE WIND" AND
THE MORE I THINK ABOUT IT, THE MORE I FEEL THERE IS
EXCELLENT PICTURE IN IT . . . ESPECIALLY IF THEY CAN SELL THE
VERY COLORFUL MAN'S ROLE TO GARY COOPER. WERE I WITH MGM I
BELIEVE I WOULD BUY IT NOW FOR SOME COMBINATION AS GABLE
AND JOAN CRAWFORD.
```

Two days later, he had further casting ideas about Rhett Butler:

```
. . . WHAT DO YOU THINK ABOUT RONALD COLMAN FOR THE LEAD?
SPENT LATE LAST NIGHT TALKING STORIES WITH HIM AND FOUND
MYSELF SELLING HIM THIS STORY. HE SEEMS VERY INTERESTED
INDEED, AND WE DISCUSSED MATTER OF SOUTHERN ACCENT. HE
```

THINKS HE WOULD LOVE TACKLE IT AND SAYS HE WOULD SPEND NEXT
SEVERAL MONTHS MAKING STUDY OF IT AND IS SURE HE COULD
MASTER IT. . . . FOR THE LEAD MIGHT TRY SOMEONE LIKE [MIRIAM]
HOPKINS OR [TALLULAH] BANKHEAD.

In the meantime, Margaret Mitchell, author of the novel on which the film was based, had clearly defined her own role in the film, as is evident from this 1936 telegram to Russell Birdwell, publicity manager for Selznick International Pictures:

. . . MUST SET YOU STRAIGHT ON MY CONNECTION WITH FILM JOB
STOP MY CONTRACT SPECIFICALLY PROVIDES THAT I HAVE NOTHING
TO DO WITH THE MOVIE AND I HAVE STATED PERSONALLY AND BY
LETTER TO VARIOUS SELZNICK PEOPLE THAT I WILL HAVE NOTHING
TO DO WITH TALENT SEARCH, CASTING, ADAPTATION OF STORY OR
FILMING. . . . WHEN MISS BROWN AND OTHERS COME TO ATLANTA I
WILL FEED THEM FRIED CHICKEN, SHOW THEM STONE MOUNTAIN AND
INTRODUCE THEM TO ANYBODY THEY WANT TO MEET BUT ALL PARTS
OF FILM JOB ARE ON THEIR HANDS AND NOT MINE STOP. . . .

During the casting frenzy surrounding *Gone With the Wind,* Tallulah Bankhead waged a strenuous campaign for the role of Scarlett, confronting Selznick himself and prompting a Tallulah-for-Scarlett petition. The drive culminated in a telegram to Selznick International from the governor of Georgia, reading:

WHY DON'T YOU GIVE TALLULAH BANKHEAD THE PART AND BE DONE
WITH IT.

After the roles were finally assigned, Margaret Mitchell Marsh got a grateful wire from Leslie Howard, who played Ashley Wilkes:

DEAR MRS MARSH: I AM NOT AT ALL ENVIOUS OF RHETT BECAUSE
THANKS TO YOU, IT WAS MELANIE, MA'AM THAT I WANTED. BUT
SERIOUSLY, I FEEL IT A GREAT HONOR TO HAVE BEEN SELECTED TO
ENACT ONE OF THE ROLES OF YOUR BOOK, THE TITLE OF WHICH
ESCAPES ME AT THE MOMENT.

In this telegram of October 11, 1939, when shooting of the film was almost completed, Selznick put the pressure on Ben Hecht to write the on-screen titles—even though Hecht was sick at home in Nyack, New York:

> . . . CAN'T YOU SWALLOW A BOTTLE OF THYROID AND A COUPLE OF
> BENZEDRINES. MY OWN METABOLISM WAS ABOUT MINUS THIRTY
> BEFORE WIND STARTED. GOD KNOWS WHAT IT IS NOW.

Before another classic film, *Casablanca,* was released in 1942, an advance print was shown to Selznick, who had lent costar Ingrid Bergman to Warner Bros. to appear in it. Selznick wired his thoughts to producer Hal Wallis:

> SAW "CASABLANCA" LAST NIGHT. THINK IT IS A SWELL MOVIE AND
> AN ALL-AROUND FINE JOB OF PICTURE MAKING. TOLD JACK
> [WARNER] AS FORCIBLY AS I COULD THAT I THOUGHT IT WOULD BE
> A TERRIBLE MISTAKE TO CHANGE THE ENDING. . . . KNOWING WHAT
> THEY STARTED WITH, I THINK THE FIRM OF EPSTEIN, EPSTEIN AND
> KOCH DID AN EXPERT PIECE OF WRITING. EVEN THOUGH RICK'S
> PHILOSOPHY IS IN AT LEAST ONE INSTANCE WORD FOR WORD THAT
> OF RHETT BUTLER.

Following the end of World War II, preproduction work was begun on two major films at the same time: *The Best Years of Our Lives,* to be directed by William Wyler, and Frank Capra's *It's a Wonderful Life.* As they began, Wyler sent Capra a telegram:

> LAST ONE IN IS A ROTTEN EGG

When Capra won the race, Wyler allowed that he was indeed a rotten egg.

After the American release of *It's a Wonderful Life,* preparations were being made for its showing overseas when a cable came from the British censor, objecting to the film on religious grounds. The movie's director, Frank Capra, replied with a cable of his own on March 19, 1947:

...TERRIBLY DISTURBED ACTION BRITISH CENSORS AS ALL
UNITED STATES CENSOR BOARDS HAVE HAILED PICTURE AS JUST
TYPE OF CLEAN WHOLESOME ENTERTAINMENT THAT THEY ALL CRY FOR
STOP....CUTTING OUT ALL REFERENCES TO HEAVEN WINGS AND
ANGELS SECOND CLASS WOULD RUIN VERY IMPORTANT SEQUENCES
STOP....

In 1954, when director Joseph L. Mankiewicz was casting the film version of *Guys and Dolls,* Marlon Brando was a hot property after winning rave reviews for *On the Waterfront,* and Mankiewicz wanted him for the part of Sky Masterson. To allay Brando's qualms, the Hollywood veteran sent Brando this wire:

UNDERSTAND YOU'RE APPREHENSIVE BECAUSE YOU'VE NEVER DONE
MUSICAL COMEDY. YOU HAVE NOTHING REPEAT NOTHING TO WORRY
ABOUT. BECAUSE NEITHER HAVE I. LOVE, JOE

Mankiewicz had bigger problems with one of his other productions. After one of the most fraught and frustrating shoots in moviemaking history, that of the Elizabeth Taylor–Richard Burton *Cleopatra,* director Mankiewicz was among many who were fired by Darryl F. Zanuck, head of Twentieth Century Fox, at which point the enraged Mankiewicz sent off a telegram to Zanuck that ended:

...NO SELF-RESPECTING PICTURE-MAKER WOULD EVER WANT TO
WORK FOR YOUR COMPANY. THE SOONER THE BULLDOZERS RAZE YOUR
STUDIO, THE BETTER IT WILL BE FOR THE INDUSTRY.

When author Ian Fleming asked Noël Coward to play the part of Dr. No in the James Bond film, Coward replied, typically:

DR NO? NO! NO! NO!

After the filming of *Some Like It Hot,* director Billy Wilder gave a newspaper interview in which he derided the working habits of Marilyn Monroe. A few days later he received an irate telegram from the actress's then-husband, playwright Arthur Miller:

DEAR BILLY: I CANNOT LET YOUR VICIOUS ATTACK ON MARILYN GO
UNCHALLENGED. YOU WERE OFFICIALLY INFORMED BY MARILYN'S
PHYSICIAN THAT DUE TO HER PREGNANCY SHE WAS NOT ABLE TO
WORK A FULL DAY, YOU CHOSE TO IGNORE THIS FACT DURING THE
MAKING OF THE PICTURE. . . . SHE WENT ON WITH THE PICTURE OUT
OF A SENSE OF RESPONSIBILITY NOT ONLY TO HERSELF BUT TO YOU
AND THE CAST AND PRODUCER. TWELVE HOURS AFTER THE LAST
SHOOTING DAY HER MISCARRIAGE BEGAN. . . . YOUR JOKES, BILLY,
ARE NOT QUITE HILARIOUS ENOUGH TO CONCEAL THE FACT. YOU ARE
AN UNJUST MAN AND A CRUEL ONE. MY ONLY SOLACE IS THAT
DESPITE YOU HER BEAUTY AND HER HUMANITY SHINE THROUGH AS
THEY ALWAYS HAVE.

Wilder's reply read in part:

. . . OF COURSE I AM DEEPLY SORRY THAT SHE LOST HER BABY BUT
I MUST REJECT THE IMPLICATION THAT OVERWORK OR
INCONSIDERATE TREATMENT BY ME OR ANYONE ELSE ASSOCIATED
WITH THE PRODUCTION WAS IN ANY WAY RESPONSIBLE FOR IT. THE
FACT IS THAT THE COMPANY PAMPERED HER, CODDLED HER AND
ACCEDED TO ALL HER WHIMS. THE ONLY ONE WHO SHOWED ANY LACK
OF CONSIDERATION WAS MARILYN, IN HER TREATMENT OF HER CO-
STARS AND CO-WORKERS. . . . HER BIGGEST PROBLEM IS THAT SHE
DOESN'T UNDERSTAND ANYBODY ELSE'S PROBLEMS. . . . HAD YOU,
DEAR ARTHUR, BEEN NOT HER HUSBAND BUT HER WRITER AND
DIRECTOR, AND BEEN SUBJECTED TO ALL THE INDIGNITIES I WAS,
YOU WOULD HAVE THROWN HER OUT ON HER CAN, THERMOS BOTTLE
AND ALL, TO AVOID A NERVOUS BREAKDOWN. I DID THE BRAVER
THING. I HAD A NERVOUS BREAKDOWN.

After another telegram from Miller demanding an apology, Wilder
relented, albeit somewhat facetiously:

IN ORDER TO HASTEN THE BURIAL OF THE HATCHET I HEREBY
ACKNOWLEDGE THAT GOOD WIFE MARILYN IS A UNIQUE PERSONALITY

AND I AM THE BEAST OF BELSEN BUT IN THE IMMORTAL WORDS OF
JOE E. BROWN QUOTE NOBODY IS PERFECT END QUOTE.

OSCARS

THE BESTOWING of the Academy Awards always produced a flurry of
telegrams, not only of congratulations but of condolence as well.

In 1954, Judy Garland was the odds-on favorite for best actress for her
performance in *A Star Is Born*—to the point where television cameras
were set up in the hospital room in which she had just given birth to her
son, Joey Luft. After word came that the winner was Grace Kelly for *The
Country Girl,* Garland was besieged with sympathetic letters and telegrams, including this one from Groucho Marx:

DEAR JUDY, THIS IS THE BIGGEST ROBBERY SINCE BRINKS.

And when lyricist Oscar Hammerstein II won the 1941 Academy Award
for his song "The Last Time I Saw Paris," he sent a generous telegram to
Johnny Mercer, who had been nominated for "Blues in the Night":

JOHNNY, YOU WAS ROBBED.

IT IS OFTEN AMUSING to look back at some of the early impressions—both positive and negative—made by future stars when they were being considered for major roles.

And when the film *Wuthering Heights* was being cast in 1938, writer Ben Hecht screened a movie at his home in Nyack, featuring an actor known primarily for his stage roles. He became excited enough to wire Hollywood:

> I SAW LAWRENCE OLIVIER ON THE SCREEN LAST NIGHT AND THOUGHT HIM ONE OF THE MOST MAGNIFICENT ACTORS I HAVE EVER SEEN HE COULD RECITE HEATHCLIFF SITTING ON A BARREL OF HERRING AND BREAK YOUR HEART.

In 1939, when Ingrid Bergman was being considered for the American-star-buildup treatment by producer David O. Selznick, he sent the following telegram to his chief New York representative, Kay Brown, on March 18:

> I NOTE BERGMAN IS 69½ INCHES TALL. IS IT POSSIBLE SHE IS ACTUALLY THIS HIGH, AND DO YOU THINK WE WILL HAVE TO USE STEPLADDERS WITH LESLIE HOWARD?

On May 21, 1942—a few days before the filming of *Casablanca* was to begin—the previously skeptical Jack Warner wired his publicity department following the preview of the film *Across the Pacific*:

> REACTION OF AUDIENCE . . . CONVINCES ME BEYOND A SHADOW OF DOUBT THAT HUMPHREY BOGART IS ONE OF OUR BIGGEST STARS. . . . IN BOGART WE HAVE WHAT I HONESTLY CONSIDER THE EQUIVALENT OF CLARK GABLE.

When the casting process began for the movie version of John Steinbeck's novel *East of Eden* in 1954, director Elia Kazan thought he had discovered the perfect young actor for the leading role of Cal and wired studio head Jack Warner on February 5:

FOUND NEW BOY THAT I MOST ENTHUSIASTIC ABOUT AND WHO COULD MAKE PICTURE THIS SPRING . . .

and again on February 23:

SCREENED JAMES DEAN TEST YESTERDAY AND I AM SURE HE'S THE BOY FOR CAL. . . . WILL SEND YOU DEAN TEST TONIGHT AND WILL EAGERLY AWAIT YOUR REACTION . . .

But a year later, the bloom was off the rose, as revealed in this wire sent by a studio executive:

RE DEAN. HE HAS BEEN ABSOLUTELY IMPOSSIBLE. HAS BEEN EXTREMELY UNCOOPERATIVE . . . FINALLY CONVINCED HIM TO SIT FOR INTERVIEWS WHEREUPON HE FOULED HIMSELF UP AND GOT ONE MAGAZINE WRITER SORE AS BLAZES. HAVE ASKED KAZAN GIVE US ASSIST AND CONFIDENTIALLY GADGE [KAZAN] SAYS HE DOESN'T WANT TO BE FATHER CONFESSOR TO THIS KID. COULD HAVE USED DEAN TO GREAT ADVANTAGE FOR [EAST OF] EDEN BUT WAY HE IS ACTING HE CAN DO US MORE HARM THAN GOOD. HE NEEDS GOOD SCRUBBING BEHIND EARS.

Another of the many future stars who did not make a stellar early impression was Michael Caine. After seeing the rushes for the 1964 film *Zulu,* in which Caine played the aristocratic Lieutenant Gonville Bromhead—in a performance reputedly modeled after Prince Philip—a senior executive at Paramount Studios in London wired back to the home office:

ACTOR PLAYING BROMHEAD SO BAD HE DOESN'T EVEN KNOW WHAT TO DO WITH HANDS . . . SUGGEST YOU REPLACE HIM.

BIG BREAKS

LUCILLE LESUEUR, soon to be known as Joan Crawford, thanks to a movie magazine naming contest, had a none-too-promising start. Her first break came in the form of a December 25, 1924, Christmas-present telegram from the MGM studios, which read:

> YOU ARE PUT UNDER A FIVE-YEAR CONTRACT STARTING AT SEVENTY-FIVE DOLLARS A WEEK. LEAVE IMMEDIATELY FOR CULVER CUTY, CALIFORNIA. CONTACT MGM KANSAS CITY OFFICE FOR TRAVEL EXPENSES.

The year 1937 was a crucial one in the careers of two of Hollywood's most enduring personalities. While Ronald Reagan was still working as an announcer at Iowa radio station WHO, he halfheartedly took a screen test at Warner Bros. To his surprise, on March 22, 1937, he received a telegram from the William Meiklejohn Agency in Hollywood with an offer from Warner Bros. for seven years starting at $200 a week. When Meiklejohn asked how he should proceed, Reagan wasted no time in wiring this reply:

> . . . SIGN BEFORE THEY CHANGE THEIR MINDS. DUTCH REAGAN

Reagan claimed he had "got the telegram worn to a frazzle."

By 1937, Bob Hope had been featured in several Broadway musicals and made a few short films but was by no means a movie star. When offered a lead in the production that would indeed make him one, he almost turned it down, as reflected in this exchange of telegrams on two consecutive days—July 14 and 15—between his two agents:

> PARAMOUNT MADE DEFINITE OFFER BOB HOPE SIX WEEKS MINIMUM GUARANTEE TWO THOUSAND PER WEEK . . . TO PLAY LEAD IN BIG BROADCAST PLEASE ADVISE BOB THIS IS THE GREAT OPPORTUNITY HE HAS BEEN WAITING FOR AND WE SHOULDNT LET MONEY STAND IN THE WAY AS WE CANT AFFORD TO LOSE THIS PROPSITION ON ACCOUNT OF A FEW THOUSAND DOLLARS. . . .

ADVISE BOB HOPE PART PARAMOUNT HAS FOR HIM IN BIG BROADCAST
IS LIGHT COMEDY LEAD AND WILL GIVE HIM EVERY OPPORTUNITY TO
SHOW HIS ABILITY AS COMEDIAN AND CHANCE TO SING SEVERAL
SONGS. . . .

Obviously persuaded, Hope took the part.

EINSTEIN'S THEORY OF TELEGRAPHY
Albert Einstein once said, "The telegraph wire is a kind of very, very
long cat. You pull his tail in New York and his head is meowing in Los
Angeles."

FAMED AUSTRIAN COMPOSER Gustav Mahler was born a Jew, then later converted to Christianity. As a young man he applied for a position at a theater but was rejected, he later learned, because of what was termed his "Jewish nose." Several years later, after he had gained a reputation, he was offered the same position by the same theater. He responded with this telegram:

CANNOT ACCEPT POSITION. NOSE THE SAME.

Every Christmas, opera composer Giacomo Puccini would have the sweet cake called panettone baked for each of his friends. But one year, he had a quarrel with conductor Arturo Toscanini just before the holiday and tried to cancel the delivery of his gift. When he found that it was too late and the cake had already been sent, Puccini wired:

PANETTONE SENT BY MISTAKE

To which the maestro supposedly replied:

PANETTONE EATEN BY MISTAKE

Immediately following the Italian premiere of Claude Debussy's opera *Pelléas et Mélisande,* conducted by Toscanini at La Scala on April 2, 1908, the conductor wired the composer:

I AM HAPPY PELLEAS HAS WON IT HAS WON HEROICALLY AND
DESPITE AN IGNORANT COWARDLY HOSTILE PART OF THE AUDIENCE
OF SUBSCRIBERS PROVOKING SCANDAL OPERA ENDED IN A TRIUMPH
FOR YOU FOR YOUR INCOMPARABLE ART

Even after George Gershwin had composed such classics as *Porgy and Bess* and *Rhapsody in Blue,* he was protesting to his agent:

. . . RUMORS ABOUT HIGHBROW MUSIC RIDICULOUS STOP. AM OUT TO
WRITE HITS.

While listening to the radio broadcast of his protégé Leonard Bernstein's

Carnegie Hall debut on November 12, 1943, Serge Koussevitzky, conductor of the Boston Symphony, shot off this approbatory telegram:

LISTENING NOW WONDERFUL

In the spring of 1944, Broadway producer/entrepreneur Billy Rose offered the distinguished classical composer Igor Stravinsky a fee of $5,000 for a fifteen-minute ballet suite to be incorporated into a stage production. After the score was completed and submitted, there was a well-publicized exchange of telegrams between the two when Rose asked for a bit of third-party tweaking:

YOUR MUSIC GREAT SUCCESS STOP COULD BE SENSATIONAL
SUCCESS IF YOU WOULD AUTHORIZE ROBERT RUSSELL BENNETT
RETOUCH ORCHESTRATION STOP BENNETT ORCHESTRATES EVEN
THE WORKS OF COLE PORTER

To which the composer replied:

SATISFIED WITH GREAT SUCCESS.

Although the following telegram is sometimes attributed to showman Mike Todd, it was actually sent by columnist Walter Winchell's right-hand woman after she had seen the revolutionary Rodgers and Hammerstein musical *Oklahoma!* in a New Haven tryout:

NO LEGS. NO SEX. NO CHANCE.

The process of constructing a lyric comes alive in this pair of telegrams sent by Cole Porter to MGM musical director Roger Edens in 1947, when they were putting together the songs for *The Pirate,* starring Judy Garland and Gene Kelly, who would sing and dance the final "Niña."

IN NINA. CHANGE LINE YOU BROKE MY HEART EITHER TO YOU
STOPPED MY HEART OR YOU HIT MY HEART

NINA/NINA NINA NINA/ YOU'RE THE PRIZE GARDENIA/OF THE
SPANISH MAIN./ NINA/ WHILE MY THEME SONG I SING/ DON'T BE

SO ENTICING/ OR I'LL GO INSANE,/ NINA—TILL ALAS I GAZED IN
YOUR EYES/ NINA I WAS MENTALLY FINE/ BUT SINCE I'VE SEEN
YUH NINA NINA NINA/ I'LL BE HAVING SCHIZOPHRENIA/ TILL I
MAKE YOU MINE STOP

Although succinctness was usually the objective of most telegrammers, there was one instance when maximum length was the goal. Famed concert violinist Mischa Elman, like many of his fellow musicians, resented the practice of concert managers' charging unnecessary communications to his account, and he tried to retaliate by sending this detailed telegram to his managers—collect:

AM SITTING IN THE DINING ROOM OF MY HOTEL HAVING FRENCH
ONION SOUP, WHOLEWHEAT TOAST, FILET MIGNON MEDIUM RARE,
MIXED SALAD WITH THOUSAND ISLAND DRESSING, FRENCH APPLE PIE
A LA MODE, COFFEE WITHOUT CREAM AND SUGAR. WEATHER
MARVELOUS. HAVE SPLENDID ROOM WITH MAGNIFICENT VIEW. NOW
HOW DO YOU LIKE COLLECT TELEGRAMS? YOURS CORDIALLY, MISCHA
ELMAN

GOOD SPORTS

A FEW improbable wires from the athletic field:

In 1914, Ethel Barrymore, a devout sports fan, wired theater critic Ashton Stevens:

IN FOUR HOURS I SHALL BE IN THE DEGRADING ACT OF ENTRAINING
FOR LINCOLN, NEBRASKA. MEANTIME WILL YOU PLEASE WIRE ME HOW
MANY ROUNDS AND WHO WON TONIGHT'S FIGHTS? YOURS FOR THE
HIGHER EDUCATION OF WOMEN, E.B.

Joe DiMaggio kisses the telegram informing him that he is the American League's Most Valuable Player for 1947.

The World Series was only sixteen years old in 1919, but it was already the focus of widespread gambling, which led to its most devastating scandal. Eight players—including the great "Shoeless" Joe Jackson, from the Chicago White Sox, who were competing against the Cincinnati Reds—were indicted for having been paid by a group of Chicago gamblers, probably joined by New York gangster Arnold Rothstein, to throw the Series. Despite being acquitted of criminal charges, all eight were banned from professional baseball for life. On September 28, 1920, they were sent this collective wire from the club's owner, Charles Comiskey:

> YOU AND EACH OF YOU ARE HEREBY NOTIFIED OF YOUR INDEFINITE
> SUSPENSION AS A MEMBER OF THE CHICAGO AMERICAN LEAGUE
> BASEBALL CLUB. YOUR SUSPENSION IS BROUGHT ABOUT BY

INFORMATION WHICH HAS JUST COME TO ME, DIRECTLY INVOLVING YOU AND EACH OF YOU IN THE BASEBALL SCANDAL NOW BEING INVESTIGATED BY THE GRAND JURY OF COOK COUNTY, RESULTING FROM THE WORLD SERIES OF 1919. IF YOU ARE INNOCENT OF ANY WRONGDOING, YOU AND EACH OF YOU WILL BE REINSTATED; IF YOU ARE GUILTY, YOU WILL BE RETIRED FROM BASEBALL FOR THE REST OF YOUR LIVES IF I CAN ACCOMPLISH IT. UNTIL THERE IS A FINALITY TO THIS INVESTIGATION, IT IS DUE TO THE PUBLIC THAT I TAKE THIS ACTION EVEN THOUGH IT COSTS CHICAGO THE PENNANT.

Baseball immortal Babe Ruth was also a man who indulged his appetite for food and women, and one of his favorite playmates in these pursuits was pitcher Waite Hoyte. At one point, the heavy-drinking Hoyte checked into a hospital for a drying-out session, although the Yankee organization disguised his problem publicly as, of all things, amnesia. Amused, Ruth sent off a telegram to Hoyte:

READ ABOUT YOUR CASE OF AMNESIA. MUST BE A NEW BRAND.

As with e-mail, multiple messages could be sent at one time. The sender had only to make one copy of the message and hand it to the telegrapher with a list of addresses and, at no charge for the special handling of what they called "books" of telegrams, they would be sent out. One New York company dispatched a mass wiring of more than 200,000 telegrams in the 1920s.

The Sultan of Swat was almost as enthusiastic about golf as he was about baseball, as was one of his rivals, the mean-spirited Ty Cobb. In 1941, Fred Corcoran, who was running the predecessor of the PGA Tour, brought the two together for a charity match in Boston, at which Bette

Davis was to present the winner with a silver cup. When Cobb hesitated before accepting the challenge, Ruth sent him a telegram:

IF YOU WANT TO COME HERE AND GET YOUR BRAINS KNOCKED OUT, COME AHEAD.

Harry Truman was an avid baseball supporter, attending more games while in office than any other president, and was the first to attend a night game. He was a good friend of Washington Senators owner Clark Griffith (who once said, "Everyone is against Harry except the people"), sending Griffith this telegram on opening day of the first post–World War II season:

BEST OF LUCK TO YOU ON OPENING DAY AND EVERY DAY. WATCH OUT FOR THAT NIXON. DON'T LET HIM THROW YOU A CURVE.

When Johnny Bench broke Yogi Berra's record for the most home runs by a catcher, Berra sent him this characteristically Yogiesque telegram:

CONGRATULATIONS ON BREAKING MY RECORD. I ALWAYS THOUGHT THE RECORD WOULD STAND UNTIL IT WAS BROKEN.

PART TWO

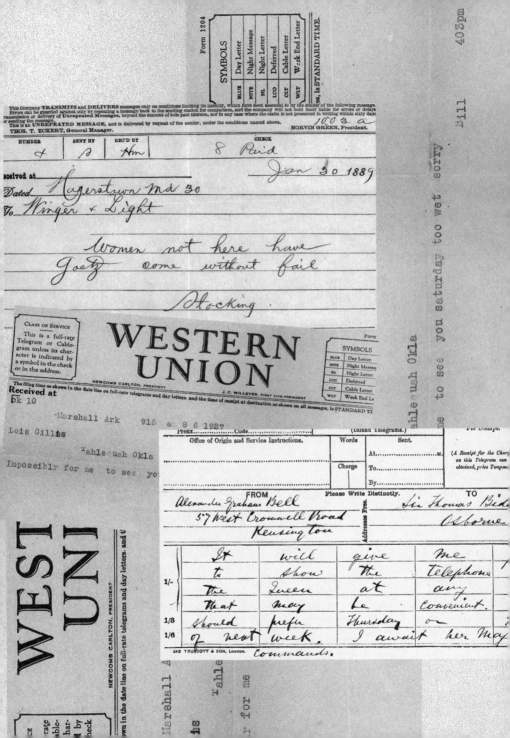

403pm

Bill

This Company TRANSMITS and DELIVERS messages only on conditions limiting its liability, which have been assented to by the sender of the following message. Errors can be guarded against only by repeating a message back to the sending station for comparison, and the company will not hold itself liable for errors or delays in transmission or delivery of Unrepeated Messages, beyond the amount of tolls paid thereon, nor in any case where the claim is not presented in writing within sixty days after sending the message.
This is an UNREPEATED MESSAGE, and is delivered by request of the sender, under the conditions named above.

THOS. T. ECKERT, General Manager.   NORVIN GREEN, President.

1003 a

NUMBER	SENT BY	REC'D BY	CHECK
4	D	Hm	8 Paid

Jan 30 1889

Received at Hagerstown Md 30

To Winger & Light

Women not here have
Goetz come without fail

Stocking

ahlequah Okla

me to see you saturday too wet sorry

Received at
Bk 10

Marshall Ark   915   a 8 6 1927

Lois Gillis

Tahlequah Okla

Imposeibly for me   to see yo

Prefix	Code	(Inland Telegrams.)		For Stamps.
Office of Origin and Service Instructions,		Words	Sent.	
			At..........M.	(A Receipt for the Charge on this Telegram can obtained, price Twopence
		Charge	To..........	
			By..........	

FROM   Please Write Distinctly.   TO

Alexander Graham Bell   Sir Thomas Bidd
57 West Cromwell Road   Osborne
Kensington

	It	will	give	me
	to	show	the	Telephone
1/-	the	Queen	at	any
	that	may	be	convenient.
1/3	should	prefer	Thursday	or
1/6	of next	week.	I await	her May

JAS TRUSCOTT & SON, LONDON.   Commands.

ahle
for me

Marshall A
is   Tahle
r for me

LINCOLN IN THE TELEGRAPH OFFICE

ABRAHAM LINCOLN spent a great deal of his time during the Civil War in the military telegraph office of the War Department—so much time, in fact, that one of its three rooms came to be called "the President's room." The first U.S. commander in chief who could communicate instantaneously with his distant armies, he would walk over to the telegraph office every morning, afternoon, and evening to receive the latest news from the front, even staying all night in periods of crisis. David Homer Bates, a young telegrapher in the office at the time, reported, "His tall, homely form could be seen crossing the well-shaded lawn between the White House and the War Department day after day with unvaried regularity." On those occasions, he would spend hours with his secretary of war, Edwin M. Stanton, so that he could read the telegrams as soon as they were received, peering over the shoulders of the cipher operators when he knew some particularly important message was in the process of being decoded.

The department's practice was to make three copies of all messages received, one "hard copy," saved for the records of the War Department, then two copies on yellow tissue paper, one for Lincoln and one for Stanton. Lincoln's routine was to go straight to the small desk drawer in which his copies were stored and begin reading them, starting at the top with the most recent, then stopping when he came to the last one he had seen on his previous visit. Bates recalled that when there was a lull, the president might begin to read aloud from the pocket edition of Shakespeare he carried with him or entertain the small staff with humorous anecdotes. It was also in the cipher room of the War Department telegraph office, his refuge from the hurly-burly of the White House (he often said, "I come here to escape my persecutors"), that Lincoln wrote the first draft of the Emancipation Proclamation, laboring over it painstakingly for a period of several weeks.

The files are full of the telegrams sent between Abraham Lincoln and such officers of the Union army as Grant, McClellan, Sherman, Halleck, Rosecrans, Butterfield, Hooker, Meade, Fremont, Fisk, and Dodge; what follows is a small sampling. On October 24, 1862, Lincoln

Confederate soldiers attempt to disrupt Union communication.

responded to one of General George McClellan's frequent complaints about inadequate forces, animals, and supplies:

I HAVE JUST READ YOUR DESPATCH ABOUT SORE TONGUED AND FATIGUED HORSES. WILL YOU PARDON ME FOR ASKING WHAT THE HORSES OF YOUR ARMY HAVE DONE SINCE THE BATTLE OF ANTIETAM THAT FATIGUE ANYTHING?

and again on the twenty-seventh:

YOURS OF YESTERDAY RECEIVED. MOST CERTAINLY I INTEND NO INJUSTICE TO ANY; AND IF I HAVE DONE ANY, I DEEPLY REGRET IT. TO BE TOLD AFTER MORE THAN FIVE WEEKS TOTAL INACTION OF THE ARMY, AND DURING WHICH PERIOD WE HAD SENT TO THAT ARMY EVERY FRESH HORSE WE POSSIBLY COULD, AMOUNTING IN THE WHOLE TO 7918, THAT THE CAVALRY HORSES WERE TOO FATIGUED TO MOVE, PRESENTED A VERY CHEERLESS, ALMOST HOPELESS, PROSPECT FOR THE FUTURE, AND IT MAY HAVE FORCED SOMETHING OF IMPATIENCE INTO MY DESPATCHES. IF NOT RECRUITED AND RESTED THEN, WHEN COULD THEY EVER BE? I SUPPOSE THE RIVER IS RISING, AND I AM GLAD TO BELIEVE YOU ARE CROSSING.

Vicksburg, Mississippi, vital for control of the Mississippi River, was the site of a key battle in the Civil War. In May of 1863, General Ulysses S. Grant opened siege there, and after six weeks of defense, the Confederates finally surrendered. On the twenty-fourth of May, Lincoln wired Anson Stager, head of the U.S. Military Telegraph command structure, in Cleveland, for clarification:

LATE LAST NIGHT FULLER TELEGRAPHED YOU, AS YOU SAY, THAT "THE STARS AND STRIPES FLOAT OVER VICKSBURG AND THE VICTORY IS COMPLETE." DID HE KNOW WHAT HE SAID, OR DID HE SAY IT WITHOUT KNOWING IT? YOUR DISPATCH OF THIS AFTERNOON THROWS DOUBT UPON IT.

Two weeks later, the president showed his concern about General William T. Sherman, who had distinguished himself at Vicksburg, and also how carefully he followed the newspaper coverage, in this June 8, 1863, telegram to Major General Dix:

> . . . WE KNEW THAT GENERAL SHERMAN WAS WOUNDED, BUT WE HOPED NOT SO DANGEROUSLY AS YOUR DISPATCH REPRESENTS. WE STILL HAVE NOTHING OF THAT RICHMOND NEWSPAPER STORY OF KIRBY SMITH CROSSING AND OF BANKS LOSING AN ARM.

Then, at the conclusion of the battle in July:

> THERE IS NO DOUBT THAT GENERAL MEADE, NOW COMMANDING THE ARMY OF THE POTOMAC, BEAT LEE AT GETTYSBURG, PA., AT THE END OF A THREE DAYS' BATTLE, AND THAT THE LATTER IS NOW CROSSING THE POTOMAC AT WILLIAMSPORT OVER THE SWOLLEN STREAM AND WITH POOR MEANS OF CROSSING, AND CLOSELY PRESSED BY MEADE. WE ALSO HAVE DISPATCHES RENDERING IT ENTIRELY CERTAIN THAT VICKSBURG SURRENDERED TO GRANT ON THE GLORIOUS OLD 4TH.

Lincoln kept his wife apprised of the military situation, as seen in this August 29, 1863, wire, sent to Mary Lincoln in Manchester, New Hampshire:

> ALL QUITE WELL. FORT SUMTER IS CERTAINLY BATTERED DOWN AND UTTERLY USELESS TO THE ENEMY AND IT IS BELIEVED HERE, BUT NOT ENTIRELY CERTAIN THAT BOTH SUMTER AND FORT WAGNER ARE OCCUPIED BY OUR FORCES. IT IS ALSO CERTAIN THAT GENERAL GILMORE HAS THROWN SOME SHOT INTO THE CITY OF CHARLESTON

Abraham Lincoln was inordinately fond of animalistic metaphor, as shown in the following three telegrams. In the first, sent to General Joseph Hooker on June 5, 1863, after offering some tactical suggestions, he writes:

> . . . I WOULD NOT TAKE ANY RISK OF BEING ENTANGLED UPON THE RIVER, LIKE AN OX JUMPED HALF OVER A FENCE, AND LIABLE TO BE TORN BY DOGS, FRONT AND REAR, WITHOUT A FAIR CHANCE TO GORE ONE WAY OR KICK THE OTHER. . . .

Nine days later, he again wrote to General Hooker:

> . . . IF THE HEAD OF LEE'S ARMY IS AT MARTINSBURG AND THE
> TAIL OF IT ON THE PLANK ROAD BETWEEN FREDRICKSBURG &
> CHANCELLORSVILLE, THE ANIMAL MUST BE VERY SLIM SOMEWHERE.
> COULD YOU NOT BREAK HIM?

And similarly, in this August 1864 dispatch sent to General Grant in City Point, Virginia:

> I HAVE SEEN YOUR DISPATCH EXPRESSING YOUR UNWILLINGNESS TO
> BREAK YOUR HOLD WHERE YOU ARE. NEITHER AM I WILLING. HOLD
> ON WITH A BULL-DOG GRIP, AND CHEW AND CHOKE, AS MUCH AS
> POSSIBLE.

Abraham Lincoln demonstrated a uniquely personal and compassionate interest in the people he served, at times intervening in their behalf. This benevolent side is shown in a telegram he sent to General Meade on October 8, 1863:

> I AM APPEALED TO IN BEHALF OF AUGUST BLITTERSDORF, AT
> MITCHELLS STATION, VA. TO BE SHOT TO-MORROW, AS A DESERTER.
> I AM UNWILLING FOR ANY BOY UNDER EIGHTEEN TO BE SHOT; AND
> HIS FATHER AFFIRMS THAT HE IS YET UNDER SIXTEEN. . . .

And again, in a telegram sent to Meade on November 20, 1863:

> AN INTELLIGENT WOMAN IN DEEP DISTRESS CALLED THIS MORNING,
> SAYING HER HUSBAND, A LIEUTENANT IN THE ARMY OF THE
> POTOMAC, WAS TO BE SHOT NEXT MONDAY FOR DESERTION, AND
> PUTTING A LETTER IN MY HAND, UPON WHICH I RELIED FOR
> PARTICULARS, SHE LEFT WITHOUT MENTIONING A NAME OR OTHER
> PARTICULAR BY WHICH TO IDENTIFY THE CASE. ON OPENING THE
> LETTER I FOUND IT EQUALLY VAGUE, HAVING NOTHING TO IDENTIFY
> IT, EXCEPT HER OWN SIGNATURE, WHICH SEEMS TO BE MRS.
> A____S. K_____. I COULD NOT AGAIN FIND HER. IF YOU HAVE A
> CASE WHICH YOU THINK IS PROBABLY THE ONE INTENDED, PLEASE
> APPLY MY DESPATCH OF THIS MORNING TO IT.

A telegrapher sends coffee quotations over stock ticker circuit. Telegraphy was one of the pioneer industries to offer opportunities to women.

And another sent to Major General Butler on December 29, 1864:

THERE IS A MAN IN COMPANY I, ELEVENTH CONNECTICUT
VOLUNTEERS . . . AT CHAPIN'S FARM, VA, UNDER THE ASSUMED NAME
OF WILLIAM STANLEY, BUT WHOSE REAL NAME IS FRANK R. JUDD,
AND WHO IS UNDER ARREST AND PROBABLY ABOUT TO BE TRIED FOR
DESERTION. HE IS THE SON OF OUR PRESENT MINISTER TO
PRUSSIA, WHO IS A CLOSE PERSONAL FRIEND OF SENATOR TRUMBELL
AND MYSELF. WE ARE NOT WILLING FOR THE BOY TO BE SHOT, BUT
WE THINK IT AS WELL THAT HIS TRIAL GO REGULARLY ON,
SUSPENDING EXECUTION UNTIL FURTHER ORDERS FROM ME AND
REPORTING TO ME.

One of numerous telegrams Lincoln sent pardoning Confederate prisoners, this December 31, 1864, example has a special resonance in our time:

SUSPEND EXECUTION OF JOHN LENNON UNTIL FURTHER ORDER FROM
ME. . . .

His pacifying instinct is evident in this telegram to Major General Dodge
in St. Louis on January 15, 1865:

IT IS REPRESENTED TO ME THAT THERE IS SO MUCH IRREGULAR
VIOLENCE IN NORTHERN MISSOURI AS TO BE DRIVING AWAY THE
PEOPLE AND ALMOST DEPOPULATING IT. PLEASE GATHER
INFORMATION, AND CONSIDER WHETHER AN APPEAL TO THE PEOPLE
THERE TO GO TO THEIR HOMES AND LET ONE ANOTHER ALONE—
RECOGNIZING AS A FULL RIGHT OF PROTECTION FOR EACH THAT HE
LETS OTHERS ALONE, AND BANNING ONLY HIM WHO REFUSES TO LET
OTHERS ALONE—MAY NOT ENABLE YOU TO WITHDRAW THE TROOPS,
THEIR PRESENCE ITSELF A CAUSE OF IRRITATION AND CONSTANT
APPREHENSION, AND THUS RESTORE PEACE AND QUIET, AND
RETURNING PROSPERITY.

This March 30, 1865, telegram sent from City Point, Virginia, to the
secretary of war demonstrates the president's remarkable emotive power:

I BEGIN TO FEEL THAT I OUGHT TO BE AT HOME AND YET I
DISLIKE TO LEAVE WITHOUT SEEING NEARER TO THE END OF
GENERAL GRANT'S PRESENT MOVEMENT. . . . LAST NIGHT AT 10:15
P.M. WHEN IT WAS DARK AS A RAINY NIGHT WITHOUT A MOON COULD
BE, A FURIOUS CANNONADE SOON JOINED IN BY A HEAVY MUSKETRY
FIRE OPENED NEAR PETERSBURG AND LASTED ABOUT TWO HOURS. THE
SOUND WAS VERY DISTINCT HERE AS ALSO WERE THE FLASHES OF
THE GUNS UP THE CLOUDS. IT SEEMED TO ME A GREAT BATTLE, BUT
THE OLDER HANDS HERE SCARCELY NOTICED IT AND SURE ENOUGH
THIS MORNING IT WAS FOUND THAT VERY LITTLE HAD BEEN DONE.

THE CIVIL WAR

ALTHOUGH THE TELEGRAPH had been used in the Crimean War, it was during the War Between the States that it proved its military value for intelligence and troop deployment, uniting the Union forces in particular. By the end of September 1861, at least a dozen generals, including McClellan and Hooker, had attached telegraph tents to their commands. More than 15,000 miles of lines were erected strictly for military purposes.

Ulysses S. Grant made particularly heavy tactical and strategic use of the service: from his headquarters with Meade's army in Virginia in 1864, he wired daily orders, and later, he directed forces exceeding half a million soldiers. The operators of the military telegraph service worked under conditions of great personal danger—more than 300 of them died in the line of duty. A fairly complete history of the Civil War could be told through the telegraphic correspondence of its leaders. Here is just a small selection. Note that with no economic strictures, full sentences and punctuation were used; the constricted language of telegramese would develop years later.

In late 1860 and early 1861, there was a flurry of wires between Georgia Governor Joseph E. Brown and other southern governors concerning the question of secession. But even the immediacy of telegraphs was not always sufficient, as when one was sent warning against surrendering the Little Rock arsenal. The reply read:

SPOKE TOO LATE, LIKE IRISHMAN WHO SWALLOWED AN EGG. ARSENAL IS NOW IN HANDS OF GOVERNOR.

General Pierre G. T. Beauregard was the Confederate general who commanded the bombardment of Fort Sumter in the Charleston, South Carolina, harbor, the first major attack of the war in April of 1861. Early on, Beauregard sent this dispatch to the South's secretary of war, L. P. Walker, in Charleston:

A typical Civil War field telegraph station, at Wilcox's Landing, Virginia.

AN AUTHORISED MESSENGER FROM PRESIDENT LINCOLN HAS JUST
INFORMED GENERAL PICKENS AND MYSELF THAT SEVERAL HAMPERS OF
CANVAS-BACK DUCKS, WILD TURKEYS, CORN CAKES, AND MATERIALS
FOR BRANDY-SMASHES AND COCK-TAILS WILL BE SENT TO FORT
SUMTER PEACEABLY OR OTHERWISE.

Acknowledging the flag of truce hoisted by Union leader Major Robert
Anderson, Beauregard sent the following civilized wire:

I SEE YOUR CONDITION THROUGH MY TELESCOPE. WE HAVE
INTERCEPTED YOUR SUPPLIES. GIVE IN LIKE A GOOD FELLOW, AND

BRING YOUR GARRISON TO DINNER, AND BEDS AFTERWARDS. NOBODY
INJURED, I HOPE?

The first widespread use of aeronautics for military purposes took place early in the Civil War, when hot-air and hydrogen-filled balloons were employed for aerial reconnaissance. Thaddeus Lowe, a leading balloonist, took up the hydrogen gas balloon *Enterprise,* equipped with a telegraph unit, on June 16, 1861, sending President Lincoln a telegram reading:

THIS POINT OF OBSERVATION COMMANDS AN AREA NEAR FIFTY MILES
IN DIAMETER. THE CITY WITH ITS GIRDLE OF ENCAMPMENTS
PRESENTS A SUPERB SCENE. I HAVE PLEASURE IN SENDING YOU
THIS FIRST DISPATCH EVER TELEGRAPHED FROM AN AERIAL STATION
AND IN ACKNOWLEDGING INDEBTEDNESS TO YOUR ENCOURAGEMENT FOR
THE OPPORTUNITY OF DEMONSTRATING THE AVAILABILITY OF THE
SCIENCE OF AERONAUTICS IN THE MILITARY SERVICE.

On May 31, 1862, Lowe was flying in the balloon *Intrepid* from which he supplied intelligence that is credited with saving the Union army at the Battle of Fair Oaks. As in most conflicts, there was widespread rowdiness, brutality, and debauchery during the Civil War, as seen in these wires sent back to Washington from the front in 1861:

A MOST WANTON MURDER WAS COMMITTED HERE TODAY ABOUT TEN
O'CLOCK BY WILLIAM MURRAY. . . . THE VICTIM WAS AN
UNFORTUNATE WOMAN NAMED MARY BUTLER LIVING IN THE LOW PART
OF THE CITY. MURRAY, WHO WAS DRUNK, ACCOSTED HER IN THE
STREET AND AFTER EXCHANGING A FEW WORDS DELIBERATELY SHOT
HER WITH HIS MUSKET. THE BALL PASSED THROUGH HER BODY AND
CAUSED DEATH IN A FEW MOMENTS. THE CONDUCT OF THE SOLDIERS
IN ALEXANDRIA TODAY HAS EXCEEDED IN OUTRAGE ALL PRECEDENT.
DRUNKENNESS HAS BEEN PREDOMINANT AND THE SLAVE PEN AND JAIL
ARE NEARLY FULL.

And another sent from Centreville, Virginia:

PLEASE SEND US PIECE ARTILLERY FOR FEW DAYS ALL DRUNK HERE.

Leaders of the Confederate forces also sent graphic telegrams back from the field, such as this one from Jefferson Davis to Samuel Cooper in Richmond after First Manassas—also known as the Battle of Bull Run—on July 21, 1861:

NIGHT HAS CLOSED UPON A HARD FOUGHT FIELD. . . . OUR FORCES
HAVE WON A GLORIOUS VICTORY THE ENEMY WAS ROUTED & FLED
PRECIPITATELY ABANDONING A VERY LARGE AMOUNT OF ARMS
MUNITIONS KNAPSACKS AND BAGGIGE—THE GROUND WAS STREWN FOR
MILES WITH THOSE KILLED & THE FARM HOUSES AND GROUNDS
AROUND WERE FILLED WITH THE WOUNDED.

Ever the self-promoter, Union General George B. McClellan did not hesitate to take credit for victories, even those that were not his. In this case, in July of 1861, he wired the War Department regarding credit for defeat of the Confederate forces near Rich Mountain in Ohio, a victory actually achieved by Brigadier General William S. Rosecrans:

HAVE MET WITH COMPLETE SUCCESS; CAPTURED THE ENEMY'S ENTIRE
CAMP, GUNS, TENTS, WAGONS, ETC. MANY PRISONERS, AMONG WHOM
SEVERAL OFFICERS. ENEMY'S LOSSES SEVERE, OURS VERY SMALL.
NO OFFICERS LOST ON OUR SIDE. I TURNED THE POSITION. ALL
WELL.

Confederate General Thomas Jonathan Jackson earned the sobriquet "Stonewall" at the first battle of Bull Run, where he and his men stood "like a stone wall." He led the brilliant Shenandoah Valley campaign in May and June of 1862, sending the following collect telegram to his wife on May 9:

YESTERDAY GOD CROWNED OUR ARMS WITH SUCCESS. THE ENEMY IS
RETREATING.

On June 28, 1862, during the Seven Days' Battles, General McClellan sent a long, somewhat inaccurate, somewhat disrespectful, defensive, and self-serving telegram to Secretary of War Edwin M. Stanton. The last sentence so offended Edward Sanford of the telegraphic office that he deleted it from the copy he delivered to Stanton. It read in part:

> . . . ON THIS SIDE OF THE RIVER (THE RIGHT BANK) WE REPULSED
> SEVERAL STRONG ATTACKS. ON THE LEFT BANK OUR MEN DID ALL
> THAT MEN COULD DO, ALL THAT SOLDIERS COULD ACCOMPLISH, BUT
> THEY WERE OVERWHELMED BY VASTLY SUPERIOR NUMBERS. . . . THE
> LOSS ON BOTH SIDES IS TERRIBLE. I BELIEVE IT WILL PROVE TO
> BE THE MOST DESPERATE BATTLE OF THE WAR. THE SAD REMNANTS
> OF MY MEN BEHAVE AS MEN. . . . MY REGULARS WERE SUPERB AND I
> COULD UPON WHAT ARE LEFT TO TURN ANOTHER BATTLE. . . . HAD I
> 20,000 OR EVEN 10,000 FRESH TROOPS TO USE TO-MORROW I COULD
> TAKE RICHMOND, BUT I HAVE NOT A MAN IN RESERVE, AND SHALL
> BE GLAD TO COVER MY RETREAT. . . . IF WE HAVE LOST THE DAY WE
> HAVE YET PRESERVED OUR HONOR, AND NO ONE NEED BLUSH FOR THE
> ARMY OF THE POTOMAC. I HAVE LOST THIS BATTLE BECAUSE MY
> FORCE WAS TOO SMALL.
>
> I AGAIN REPEAT THAT I AM NOT RESPONSIBLE FOR THIS, AND I
> SAY IT WITH THE EARNESTNESS OF A GENERAL WHO FEELS IN HIS
> HEART THE LOSS OF EVERY BRAVE MAN WHO HAS BEEN NEEDLESSLY
> SACRIFICED TO-DAY. I STILL HOPE TO RETRIEVE OUR FORTUNES
> BUT TO DO THIS THE GOVERNMENT . . . MUST SEND ME VERY LARGE
> RE-ENFORCEMENTS, AND SEND THEM AT ONCE. . . .
>
> . . . I ONLY WISH TO SAY TO THE PRESIDENT THAT I THINK HE IS
> WRONG IN REGARDING ME AS UNGENEROUS WHEN I SAID THAT MY
> FORCE WAS TOO WEAK. . . . I HAVE SEEN TOO MANY DEAD AND
> WOUNDED COMRADES TO FEEL OTHERWISE THAN THAT THE GOVERNMENT
> HAS NOT SUSTAINED THIS ARMY. IF YOU DO NOT DO SO NOW THE
> GAME IS LOST. IF I SAVE THIS ARMY NOW, I TELL YOU PLAINLY
> THAT I OWE NO THANKS TO YOU OR ANY OTHER PERSONS IN
> WASHINGTON. YOU HAVE DONE YOUR BEST TO SACRIFICE THIS ARMY.

On August 30, 1862, General Robert E. Lee, after winning the significant second Battle of Manassas, sent this message to be telegraphed to

Confederate President Jefferson Davis, to reassure the anxious Southern people:

THIS ARMY TODAY ACHIEVED ON THE PLAINS OF MANASSAS A SIGNAL VICTORY OVER COMBINED FORCES OF GENLS. MCCLELLAN AND POPE. ON THE 28TH AND 29TH EACH WING UNDER GENLS. LONGSTREET AND JACKSON REPULSED WITH VALOUR ATTACKS MADE ON THEM SEPARATELY. WE MOURN THE LOSS OF OUR GALLANT DEAD IN EVERY CONFLICT YET OUR GRATITUDE TO ALMIGHTY GOD FOR HIS MERCIES RISES HIGHER AND HIGHER EACH DAY, TO HIM AND TO THE VALOUR OF OUR TROOPS A NATION'S GRATITUDE IS DUE.

During the Civil War, the telegraph contributed to the failure of a Confederate attack when the assault force under General James Longstreet got tangled in Union telegraph wires strung between two tree stumps at Fort Sanders in Knoxville, Tennessee.

In a military telegraph sent to Elihu B. Washburne on September 21, 1864, giving President Lincoln permission to use anything Ulysses S. Grant had written to him for political purposes, Grant exhibits both a sense of humor and a flare for simile equal to Lincoln's:

I HAVE NO OBJECTION TO THE PRESIDENT USING ANYTHING I HAVE EVER WRITTEN TO HIM AS HE SEES FIT. I THINK HOWEVER FOR HIM TO ATTEMPT TO ANSWER ALL THE CHARGES THE OPPOSITION WILL BRING AGAINST HIM WILL BE LIKE SETTING A MAIDEN TO WORK TO PROVE HER CHASTITY.

In a brutal 1864 battle in which the Union forces succeeded in protecting the Western & Atlantic Railroad at Allatoona Pass in Georgia but lost a considerable percentage of their men, General John Murray Corse sent this greatly exaggerated telegram to General William Tecumseh Sherman:

I AM SHORT ONE CHEEKBONE AND ONE EAR, BUT AM ABLE TO WHIP
ALL HELL YET.

In reality, Corse was only slightly scratched.

On December 20, 1864, Savannah fell to the Union forces, dealing a severe blow to the Southern forces and population. Two days later, Union General Sherman sent the following famous telegram to the president:

I BEG TO PRESENT TO YOU AS A CHRISTMAS GIFT THE CITY OF
SAVANNAH, WITH ONE HUNDRED AND FIFTY HEAVY GUNS AND PLENTY
OF AMMUNITION, ALSO ABOUT TWENTY-FIVE THOUSAND BALES OF
COTTON.

The longest Morse code telegram ever sent was dispatched in 1864 when, in order to meet a deadline for statehood, the entire constitution of Nevada was wired from Carson City to Washington, D.C., taking several hours and costing $3,400.

One of the key documents of the Civil War was sent via Morse telegraph on April 9, 1865, after the decisive conference held between opposing generals Ulysses S. Grant and Robert E. Lee. Shortly after leaving the McLean house in Appomattox in which it took place, Grant dismounted from his horse, sat down on a rock beside the road, and wrote out this message to Secretary of War Edwin M. Stanton:

GENERAL LEE SURRENDERED THE ARMY OF NORTHERN VIRGINIA THIS
AFTERNOON ON TERMS PROPOSED BY MYSELF THE ACCOMPANYING
ADDITIONAL CORRESPONDENCE WILL SHOW THE CONDITIONS FULLY.

ON JUNE 25, 1876, the headstrong George Armstrong Custer led his Seventh Cavalry against a massive force of Sioux and Cheyenne, who annihilated the attacking troops in the Battle of Little Bighorn. The same recklessness had caused problems a month before the battle, as seen in this telegraph from General Sheridan to General Townsend:

```
I AM SORRY LIEUTENANT COLONEL CUSTER DID NOT MANIFEST AS
MUCH INTEREST BY STAYING AT HIS POST TO ORGANIZE AND GET
READY HIS REGIMENT . . . AS HE DOES NOW TO ACCOMPANY IT. ON A
PREVIOUS OCCASION . . . I ASKED EXECUTIVE CLEMENCY FOR
GENERAL CUSTER TO ENABLE HIM TO ACCOMPANY HIS REGIMENT
AGAINST THE INDIANS, AND I SINCERELY HOPE IF GRANTED THIS
TIME IT WILL HAVE SUFFICIENT EFFECT TO PREVENT HIM FROM
```

The bustling main operating room of Western Union in New York.

AGAIN ATTEMPTING TO THROW DISCREDIT ON HIS PROFESSION AND
HIS BROTHER OFFICERS.

On May 8, 1876, came this wire from Sherman to General Alfred H.
Terry:

ADVISE CUSTER TO BE PRUDENT NOT TO TAKE ALONG ANY NEWSPAPER
MEN WHO ALWAYS WORK MISCHIEF, AND TO ABSTAIN FROM ANY
PERSONALITIES IN THE FUTURE. TELL HIM I WANT HIM TO CONFINE
HIS WHOLE MIND TO HIS LEGITIMATE OFFICE, AND TRUST TO TIME.

And following the final debacle, General Terry reported to Sheridan:

IT IS MY PAINFUL DUTY TO REPORT THAT DAY BEFORE
YESTERDAY . . . A GREAT DISASTER OVERTOOK GENERAL CUSTER AND
THE TROOPS UNDER HIS COMMAND. . . . OF THE MOVEMENTS OF
GENERAL CUSTER AND THE FIVE COMPANIES UNDER HIS IMMEDIATE
COMMAND, SCARCELY ANYTHING IS KNOWN FROM THOSE WHO
WITNESSED THEM; FOR NO OFFICER OR SOLDIER WHO ACCOMPANIED
HIM HAS YET BEEN FOUND ALIVE. . . .

WOUNDED KNEE

WHEN THE SIOUX NATION, under the leadership of Chief Big Foot, found
its way of life being destroyed, as its members were confined to reserva-
tions and completely dependent on federal agents, many of them sought
release in a new mysticism preached by a shaman called Wovoka. He
instructed them in what he called the Ghost Dance, performed in
"Ghost Shirts" that they believed would protect them from the blue-
coats' bullets. At the time of the battle of Wounded Knee, Dr. Daniel F.

Royer, agent for the Pine Ridge Agency, sent this telegram to Washington on November 15, 1890:

INDIANS ARE DANCING IN THE SNOW AND ARE WILD AND
CRAZY. . . . THE EMPLOYEES AND THE GOVERNMENT PROPERTY AT
THIS AGENCY HAVE NO PROTECTION AND ARE AT THE MERCY OF THE
GHOST DANCERS. . . . WE NEED PROTECTION AND WE NEED IT
NOW. . . . NOTHING [SHORT] OF 1000 TROOPS WILL STOP THIS
DANCING.

AN EARLY CUBAN CRISIS

FROM EARLY 1889, when Spain responded to the growing insurrection in Cuba by sending troops to the island, newspaper publisher William Randolph Hearst featured the Cuban conflict and its devastating effects on the front pages of his papers. This 1898 telegram from Hearst to James Creelman, one of his top writers, in London shows how powerful Hearst was:

I WISH YOU WOULD AT ONCE MAKE PREPARATIONS SO THAT IN CASE
THE SPANISH FLEET ACTUALLY STARTS FOR MANILA WE CAN BUY
SOME BIG ENGLISH STEAMER AT THE EASTERN END OF THE
MEDITERRANEAN AND TAKE HER TO SOME PART OF THE SUEZ CANAL,
WHERE WE CAN THEN SINK HER AND OBSTRUCT THE PASSAGE OF THE
SPANISH WARSHIPS. THIS MUST BE DONE IF THE AMERICAN
MONITORS SENT FROM SAN FRANCISCO HAVE NOT REACHED DEWEY AND
HE SHOULD BE PLACED IN A CRITICAL POSITION BY THE APPROACH
OF CAMARA'S FLEET. . . .

On February 15, 1898, the U.S. battleship *Maine* was blown up in Havana harbor, resulting in the deaths of 260 crew members, and prompting the slogan "Remember the *Maine.*" The captain of the ship, Charles D. Sigsbee, dashed off a telegram to Washington:

MAINE BLOWN UP IN HAVANA HARBOR AT NINE FORTY TONIGHT AND DESTROYED. MANY WOUNDED AND DOUBTLESS MORE KILLED OR DROWNED. . . . PUBLIC OPINION SHOULD BE SUSPENDED UNTIL FURTHER REPORT. . . .

A declaration of war followed two months later.

As for the infamous wire Hearst supposedly sent to artist Frederic Remington, who was covering the event,

PLEASE REMAIN. YOU FURNISH THE PICTURES, AND I'LL FURNISH THE WAR

historians now have serious doubts as to its existence—it may well have been a case of Hearst trying to convince the public of his extraordinary influence. The line between fact and fiction blurred even further in a scene in *Citizen Kane.* When the following telegram from one of his reporters in Cuba is read to Charles Foster Kane: "Girls delightful in Cuba stop. Could send you prose poems about scenery but don't feel right spending your money stop. There is no war in Cuba," Kane dictates the response, "You provide the prose poems, I'll provide the war."

ELECTIONS

IN 1860, the leading Republican presidential hopefuls were William Seward and Abraham Lincoln, with Seward the favorite. Lincoln decided not to attend the nominating convention in Chicago, but two of his supporters, Judge Davis and Jesse Dubois, kept him updated by telegram:

The scene inside the telegraph office of Underwood & Underwood, 1904.

On May 14, they wired:

DON'T COME UNLESS WE SEND FOR YOU.

And the following day:

WE ARE QUIET BUT MOVING HEAVEN AND EARTH. NOTHING WILL BEAT US BUT OLD FOGEY POLITICIANS. THE DIEHARTS OF THE DELEGATES ARE WITH US.

Lincoln was nominated on the eighteenth.

Following his reelection in 1864, Abraham Lincoln got this wire of congratulations and advice from his "friend and supporter" Jesse H. Robinson in Chattanooga, Tennessee, regarding the state of the union on the hopeful ending of the Civil War:

DEAR SIR, ALLOW ME TO CONGRATULATE YOU ON BEING REELECTED
BY SUCH A LARGE MAJORITY. THE COUNTRY IS SO FAR WITH YOU
FOR HER PILOT I THINK THE SAME AS YOUR HONORABLE SECY OF
STATE THE PAST SHOULD BE FORGOTTEN LET THE DEMOCRATS JOIN
HANDS WITH US AND HAVE BUT ONE PARTY AND THAT PARTIES
OBJECT TO BE TO CRUSH THE REBELLION AND EXTERMINATE HUMAN
SLAVERY FROM THE LAND TO ACCOMPLISH THE UNANIMOUS ACTION OF
THE TWO PARTIES WE MUST BE MAGNANIMOUS TOWARDS OUR DEFEATED
BRETHREN. . . . IN MY JUDGMENT I THINK THE WAY TO SHOW OUR
MAGNANMITY WOULD BE TO GIVE MCCLELLAN AN ACTION COMMAND
THAT IN YOUR JUDGMENT WOULD BE SUITABLE TO HIS CAPACITY. DO
THIS AND YOU MAY DEPEND UPON IT THE INTELLIGENT PORTION OF
THE DEMOCRATS WILL JOIN HANDS WITH US CHEERFULLY. THIS IS
NO TIME FOR ANY PARTY BUT ONE AND THAT ONE SHOULD BE FOR
THE UNION OUT AND OUT. WE MAY DIFFER ON SOME TRIFLING
THINGS BUT FOR THE LOVE OF GOD AND OUR COUNTRY LET US BE A
UNIT ON THE CRUSHING OF THE REBELLION.

Civil War General William Tecumseh Sherman, most famous for his March to the Sea, retired from the army in 1883. The following year, he was being recruited to run as the Republican candidate for president. His reply was sent in the form of a historic telegram:

I WILL NOT ACCEPT IF NOMINATED, AND WILL NOT SERVE IF
ELECTED

After he had served as a Republican president for two terms, Theodore Roosevelt became alarmed by the conservatism of his Republican successor, William Howard Taft, and formed the Progressive, or Bull Moose, party. When he ran (unsuccessfully) for the presidency on this ticket in 1912, TR's nomination was seconded by social reformer Jane Addams, then vice president of the National American Woman Suffrage Alliance. On August 12 of that year, he sent her a telegram of thanks, which began:

I PRIZED YOUR ACTION NOT ONLY BECAUSE OF WHAT YOU ARE AND
STAND FOR, BUT BECAUSE OF WHAT IT SYMBOLIZED FOR THE NEW
MOVEMENT. IN THIS GREAT NATIONAL CONVENTION STARTING THE
NEW PARTY WOMEN HAVE THEREBY BEEN SHOWN TO HAVE THEIR PLACE
TO FILL PRECISELY AS MEN HAVE, AND ON AN ABSOLUTE EQUALITY.
IT IS NOW IDLE TO ARGUE WHETHER WOMEN CAN PLAY THEIR PART
IN POLITICS, BECAUSE IN THIS CONVENTION WE SAW THE
ACCOMPLISHED FACT. . . . THE WOMEN WHO HAVE ACTIVELY
PARTICIPATED IN THIS WORK OF LAUNCHING THE NEW PARTY
REPRESENT ALL THAT WE ARE MOST PROUD TO ASSOCIATE WITH
AMERICAN WOMANHOOD. . . .

Feisty Jack London offered his typically acrimonious response to a query
from the *New York World* newspaper about the coming election in October of 1916:

I HAVE NO CHOICE FOR PRESIDENT. WILSON HAS NOT ENAMORED
ME WITH PAST PERFORMANCES. HUGHES HAS NOT ENAMORED ME
WITH PROMISE OF FUTURE PERFORMANCE. THERE IS NOTHING TO
HOPE FOR FROM EITHER OF THEM EXCEPT THAT THEY WILL
BRILLIANTLY GUIDE THE UNITED STATES DOWN HER FAT HELPLESS
LONELY UNHONORABLE PROFIT-SEEKING WAY TO THE SHAMBLES
THAT HER SHAMELESS UNPREPAREDNESS IS LEADING HER. . . . WE
STAND FOR NOTHING EXCEPT FAT. WE ARE BECOMING THE FAT MAN
WHOM NO NATION LOVES. ALL NATIONS WILL DELIGHT IN THE
SPECTACLE OF SEEING ANY NATION STICK US UP AND BLEED
US. . . .

In August of 1922, Louis Howe, FDR's right-hand man, sent his boss
a telegram reporting on the outcome of the New York State
Democratic convention, in which Roosevelt backed Al Smith:

AL NOMINATED WITH GREAT ENTHUSIASM. MORGENTHAU AND YOUR
MISSUS LED THE DUTCHESS COUNTY DELEGATION WITH THE BANNER
THREE TIMES AROUND THE HALL. . . .

As the 1932 election approached, Franklin D. Roosevelt was considered such a shoo-in against the incumbent Herbert Hoover that one voter wired Hoover:

VOTE FOR ROOSEVELT AND MAKE IT UNANIMOUS.

Joseph P. Kennedy and Franklin D. Roosevelt had a mercurial but usually congenial relationship, as can be seen from the following wire sent by Kennedy from Connecticut to the president on March 14, 1933:

I JUST STOPPED OFF AT PROVIDENCE TO SEE MY OLDEST DAUGHTER
AT THE SACRED HEART CONVENT. THE MOTHER SUPERIOR OF THE
CONVENT, A REAL SAINTLY WOMAN, SAID THE NUNS WERE PRAYING
FOR YOU AND THEN MADE A REMARKABLE STATEMENT FOR A
RELIGIOUS WOMAN TO MAKE "THAT SINCE YOUR INAUGURATION
PEACE SEEMED TO COME ON THE EARTH; IN FACT IT SEEMED LIKE
ANOTHER RESURRECTION." MORTAL MEN CAN PAY YOU NO HIGHER
COMPLIMENT.

The great heavyweight champion Joe Louis had strong political views, most significantly that the government under FDR was accruing too much power with its Works Progress Administration and other New Deal programs. Before the presidential election of 1940, Louis telegraphed opposing Republican candidate Wendell Willkie:

WIN BY A KNOCKOUT. IT WILL MEAN FREEDOM FROM THE WPA AND
FOR AMERICAN NEGRO RIGHTS.

During the campaign of 1944, FDR gave a speech in Chicago in which he set as his postwar goal full employment and sixty million jobs. His departing vice president, Henry A. Wallace, predicted Roosevelt would carry thirty-six states with a popular majority of 3 million. (He would be right on the nose on the thirty-six states, 600,000 short on the popular vote.) On November 1, Roosevelt wired Wallace:

GLAD YOU LIKED THE CHICAGO SHOW. I PROMISE TO MAKE GOOD ON
THE SIXTY MILLION JOBS IF YOU WILL DO THE SAME ON YOUR

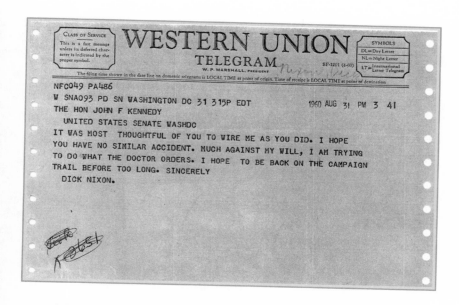

WESTERN UNION
TELEGRAM
W. P. MARSHALL, PRESIDENT

The filing time shown in the date line on domestic telegrams is LOCAL TIME at point of origin. Time of receipt is LOCAL TIME at point of destination

SF-1201 (4-60)

NFC049 PA486

W SNA093 PD SN WASHINGTON DC 31 315P EDT   1960 AUG 31 PM 3 41
THE HON JOHN F KENNEDY
   UNITED STATES SENATE WASHDC
   IT WAS MOST THOUGHTFUL OF YOU TO WIRE ME AS YOU DID. I HOPE
   YOU HAVE NO SIMILAR ACCIDENT. MUCH AGAINST MY WILL, I AM TRYING
   TO DO WHAT THE DOCTOR ORDERS. I HOPE TO BE BACK ON THE CAMPAIGN
   TRAIL BEFORE TOO LONG. SINCERELY
      DICK NIXON.

Richard Nixon to John F. Kennedy, August 31, 1960, in response to a wire
from Kennedy promising to halt his presidential campaign
until Nixon had recovered from an injury.

PREDICTIONS REGARDING THE THIRTY-SIX STATES, THE POPULAR
AND ELECTORAL COLLEGE MAJORITIES. . . .

Orson Welles was an ardent supporter of and tireless campaigner for
Franklin Roosevelt. In the final run of 1944, FDR sent the following
telegram to Welles, who lay ill in the Waldorf-Astoria hotel:

I DEEPLY APPRECIATE EVERYTHING YOU HAVE DONE AND YOU ARE
DOING. I HAVE JUST LEARNED THAT YOU ARE ILL AND I HOPE MUCH
YOU WILL FOLLOW YOUR DOCTORS ORDERS AND TAKE CARE OF
YOURSELF. THE MOST IMPORTANT THING IS FOR YOU TO GET WELL
AND BE AROUND FOR THE LAST DAYS OF THE CAMPAIGN. MY WARM
REGARDS.

THE ASSASSINATION of Archduke Francis Ferdinand, heir apparent to the Austro-Hungarian throne, by a Serbian nationalist in Sarajevo on June 28, 1914, is considered to be the event that triggered World War I. One month later, after its demands for retribution were refused, Austria-Hungary declared war on Serbia, with other declarations of war following quickly, until every major European power was drawn in by a complex and antiquated network of diplomatic alliances. On July 29, a series of telegrams in English passed between cousins Kaiser Wilhelm II, a grandson of Queen Victoria, and Czar Nicholas II—about whom Wilhelm once remarked that he was "only fit to live in a country house and grow turnips." Here are some excerpts from this remarkable exchange, known as the Willy-Nicky correspondence.

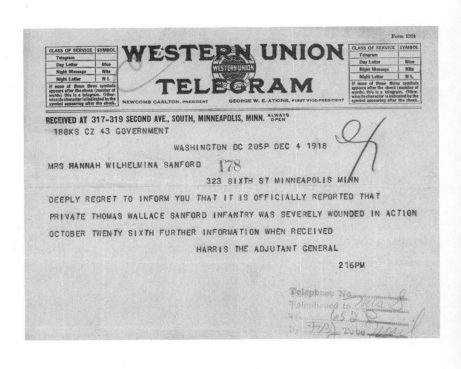

At 1 A.M. on July 29 from the czar to the kaiser:

> . . . I APPEAL TO YOU TO HELP ME. AN IGNOBLE WAR HAS BEEN
> DECLARED TO A WEAK COUNTRY. THE INDIGNATION IN RUSSIA
> SHARED FULLY BY ME IS ENORMOUS. I FORESEE THAT SOON I SHALL
> BE OVERWHELMED BY THE PRESSURE FORCED UPON ME AND BE FORCED
> TO TAKE EXTREME MEASURES WHICH WILL LEAD TO WAR. TO TRY AND
> AVOID SUCH A CALAMITY AS A EUROPEAN WAR I BEG YOU IN THE
> NAME OF OUR OLD FRIENDSHIP TO DO WHAT YOU CAN TO STOP YOUR
> ALLIES FROM GOING TOO FAR. . . .

On the same date, at 1:45 A.M., the kaiser was sending his own telegraph,
which crossed cables with his cousin's:

> . . . WITH REGARD TO THE HEARTY AND TENDER FRIENDSHIP WHICH
> BINDS US BOTH FROM LONG AGO WITH FIRM TIES, I AM EXERTING
> MY UTMOST INFLUENCE TO INDUCE THE AUSTRIANS TO DEAL
> STRAIGHTLY TO ARRIVE TO A SATISFACTORY UNDERSTANDING WITH
> YOU. . . .
> YOUR VERY SINCERE AND DEVOTED FRIEND AND COUSIN

From Berlin later that day, at 6:30 P.M.:

> . . . I CANNOT CONSIDER AUSTRIA'S ACTION AGAINST SERBIA AN
> "IGNOBLE" WAR. . . . IT WOULD BE QUITE IMPOSSIBLE FOR RUSSIA
> TO REMAIN A SPECTATOR OF THE AUSTRO-SERBIAN CONFLICT
> WITHOUT INVOLVING EUROPE IN THE MOST HORRIBLE WAR SHE EVER
> WITNESSED. I THINK A DIRECT UNDERSTANDING BETWEEN YOUR
> GOVERNMENT AND VIENNA POSSIBLE AND DESIRABLE. . . .

From St. Peter's Court Palace at 8:20 P.M.:

> THANKS FOR YOUR TELEGRAM CONCILIATORY AND FRIENDLY. WHEREAS
> OFFICIAL MESSAGE PRESENTED TODAY BY YOUR AMBASSADOR TO MY
> MINISTER WAS CONVEYED IN A VERY DIFFERENT TONE. . . . BEG YOU
> TO EXPLAIN THIS DIVERGENCY! . . .
> YOUR LOVING NICKY

Willy's reply, July 31:

ON YOUR APPEAL TO MY FRIENDSHIP AND YOUR CALL FOR
ASSISTANCE BEGAN TO MEDIATE BETWEEN YOUR AND THE AUSTRO-
HUNGARIAN GOVERNMENT. WHILE THIS ACTION WAS PROCEEDING YOUR
TROOPS WERE MOBILISED AGAINST AUSTRO-HUNGARY, MY ALLY.
THEREBY, AS I HAVE ALREADY POINTED OUT TO YOU, MY MEDIATION
HAS BEEN MADE ALMOST ILLUSORY. . . . THE PEACE OF EUROPE MAY
STILL BE MAINTAINED BY YOU, IF RUSSIA WILL AGREE TO STOP
THE MILIT. MEASURES. . . .

Another crossed telegram, from the czar, July 31:

I THANK YOU HEARTILY FOR YOUR MEDIATION WHICH BEGINS TO
GIVE ONE HOPE THAT ALL MAY YET END PEACEFULLY. IT IS
TECHNICALLY IMPOSSIBLE TO STOP OUR MILITARY PREPARATIONS
WHICH WERE OBLIGATORY OWING TO AUSTRIA'S MOBILIZATION, WE
ARE FAR FROM WISHING WAR. . . .

The kaiser's telegrams began to take on a more impersonal tone on
August 1:

. . . I YESTERDAY POINTED OUT TO YOUR GOVERNMENT THE WAY BY
WHICH ALONE WAR MAY BE AVOIDED. ALTHOUGH I REQUESTED AN
ANSWER FOR NOON TODAY, NO TELEGRAM . . . HAS REACHED ME AS
YET. I THEREFORE HAVE BEEN OBLIGED TO MOBILISE MY ARMY.
IMMEDIATE AFFIRMATIVE CLEAR AND UNMISTAKABLE ANSWER FROM
YOUR GOVERNMENT IS THE ONLY WAY TO AVOID ENDLESS
MISERY. . . . I MUST REQUEST YOU TO IMMEDIATLY ORDER YOUR
TROOPS ON NO ACCOUNT TO COMMIT THE SLIGHTEST ACT OF
TRESPASSING OVER OUR FRONTIERS.

That same day, Germany declared war on Russia.

One of the most infamous of all telegrams—about which historian Barbara Tuchman wrote an entire book—is known as the Zimmermann

Telegram and was a major factor in America entering the First World War. Arthur Zimmermann was the German foreign minister when, in January of 1917, he sent an encrypted cable to the German ambassador in Mexico, proposing that Mexico, with German and Japanese assistance, attack America in return for her "lost" states of New Mexico, Texas, and Arizona. Decoded by the British, it read in part:

```
WE INTEND TO BEGIN ON THE FIRST OF FEBRUARY UNRESTRICTED
SUBMARINE WARFARE. WE SHALL ENDEAVOR IN SPITE OF THIS TO
KEEP THE UNITED STATES OF AMERICA NEUTRAL. IN THE EVENT
THIS IS NOT SUCCEEDING, WE MAKE MEXICO A PROPOSAL OF
ALLIANCE ON THE FOLLOWING BASIS: MAKE WAR TOGETHER, MAKE
PEACE TOGETHER, GENEROUS FINANCIAL SUPPORT AND AN
UNDERSTANDING ON OUR PART THAT MEXICO IS TO RECONQUER THE
LOST TERRITORY IN TEXAS, NEW MEXICO, AND ARIZONA.
```

Disclosure of the contents of the Zimmermann Telegram in the United States on March 1, 1917, further inflamed American public opinion against Germany, and on April 6, President Woodrow Wilson, who had been adamant in his neutrality, asked Congress to declare war on Germany and the Central Powers. Two days later, it complied.

The use of the word "stop" came into common usage during World War I, when the government employed it widely as a precaution against having messages misunderstood as a result of the misplacement or omission of the small period dot. To ensure that vital orders would be absolutely clear, they not only used "stop" to indicate periods but spelled out "comma," "colon," "semicolon," and "query" for question mark. "Stop" was used internationally, no matter what language the telegram was written in.

THE RUSSIAN REVOLUTION

IN THE EARLY YEARS of the twentieth century, widespread discontent among the Russian peasants, workers, military, intelligentsia, and religious minorities was inflamed by the corrupt regime of Czar Nicholas II. After an abortive revolution in 1905, the events of World War I brought the situation to a head. By early 1917, there were strikes and food riots as a result of severe civilian deprivation, as reported by Michael Rodzianko, president of the Duma (Parliament) in this February 26 telegram to Nicholas:

> THE SITUATION IS SERIOUS. THE CAPITAL IS IN A STATE OF
> ANARCHY. THE GOVERNMENT IS PARALYSED; THE TRANSPORT SERVICE
> HAS BROKEN DOWN; THE FOOD AND FUEL SUPPLIES ARE COMPLETELY
> DISORGANIZED. . . . THERE IS WILD SHOOTING IN THE
> STREETS. . . . IT IS URGENT THAT SOMEONE ENJOYING THE
> CONFIDENCE OF THE COUNTRY BE ENTRUSTED WITH THE FORMATION
> OF A NEW GOVERNMENT. . . . HESITATION IS FATAL.

To which Nicholas replied on March 1:

> THERE IS NO SACRIFICE THAT I WOULD NOT BE WILLING TO MAKE
> FOR THE WELFARE AND SALVATION OF MOTHER RUSSIA. THEREFORE I
> AM READY TO ABDICATE IN FAVOUR OF MY SON, UNDER THE REGENCY
> OF MY BROTHER. . . .

A long telegram from the American consulate general in Saint Petersburg, North Winship, to his superiors at the State Department, sent on March 20, filled in the background of the Bolshevik uprising. It read in part:

> ON THE BEGINNING OF THE WEEK OF MARCH 4TH, A SHORTAGE OF
> BLACK BREAD WAS NOTICEABLE. THIS AT ONCE CAUSED UNREST
> AMONG THE LABORING CLASSES. ALL OTHER PRIME NECESSITIES
> WITHIN THE MEANS OF THE WORKING CLASSES HAD ALREADY
> GRADUALLY DISAPPEARED AS THE WINTER ADVANCED: MEAT, SUGAR,
> WHITE FLOUR, BUCKWHEAT, POTATOES, FISH, FOWLS, EGGS, MILK

CHEESE, AND BUTTER, HAD FOR A LONG TIME BEEN SO EXPENSIVE
THAT THEY WERE ONLY WITHIN THE MEANS OF THE VERY WELL-TO-
DO-CLASSES. THE UNREST FIRST TOOK VISIBLE FORM IN THE
OUTSKIRTS AND FACTORY DISTRICTS OF THE CITY WEDNESDAY,
MARCH 7TH. . . . THE NEXT DAY . . . THERE WERE SPONTANEOUS
ISOLATED DEMONSTRATIONS. IN MANY PLACES, A FEW OF THE
WORKING CLASS, MOSTLY WOMEN, TIRED OF WAITING IN THE BREAD
LINES IN THE SEVERE COLD BEGAN TO CRY, "GIVE US BREAD."
THESE GROUPS WERE IMMEDIATELY DISPERSED BY LARGE
DETACHMENTS OF MOUNTED POLICE AND COSSACKS. . . .

> "I used to be the fastest telegram messenger boy in Fresno. My nick-
> name was 'Speed.' Finally I said, 'Take back your nickname. This pace
> is killing me.'"
> —William Saroyan

Bolshevik leader Vladimir Lenin became the virtual dictator of the new
regime. The brutality of his methods is revealed in this November 1918
telegram sent to several Communist party comrades:

. . . THE REVOLT OF THE FIVE KULAK VOLOST'S MUST BE
REPRESSED WITHOUT MERCY. THE INTEREST OF THE ENTIRE
REVOLUTION DEMANDS THIS, BECAUSE WE HAVE NOW BEFORE US OUR
FINAL DECISIVE BATTLE "WITH THE KULAKS." WE NEED TO SET AN
EXAMPLE.

1. YOU NEED TO HANG (HANG WITHOUT FAIL, SO THAT THE PUBLIC
SEES) AT LEAST 100 NOTORIOUS KULAKS, THE RICH, AND THE
BLOODSUCKERS.

2. PUBLISH THEIR NAMES.

3. TAKE AWAY ALL OF THEIR GRAIN.

4. EXECUTE THE HOSTAGES. . . .

THIS NEEDS TO BE ACCOMPLISHED IN SUCH A WAY, THAT PEOPLE
FOR HUNDREDS OF MILES WILL SEE, TREMBLE, KNOW AND SCREAM
OUT: LET'S CHOKE AND STRANGLE THOSE BLOOD-SUCKING
KULAKS. . . .
P.S. USE YOUR TOUGHEST PEOPLE FOR THIS.

GANDHI

MAHATMA GANDHI endured long fasts and hunger strikes both for his own spiritual enlightenment and for the cause of Indian independence. On September 18, 1924, in reply to a telegram from Chakravarti Rajagopalachari urging him to give up his fast, "which would mean nothing short of death in view of his present health," Gandhi wired:

CANCELLATION FAST CANCELLATION SELF. AM FASTING TO LIVE NOT
DIE UNLESS GOD WILLS OTHERWISE. DON'T WORRY

THE CRASH AND THE DEPRESSION

THE OPTIMISTIC CHAIRMAN of National City Bank sent this telegram to Bernard Baruch on August 21, 1929, just two months before the great Wall Street crash:

GENERAL SITUATION LOOKS EXCEPTIONALLY SOUND WITH VERY FEW
BAD SPOTS SUCH AS RUBBER. . . . I DOUBT IF ANYTHING THAT WILL
NOT AFFECT BUSINESS CAN AFFECT THE MARKET, WHICH IS LIKE A
WEATHER-VANE POINTING INTO A GALE OF PROSPERITY.

And on October 23, 1929, exactly one day before Black Thursday, financial wizard Baruch (who had the foresight to get out of the market himself before the Crash) sent the following wire to Baltimore & Ohio Railroad director John Morron:

. . . ONLY THING UNPLEASANT IN SIGHT AT PRESENT IS PROSPECTIVE DECLINE IN BUSINESS WHICH WILL BE BAD BUT WILL BE MUCH EXAGGERATED AS THE BULLISHNESS WAS EXAGGERATED SIX MONTHS AGO. . . . BUSINESS CANNOT REMAIN VERY BAD IN THIS COUNTRY LONG.

During the Great Depression, the price of the South's main crop, "King Cotton," plunged drastically. To drive up the prices, Louisiana Governor Huey Long came up with a radical proposal, which he wired to other Southern leaders, including this one to Texas Governor Ross S. Sterling on August 16, 1931:

WE CAN RESTORE THE PROSPERITY OF THE SOUTH AND . . . THE BALANCE OF THE WORLD WITHIN LESS THAN TWO WEEKS TIME IF THE COTTON-PRODUCING STATES HAVE GOVERNORS WHO HAVE THE COURAGE TO ACT NOW AND DECISIVELY. THE ONLY WAY THAT THIS CAN BE DONE IS TO PROHIBIT BY LAW AT ONCE THE RAISING OF A SINGLE BALE OF COTTON IN ALL COTTON GROWING STATES DURING THE YEAR 1932.

DADDY WARBUCKS

At the height of the popularity of the comic strip *Little Orphan Annie,* a story line involving Annie's dog, Sandy, getting lost incited a wave of public outcry. Even flinty industrialist Henry Ford sent a telegram to artist Harold Gray imploring that Sandy be found and the girl and her dog be reunited.

In the midst of the depression, Franklin Roosevelt, then governor of New York, summoned a special session of the state legislature to consider the question of relief to the needy, proposing a twenty-million-dollar Temporary Emergency Relief Fund to underwrite municipal aid. A grateful Fiorello La Guardia, then congressman from New York, wired the governor:

> YOUR COURAGEOUS STAND ON PROVIDING REVENUE FROM TAXATION TO
> CARRY OUT PROGRAM IS INDEED TO BE COMMENDED IN THESE DAYS
> OF TIMIDITY TO FACE ISSUE AND PASS THE BUCK. . . . IN THE
> NAME OF THOUSANDS OF INNOCENT VICTIMS OF PRESENT DEPRESSION
> WITH WHOM I AM IN CONTACT THANKS.

In that time of unprecedented unemployment and poverty, Hoover-villes—squalid settlements of sheds made of boxes and scrap metal—were set up by the homeless in vacant lots, one of the largest of which sprang up not far from the White House. In the spring of 1932, a group of 20,000 World War I veterans and their families descended on Washington to claim a bonus that officially would not be due to them until 1945. When the Senate voted against this, armed soldiers, led by General Douglas MacArthur, pursued the veterans and burned their shacks. Not surprisingly, there was a massive protest, as seen in this telegram from then Representative La Guardia, to President Herbert Hoover:

> SOUP IS CHEAPER THAN TEAR BOMBS AND BREAD BETTER THAN
> BULLETS IN THESE TIMES OF DEPRESSION, UNEMPLOYMENT AND
> HUNGER. . . . REGARDLESS OF WHOM THEY MAY BE, AMERICAN
> CITIZENS MUST BE PROVIDED WITH FOOD AND SHELTER IF THEY ARE
> DESTITUTE AND HUNGRY. WHEN MEN ARE HUNGRY FOR BREAD THEY
> ARE IRRITABLE AND WILL USE FORCE.

Former General Erich Ludendorff had been a comrade of Adolf Hitler in 1923, during the Beer Hall Putsch. When he heard that Hitler had been made chancellor, in 1933, Ludendorff sent this all-too-prophetic wire to German President Paul von Hindenburg:

> BY APPOINTING HITLER CHANCELLOR OF THE REICH YOU HAVE HANDED OVER OUR SACRED GERMAN FATHERLAND TO ONE OF THE GREATEST DEMAGOGUES OF ALL TIME. I PROPHESY TO YOU THIS EVIL MAN WILL PLUNGE OUR REICH INTO THE ABYSS AND WILL INFLICT IMMEASURABLE WOE ON OUR NATION. FUTURE GENERATIONS WILL CURSE YOU IN YOUR GRAVE FOR THIS ACTION.

Within weeks, Hitler would be absolute dictator of Germany and would set in motion the chain of events that resulted in World War II.

At this time, Hitler had his supporters in England. Six days before the invasion of Poland, the Duke of Windsor sent a telegram directly to

In the 1930s, William Randolph Hearst had contracts with several world leaders to write for his papers. They included Churchill, Lloyd George, Mussolini, and even Adolf Hitler, whose first article appeared on September 28, 1930, advertised as "Hitler's Own Story: He Tells What Is the Matter with Germany and How He Proposes to Remedy It." There were problems with Hitler over meeting deadlines and hassles over exclusivity and payment rates—he was asking for $1,000 per article—but when one of Hearst's minions cabled that he didn't think they were worth more than $500, the publisher wired back that he thought an article on disarmament by Hitler would be of sufficient interest in America that if Hitler didn't agree to $500, the bid should be increased.

the Führer, urging him to use his influence to preserve the peace. On the twenty-seventh of August, 1939, Hitler replied:

YOU MAY REST ASSURED THAT MY ATTITUDE TOWARDS BRITAIN AND MY DESIRE TO AVOID ANOTHER WAR BETWEEN OUR PEOPLE REMAINS UNCHANGED.

In the same year, Noël Coward sent this uncharacteristically bleak telegram to his business manager:

GRAVE POSSIBILITY WAR WITHIN FEW WEEKS OR DAYS. IF THIS HAPPENS POSTPONEMENT REVUE INEVITABLE AND ANNIHILATION OF US ALL PROBABLE.

And a voice from the military: in September of 1940, General Douglas MacArthur sent a telegram to journalist William Allen White in response to a request for his opinion on whether the United States should continue to give aid to England:

. . . THE HISTORY OF FAILURE IN WAR CAN ALMOST BE SUMMED UP IN TWO WORDS: TOO LATE. TOO LATE IN COMPREHENDING THE DEADLY PURPOSE OF A POTENTIAL ENEMY. TOO LATE IN REALIZING MORTAL DANGER. TOO LATE IN PREPAREDNESS. TOO LATE IN UNITING ALL POSSIBLE FORCES FOR RESISTANCE. TOO LATE IN STANDING WITH ONE'S FRIENDS. VICTORY IN WAR RESULTS FROM NO MYSTERIOUS ALCHEMY OR WIZARDRY, BUT ENTIRELY UPON THE CONCENTRATION OF SUPERIOR FORCE AT THE CRITICAL POINTS OF COMBAT. . . . THE GREATEST STRATEGICAL MISTAKE IN ALL HISTORY WILL BE MADE IF AMERICA FAILS TO RECOGNIZE THAT VITAL MOMENT, IF SHE PERMITS AGAIN THE WRITING OF THAT FATAL EPITAPH "TOO LATE." . . .

Despite her later protestations to the contrary, the attitude of filmmaker Leni Riefenstahl toward the leader of the Third Reich is evident in this telegram she sent to Hitler in 1940, when his troops marched into Paris:

YOUR DEEDS EXCEED THE POWER OF HUMAN IMAGINATION. THEY ARE
WITHOUT EQUAL IN THE HISTORY OF MANKIND. HOW CAN WE EVER
THANK YOU?

In the spring of 1940, President Franklin Roosevelt sent several telegrams to Benito Mussolini, the premier of Italy, trying to persuade Il Duce not to enter into an alliance with Hitler. An excerpt from his May 14 dispatch:

... ALL OF US IN THE AMERICAS FEEL IN OUR HEARTS THAT
TONIGHT THE WHOLE WORLD FACES A THREAT WHICH OPPOSES EVERY
TEACHING OF CHRIST, EVERY PHILOSOPHY OF ALL THE GREAT
TEACHERS OF MANKIND OVER THOUSANDS OF YEARS. FORCES OF
SLAUGHTER, FORCES WHICH DENY GOD, FORCES WHICH SEEK TO
DOMINATE MANKIND BY FEAR RATHER THAN BY REASON SEEM AT THIS
MOMENT TO BE EXTENDING THEIR CONQUEST AGAINST A HUNDRED
MILLION HUMAN BEINGS WHO HAVE NO DESIRE BUT PEACE. YOU WHOM
THE GREAT ITALIAN PEOPLE CALL THEIR LEADER HAVE IT IN YOUR
OWN HANDS TO STAY THE SPREAD OF THIS WAR TO ANOTHER GROUP
OF 200,000 HUMAN SOULS.

German diplomat Joachim von Ribbentrop (who would later be executed for war crimes) sent this telegram to his Russian counterpart, Vyacheslav Molotov, concerning the proposed German–Japanese pact on September 25, 1940:

THIS ALLIANCE IS DIRECTED EXCLUSIVELY AGAINST AMERICAN
WARMONGERS. . . . ITS EXCLUSIVE PURPOSE IS TO BRING THE
ELEMENTS PRESSING FOR AMERICA'S ENTRY INTO THE WAR TO THEIR
SENSES BY CONCLUSIVELY DEMONSTRATING TO THEM IF THEY ENTER
THE PRESENT STRUGGLE THEY WILL AUTOMATICALLY HAVE TO DEAL
WITH THE THREE GREAT POWERS AS ADVERSARIES.

In 1941, when aviation hero Charles Lindbergh's isolationist America First speeches were widely interpreted as sympathetic to the Nazis, he received the following telegram from showman Billy Rose:

IF YOU ARE WILLING TO CONDEMN HITLER AND HIS GANG AND THEIR
UNSPEAKABLE BARBARITIES, I WILL ENGAGE MADISON SQUARE
GARDEN AT MY EXPENSE AND GIVE YOU AN OPPORTUNITY TO AIR
YOUR VIEWS. MY ONLY CONDITION IS THAT THE PUBLIC MELTING
DOWN OR HAMMERING OUT OF SHAPE OF YOUR NAZI MEDAL BE MADE A
FEATURE OF THE RALLY.

At the end of November 1941, when repeated Soviet assaults forced the
German troops to withdraw behind the Mius River, German reserves
earmarked for Moscow were sent to Kharkov to stem this attack, causing Hitler to send this curt telegram to Field Marshal Ewald von Kleist:

FURTHER COWARDLY RETREATS ARE FORBIDDEN.

ROOSEVELT AND CHURCHILL

FRANKLIN ROOSEVELT and Winston Churchill corresponded regularly,
largely by telegraph, before and during World War II. They formed a
grand personal alliance of their own as they shared information and
opinions. The following are a few early excerpts. In many cases,
Churchill referred to himself as Former Naval Person, and code words
were frequently employed for sensitive issues.

November 5, 1940, WC to FDR:

I DID NOT THINK IT RIGHT FOR ME AS A FOREIGNER TO EXPRESS
ANY OPINION UPON AMERICAN POLICIES WHILE THE ELECTION WAS
ON, BUT NOW I FEEL YOU WILL NOT MIND MY SAYING THAT I
PRAYED FOR YOUR SUCCESS AND THAT I AM TRULY THANKFUL FOR
IT. . . . WE ARE NOW ENTERING UPON A SOMBRE PHASE OF WHAT MUST
EVIDENTLY BE A PROTRACTED AND BROADENING WAR, AND I LOOK

FORWARD TO BEING ABLE TO INTERCHANGE MY THOUGHTS WITH YOU
IN THE CONFIDENCE AND GOOD WILL WHICH HAS GROWN UP BETWEEN
US. . . . THINGS ARE AFOOT WHICH WILL BE REMEMBERED AS LONG AS
THE ENGLISH LANGUAGE IS SPOKEN IN ANY QUARTER OF THE GLOBE,
AND IN EXPRESSING THE COMFORT I FEEL THAT THE PEOPLE OF THE
UNITED STATES HAVE ONCE AGAIN CAST THESE GREAT BURDENS UPON
YOU, I MUST AVOW MY SURE FAITH THAT THE LIGHTS BY WHICH WE
STEER WILL BRING US ALL SAFELY TO ANCHOR.

February 15, 1941, FDR to WC:

MANY DRIFTING STRAWS SEEM TO INDICATE JAPANESE INTENTION TO
MAKE WAR ON US OR DO SOMETHING THAT WOULD FORCE US TO MAKE
WAR ON THEM IN THE NEXT FEW WEEKS OR MONTHS. . . . SOME
BELIEVE THAT JAPAN IN HER PRESENT MOOD WOULD NOT HESITATE
TO COURT AN ATTEMPT TO WAGE WAR BOTH AGAINST GREAT BRITAIN
AND THE UNITED STATES. PERSONALLY, I THINK THE ODDS ARE
AGAINST THAT, BUT NO ONE CAN TELL.

November 30, 1941, WC to FDR:

IT SEEMS TO ME THAT ONE IMPORTANT METHOD REMAINS UNUSED IN
AVERTING WAR BETWEEN JAPAN AND OUR TWO COUNTRIES, NAMELY A
PLAIN DECLARATION, SECRET OR PUBLIC . . . THAT ANY FURTHER
ACT OF AGGRESSION BY JAPAN WILL LEAD IMMEDIATELY TO THE
GRAVEST CONSEQUENCES. . . . IT WOULD BE TRAGIC IF JAPAN
DRIFTED INTO WAR BY ENCROACHMENT WITHOUT HAVING BEFORE HER
FAIRLY AND SQUARELY THE DIRE CHARACTER OF ANY AGGRESSIVE
STEP. . . . WE WOULD, OF COURSE, MAKE A SIMILAR
DECLARATION. . . .

PEARL HARBOR

IN THE MONTHS PRECEDING the Japanese attack on Pearl Harbor, the United States intercepted a number of diplomatic messages telegraphed by the Japanese government presenting a picture of their attitudes, surveillance, and path toward war. Following are a few translated excerpts.

July 25, 1941, Manila to Tokyo:

THE UNITED STATES IS MAKING A CONCENTRATED EFFORT TO STRENGTHEN PHILIPPINE DEFENSES. THERE ARE AT PRESENT 460 PLANES, AND ABOUT 1300 PILOTS. ARMY FORCE NUMBERS 10,000. . . .

July 31, 1941, Tokyo to Washington:

. . . COMMERCIAL AND ECONOMIC RELATIONS BETWEEN JAPAN AND THIRD COUNTRIES, LED BY ENGLAND AND THE UNITED STATES, ARE GRADUALLY BECOMING SO HORRIBLY STRAINED THAT WE CANNOT ENDURE IT MUCH LONGER, CONSEQUENTLY, OUR EMPIRE, TO SAVE ITS LIFE, MUST TAKE MEASURES TO SECURE THE RAW MATERIALS OF THE SOUTH SEAS. OUR EMPIRE MUST IMMEDIATELY TAKE STEPS TO BREAK ASUNDER THIS EVER-STRENGTHENING CHAIN OF ENCIRCLEMENT WHICH IS BEING WOVEN UNDER THE GUIDANCE AND WITH THE PARTICIPATION OF ENGLAND AND THE UNITED STATES, ACTING LIKE A CUNNING DRAGON SEEMINGLY ASLEEP. . . .

July 31, 1941, Tokyo to Washington:

. . . I KNOW THAT THE GERMANS ARE SOMEWHAT DISSATISFIED OVER OUR NEGOTIATIONS WITH THE UNITED STATES, BUT WE WISHED AT ANY COST TO PREVENT THE UNITED STATES FROM GETTING INTO THE WAR. . . .

September 27, 1941, Tokyo to Washington:

. . . SHOULD THE UNITED STATES AND JAPAN COME TO BLOWS, THE PACIFIC, TOO, WOULD IMMEDIATELY BE THROWN INTO THE CHAOS

THAT IS WAR. WORLD CIVILIZATION WOULD THEN COME CRASHING
DOWN. NO GREATER MISFORTUNE COULD BEFALL MANKIND. . . .
MAINTENANCE OF PEACE IS JAPAN'S SOLE MOTIVATING POWER. . . .

November 10, 1941, Washington to Tokyo:

IN THE NEWSPAPERS AND MAGAZINES . . . IT IS REPORTED THAT THE
AMERICANS ARE MUCH MORE EAGER FOR A WAR WITH JAPAN THAN
THEY ARE FOR ONE WITH GERMANY. . . .

November 24, 1941, Honolulu to Tokyo:

ACCORDING TO NORMAL PRACTICE, THE FLEET LEAVES PEARL
HARBOR, CONDUCTS MANEUVERS AND FORTHWITH RETURNS. . . .

December 1, 1941, Washington to Tokyo:

. . . THE GENERAL TONE OF THESE REPORTS IS THAT ROOSEVELT
DECIDED TO CUT HIS VACATION SHORT AND RUSH BACK TO
WASHINGTON BECAUSE [SECRETARY OF STATE CORDELL] HULL

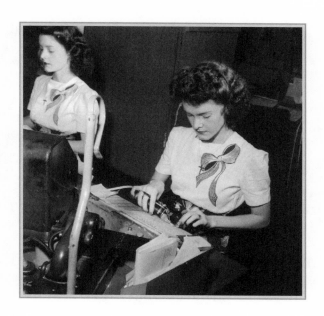

A telegraph operator
pastes up a telegram
at the Western Union
office in Washington,
June 1943.

ADVISED HIM . . . THAT PREMIER TOJO HAD MADE AN EXTREMELY
STRONG SPEECH, AND RELAYED TO HIM THAT A FAR EASTERN CRISIS
MAY BE AT HAND. . . . SOME OF THE NEWSPAPERS COMMENT THAT
SINCE JAPAN'S INVASION OF THAI HAS ALREADY BEEN DEFINITELY
MAPPED OUT, THE ABOVE IS MERELY A MEANS OF STALLING FOR
TIME SO AS TO GIVE THE JAPANESE A CHANCE TO SEIZE THE MOST
OPPORTUNE MOMENT . . . TO LAUNCH THIS ATTACK.

December 3, 1941, Tokyo to Washington:

. . . RECENTLY, BRITAIN, THE UNITED STATES, AND OTHERS HAVE
BEEN MAKING MILITARY PREPARATIONS AGAINST JAPAN AT AN EVER
INCREASING TEMPO. AT THE SAME TIME, THEY HAVE BEEN ACTING
IN A MORE AND MORE ANTAGONISTIC MANNER OF LATE. . . .

Just one day before the attack on Pearl Harbor, President Roosevelt
made a last-ditch attempt to avoid the hostilities that were imminent. His
lengthy telegram to Japan's Emperor Hirohito read in part:

ALMOST A CENTURY AGO THE PRESIDENT OF THE UNITED STATES
ADDRESSED TO THE EMPEROR OF JAPAN EXTENDING AN OFFER OF
FRIENDSHIP OF THE PEOPLE OF THE UNITED STATES TO THE PEOPLE
OF JAPAN. THAT OFFER WAS ACCEPTED, AND IN THE LONG PERIOD
OF UNBROKEN PEACE AND FRIENDSHIP WHICH HAS FOLLOWED, OUR
RESPECTIVE NATIONS, THROUGH THE VIRTUES OF THEIR PEOPLES
AND THE WISDOM OF THEIR RULERS HAVE PROSPERED AND
SUBSTANTIALLY HELPED HUMANITY. . . . DEVELOPMENTS ARE
OCCURRING IN THE PACIFIC AREA WHICH THREATEN TO DEPRIVE
EACH OF OUR NATIONS AND ALL HUMANITY OF THE BENEFICIAL
INFLUENCE OF THE LONG PEACE BETWEEN OUR TWO COUNTRIES.
THESE DEVELOPMENTS CONTAIN TRAGIC POSSIBILITIES. . . . DURING
THE PAST FEW WEEKS IT HAS BECOME CLEAR TO THE WORLD THAT
JAPANESE MILITARY, NAVAL AND AIR FORCES HAVE BEEN SENT TO
SOUTHERN INDO-CHINA IN SUCH LARGE NUMBERS AS TO CREATE A
REASONABLE DOUBT ON THE PART OF OTHER NATIONS THAT
THIS . . . IS NOT DEFENSIVE IN ITS CHARACTER. . . . THERE IS

ABSOLUTELY NO THOUGHT ON THE PART OF THE UNITED STATES OF
INVADING INDO-CHINA IF EVERY JAPANESE SOLDIER OR SAILOR
WERE TO BE WITHDRAWN THEREFROM. . . . I AM CONFIDENT THAT
BOTH OF US, FOR THE SAKE OF THE PEOPLES NOT ONLY OF OUR OWN
GREAT COUNTRIES BUT FOR THE SAKE OF HUMANITY IN NEIGHBORING
TERRITORIES, HAVE A SACRED DUTY TO RESTORE TRADITIONAL
AMITY AND PREVENT FURTHER DEATH AND DESTRUCTION IN THE
WORLD.

The next day, Japanese functionaries in Washington were wiring Tokyo:

YOUR INSTRUCTIONS . . . HAVE BEEN DULY RECEIVED AND DECODED,
AND AS SOON AS WE HAVE COMPOSED AND DISPATCHED THIS
TELEGRAM WE WILL COMMENCE THE DEMOLITION AND DESTRUCTION BY
FIRE. . . .

About nine hours before the attack, Tokyo sent a wire to its embassy in Washington, telling officials to break diplomatic relations with the United States, destroy encoding machines, burn papers, and prepare a message for U.S. officials. The intercepted message was transmitted via Western Union to Honolulu about 1¼ hours before the bombs fell; a motorcycle messenger picked it up at a telegraph office twenty minutes before the attack, got stuck in traffic, and didn't reach Admiral Husband Kimmel until seven hours after the attack. When the Japanese struck, this is the telegram that went out from the commander in chief of the Pacific fleet to all the ships in the Hawaii area:

AIR RAID ON PEARL HARBOR. THIS IS NO DRILL.

THE FOLLOWING DAY, President Roosevelt informed Churchill by telegram:

> THE SENATE PASSED THE ALL-OUT DECLARATION OF WAR EIGHTY-TWO TO NOTHING, AND THE HOUSE HAS PASSED IT THREE HUNDRED EIGHTY-EIGHT TO ONE. TODAY ALL OF US ARE IN THE SAME BOAT WITH YOU AND THE PEOPLE OF THE EMPIRE AND IT IS A SHIP WHICH WILL NOT AND CANNOT BE SUNK.

On the same day, the Axis forces were mobilizing, as seen in this telegram from the Japanese ambassador in Berlin to Tokyo:

> AT 1:00 P.M. TODAY I CALLED ON FOREIGN MINISTER RIBBENTROP AND TOLD HIM OUR WISH WAS TO HAVE GERMANY AND ITALY ISSUE FORMAL DECLARATIONS OF WAR ON AMERICA AT ONCE. . . . HITLER WAS THEN IN THE MIDST OF A CONFERENCE DISCUSSING HOW THE FORMALITIES OF DECLARING WAR COULD BE CARRIED OUT SO AS TO MAKE A GOOD IMPRESSION ON THE GERMAN PEOPLE. . . . RIBBENTROP TOLD ME THAT ON THE MORNING OF THE 8TH HITLER ISSUED ORDERS TO THE ENTIRE GERMAN NAVY TO ATTACK AMERICAN SHIPS WHENEVER AND WHEREVER THEY MAY MEET THEM. . . .

Almost immediately following what he termed "the dastardly Japanese attack," oil magnate and ardent patriot J. Paul Getty was moved to fire off a telegram to Navy Secretary James V. Forrestal stating that although he was forty-nine years old, he was an experienced yachtsman in good health and offering his services to the navy in any capacity.

As the war progressed, the Roosevelt-Churchill telegraphic correspondence continued, sometimes including confidential remarks concerning

TELEGRAM

OFFICIAL BUSINESS—GOVERNMENT RATES

FROM **The White House**
Washington

January 1, 1942.

H. M. GEORGE VI
LONDON

We are with you in spirit on this New Year's Day and there can be no doubt that with joined hands our two nations will win through and save the civilization we have prized so long

FRANKLIN D. ROOSEVELT

their other Allies, as in this September 16, 1942, example that was written by Roosevelt but never sent:

> I AGREE FULLY AND CONSIDER IT ESSENTIAL THAT DE GAULLE BE KEPT OUT OF THE PICTURE AND BE PERMITTED TO HAVE NO REPEAT NO INFORMATION WHATEVER REGARDLESS OF HOW IRRITATING HE MAY BECOME.

And another from Roosevelt that *was* sent on October 5, 1942:

> . . . PLEASE LET ME KNOW WHEN YOU SEND MESSAGE TO STALIN AND I WILL IMMEDIATELY SEND HIM A SIMILAR MESSAGE, BUT I AM CERTAIN BOTH OUR MESSAGES SHOULD BE SO PHRASED AS TO LEAVE A GOOD TASTE IN HIS MOUTH.

De Gaulle continued to rile both Roosevelt and Churchill. FDR accused the French leader of having a messianic complex and of fomenting racial discord, negative feelings that were shared by Churchill who,

TELEGRAM

𝕿𝖍𝖊 𝖂𝖍𝖎𝖙𝖊 𝕳𝖔𝖚𝖘𝖊

WB156 CABLE BRITGOVT

𝖂𝖆𝖘𝖍𝖎𝖓𝖌𝖙𝖔𝖓   [2]

LONDON 118 128A JANUARY 1 1941

THE PRESIDENT OF THE UNITED STATES OF AMERICA

THE WHITE HOUSE

AT THE OPENING OF A NEW YEAR WHICH FINDS THE PEOPLE OF YOUR GREAT COUNTRY AT THE SIDE OF THE BRITISH PEOPLES IN A WAR FORCED ON THEM BY THE ENEMIES OF FREEDOM I SEND YOU MR. PRESIDENT MY HEARTFELT GOOD WISHES FOR YOUR HEALTH AND WELFARE. WHATEVER CHANGES AND CHANCES THE COMING YEAR MAY BRING, I HAVE ENTIRE CONFIDENCE, WHICH I KNOW YOU SHARE, THAT OUR TWO PEOPLES AND THOSE ASSOCIATED WITH THEM WILL IN THE END OVERTHROW UTTERLY THE EVIL FORCES WHICH HAVE ATTACKED CIVILIZATION AND HAVE ALREADY IMPOSED SO MUCH SUFFERING ON THE PEACE LOVING NATIONS OF THE EARTH

GEORGE R I

1100P

King George VI of England to President Franklin Roosevelt on January 1, 1941, expressing New Year's greetings.

⟨∘⟩

on May 21, 1943, sent a "Most Secret and Personal" telegram to Deputy Prime Minister Clement Attlee and Foreign Secretary Anthony Eden:

. . . DE GAULLE IS, IN MY OPINION, ABSORBED IN HIS OWN PERSONAL CAREER WHICH DEPENDS ON A VAIN ENDEAVOR TO MAKE HIMSELF THE ARBITER OF THE CONDUCT OF EVERY FRENCHMAN FOLLOWING THE MILITARY DEFEAT. I ASK MY COLLEAGUES NOW TO

CONSIDER URGENTLY WHETHER WE SHOULD NOT ELIMINATE DE GAULLE
AS A POLITICAL FORCE. . . . HE HATES ENGLAND AND HAS LEFT A
TRAIL OF ANGLOPHOBIA BEHIND HIM EVERYWHERE. . . .

In September of 1943, General Dwight D. Eisenhower tried to convince
the Italians to sever their coalition with the Germans and join the Allies,
as expressed in this cable to Marshal Pietro Badoglio:

. . . THE GERMANS HAVE DEFINITELY AND DELIBERATELY TAKEN THE
FIELD AGAINST YOU. THEY HAVE BOMBED YOUR FLEET AND SUNK ONE
OF YOUR SHIPS, THEY HAVE ATTACKED YOUR SOLDIERS AND SEIZED
YOUR PORTS. THE GERMANS ARE NOW BEING ATTACKED BY LAND AND
SEA AND ON AN EVER INCREASING SCALE FROM THE AIR. NOW IS
THE TIME TO STRIKE. IF ITALY RISES NOW AS ONE MAN WE SHALL
SEIZE EVERY GERMAN BY THE THROAT. . . .

As in every conflict since the Civil War, the telegram was the primary
form of communication between leaders during World War II. General
Eisenhower, commander of the Allied invasion of Europe and all the
Allied armies in the West, was in constant contact with Army Chief of
Staff General George C. Marshall, British Field Marshal Bernard Montgomery, Winston Churchill, and others. In addition to battling the Axis
forces, Eisenhower had to deal with the peccadilloes of some of his own
officers, particularly the erratic General George Patton, as he wired Marshall on numerous occasions.

On November 24, 1943, referring to the Sicilian campaign:

. . . IN THE CAMPAIGN HE DROVE HIMSELF AS HARD AS HE DID THE
MEMBERS OF HIS ARMY AND, AS A RESULT, HE BECAME ALMOST
RUTHLESS IN HIS DEMANDS UPON INDIVIDUAL MEN. IN TWO
INSTANCES WHILE HE WAS VISITING WOUNDED IN HOSPITALS, HE
ENCOUNTERED TWO . . . PATIENTS WHO HAD BEEN EVACUATED FOR . . .
WHAT IS COMMONLY KNOWN AS "BATTLE ANXIETY." IN ADDITION ONE
MAN HAD A TEMPERATURE. IN THESE TWO INSTANCES HE
MOMENTARILY LOST HIS TEMPER AND UPBRAIDED THE INDIVIDUALS
IN AN UNSEEMLY AND INDEFENSIBLE MANNER, AND IN ONE OF THE

CASES HE CUFFED THE INDIVIDUAL INVOLVED SO THAT THE MAN'S
HELMET ROLLED OFF HIS HEAD. . . .

April 29, 1944:

. . . APPARENTLY HE IS UNABLE TO USE REASONABLY GOOD SENSE
IN ALL THESE MATTERS WHERE SENIOR COMMANDERS MUST
APPRECIATE THE EFFECT OF THEIR OWN ACTIONS UPON PUBLIC
OPINION AND THIS RAISES DOUBTS AS TO THE WISDOM OF
RETAINING HIM IN HIGH COMMAND DESPITE HIS DEMONSTRATED
CAPACITY IN BATTLE LEADERSHIP. . . . HIS ACTUAL WORDS,
ACCORDING TO MY REPORTS WERE, "SINCE IT SEEMS TO BE THE
DESTINY OF AMERICA, GREAT BRITAIN AND RUSSIA TO RULE THE
WORLD, THE BETTER WE KNOW EACH OTHER THE BETTER OFF WE WILL
BE." . . .

And on April 30, 1944:

. . . AFTER A YEAR AND A HALF OF WORKING WITH HIM IT APPEARS
HOPELESS TO EXPECT THAT HE WILL EVER COMPLETELY OVERCOME
HIS LIFELONG HABIT OF POSING AND SELF-DRAMATIZATION WHICH
CAUSES HIM TO BREAK OUT IN THESE EXTRAORDINARY WAYS. . . .

By 1943, things were not going well for the German forces on the Russian front. On the morning of February 1, Field Marshal Paulus sent the following telegram to Berlin:

MEIN FUHRER. THE SIXTH ARMY HAS KEPT FAITH. WE HAVE FOUGHT
TO THE LAST MAN, LAST BULLET, AS YOU ORDERED. WE HAVE NO
MORE ARMS, NO MORE AMMUNITION, NO MORE FOOD. THE FOLLOWING
DIVISIONS HAVE BEEN TOTALLY WIPED OUT: 14TH, 16TH AND 24TH
PANZER DIVISIONS; 9TH FLAK DIVISION; 30TH MOTORIZED
DIVISION; 44TH, 71ST AND 176TH INFANTRY DIVISIONS, 100TH
RIFLE DIVISION. HEIL HITLER! LONG LIVE GERMANY!

As the war was drawing to a close, on May 5, 1945, Winston Churchill
expressed his conflicted feelings to his wife:

...IT IS ASTONISHING ONE IS NOT IN A MORE BUOYANT FRAME OF MIND. . . . DURING THE LAST THREE DAYS WE HAVE HEARD OF THE DEATH OF MUSSOLINI AND HITLER, ALEXANDER HAS TAKEN A MILLION PRISONERS OF WAR, MONTGOMERY TOOK 500,000 ADDITIONAL YESTERDAY AND FAR MORE THAN A MILLION TO-DAY; ALL NORTH-WEST GERMANY, HOLLAND AND DENMARK ARE TO BE SURRENDERED EARLY TOMORROW MORNING WITH ALL TROOPS AND SHIPS, ETC; THE NEXT DAY NORWAY, AND THE U-BOATS WILL, I BELIEVE, GIVE IN; AND WE ARE ALL OCCUPIED HERE WITH PREPARATIONS FOR VICTORY-EUROPE DAY. MEANWHILE I NEED SCARCELY TELL YOU THAT BENEATH THESE TRIUMPHS LIE POISONOUS POLITICS AND DEADLY INTERNATIONAL RIVALRIES.

THE HOLOCAUST

LIKE THE JEWS, Gypsies were singled out by the Nazis for persecution and annihilation, sent to extermination camps, put before firing squads, used as medical guinea pigs, and injected with lethal substances. This was made clear in a telegram sent by strategist Adolf Eichmann from Vienna to the Gestapo, in reply to a question of just how these people were to be "expedited":

REGARDING TRANSPORT OF GYPSIES BE INFORMED THAT ON FRIDAY, OCTOBER 20, 1939, THE FIRST TRANSPORT OF JEWS WILL DEPART VIENNA. TO THIS TRANSPORT 3–4 CARS OF GYPSIES ARE TO BE ATTACHED. . . . THE SIMPLEST METHOD IS TO ATTACH SOME CARLOADS OF GYPSIES TO EACH TRANSPORT. BECAUSE THESE TRANSPORTS MUST FOLLOW SCHEDULE, A SMOOTH EXECUTION OF THIS MATTER IS EXPECTED.

Sometimes a telegram took on great historic importance because it was *not* sent or received or acknowledged. This is the case for one known as the Riegner Telegram. Gerhart Riegner was secretary of the World Jewish Congress in Switzerland in 1942 when a phone call from a friend informed him of a plan being discussed by Hitler to exterminate all the Jews of Europe. Although reports of Nazi atrocities had been trickling out of Europe since 1941, their scope was not known. Riegner sent a telegram to the U.S. government, warning that the Jews of Europe were to be annihilated by gas, asking that copies of his message—the first authoritative word that the Nazis actually had a coordinated extermination plan—be sent to Jewish leaders, including the highly influential Rabbi Stephen Wise, president of the WJC and a personal friend of President Roosevelt. One State Department official instructed that it not be sent to Wise because of the "fantastic nature of the allegation," which he regarded as "a wild rumor inspired by Jewish fears," but it finally reached Wise on August 28, 1942. It wasn't until November 24, however, that Wise called a press conference announcing the mass slaughter taking place, and even then the news created little stir in the press. Riegner's telegram, sent on August 12, 1942, read:

> RECEIVED ALARMING REPORT STATING THAT, IN THE FUEHRER'S HEADQUARTERS, A PLAN HAS BEEN DISCUSSED, AND IS UNDER CONSIDERATION, ACCORDING TO WHICH ALL JEWS OCCUPIED OR CONTROLLED BY GERMANY NUMBERING 3½ TO 4 MILLIONS SHOULD, AFTER DEPORTATION AND CONCENTRATION IN THE EAST, BE AT ONE BLOW EXTERMINATED IN ORDER TO RESOLVE, ONCE AND FOR ALL THE JEWISH QUESTION IN EUROPE. ACTION IS REPORTED TO BE PLANNED FOR THE AUTUMN. WAYS OF EXECUTION ARE STILL BEING DISCUSSED INCLUDING THE USE OF PRUSSIC ACID. . . .

For the rest of his life, Riegner was haunted by the knowledge that many of the six million Jews killed in Nazi concentration camps could have been saved if the United States and England had acted promptly on his warning.

HITLER'S DEMISE

FAR FROM CUT OFF in his underground bunker in April of 1945, Adolf Hitler continued to communicate with his henchmen by wire. On April 23, he was enraged to receive this telegram from his former deputy Hermann Göring, who had reached safety near Berchtesgaden.

MY FUHRER!

IN VIEW OF YOUR DECISION TO REMAIN IN THE FORTRESS OF
BERLIN, DO YOU AGREE THAT I TAKE OVER AT ONCE THE TOTAL
LEADERSHIP OF THE REICH, WITH FULL FREEDOM AT HOME AND
ABROAD AS YOUR DEPUTY, IN ACCORDANCE WITH YOUR DECREE OF
JUNE 29, 1941? IF NO REPLY IS RECEIVED BY 10 O'CLOCK
TONIGHT, I SHALL TAKE IT FOR GRANTED THAT YOU HAVE LOST
YOUR FREEDOM OF ACTION, AND SHALL CONSIDER THE CONDITIONS
OF YOUR DECREE AS FULFILLED, AND SHALL ACT FOR THE BEST
INTERESTS OF OUR COUNTRY AND OUR PEOPLE. YOU KNOW WHAT I
FEEL FOR YOU IN THIS GRAVEST HOUR OF MY LIFE. . . . MAY GOD
PROTECT YOU, AND SPEED YOU QUICKLY HERE IN SPITE OF ALL.

Goaded on by Göring's rival, Heinrich Himmler, Hitler sent a return message accusing Göring of high treason but assuring him that even though the penalty for this was death, he would be spared due to his years of loyal service if he would immediately resign all of his offices. Göring was arrested by the SS on the morning of April 25.

Soon after Hitler committed suicide in his bunker, Joseph Goebbels, the Nazi minister of propaganda, sent this telegram from the Fuehrerbunker to his successor, Admiral Karl Dönitz, on May 1, 1945:

THE FUEHRER DIED YESTERDAY AT 15:30 HOURS. TESTAMENT OF
APRIL 29TH APPOINTS YOU AS REICH PRESIDENT, REICH MINISTER
DR. GOEBBELS AS REICH CHANCELLOR, REICHSLEITER BORMANN AS
PARTY MINISTER. . . . BY ORDER OF THE FUEHRER, THE TESTAMENT
HAS BEEN SENT OUT OF BERLIN TO YOU. . . . FOR PRESERVATION

HIROSHIMA

ON AUGUST 6, 1945, an American B-29 dropped an atomic bomb on Hiroshima, the seventh largest city in Japan. Among the first neutral witnesses to arrive on the scene was an International Red Cross committee delegate, who described the apocalyptic disaster in a telegram he sent on August 30.

> . . . CONDITIONS APPALLING STOP CITY WIPED OUT, EIGHTY PERCENT ALL HOSPITALS DESTROYED OR SERIOUSLY DAMAGED; CONDITIONS BEYOND DESCRIPTION FULL STOP EFFECT OF BOMB MYSTERIOUSLY SERIOUS STOP MANY VICTIMS, APPARENTLY RECOVERING, SUDDENLY SUFFER FATAL RELAPSE DUE TO DECOMPOSITION OF WHITE BLOOD CELLS AND OTHER INTERNAL INJURIES, NOW DYING IN GREAT NUMBERS STOP ESTIMATED . . . OVER ONE HUNDRED THOUSAND WOUNDED IN EMERGENCY HOSPITALS. . . .

Albert Einstein had strongly advised President Roosevelt to begin an atomic research project as early as 1939. However, after nuclear bombs were unleashed on Hiroshima and Nagasaki in 1945, he sent a telegram on behalf of the Emergency Committee of Atomic Sciences to several hundred prominent Americans, and which appeared in the *New York Times* on May 25, 1946. Part of it read:

> THE UNLEASHED POWER OF THE ATOM HAS CHANGED EVERYTHING SAVE OUR MODES OF THINKING AND WE THUS DRIFT TOWARD UNPARALLELED CATASTROPHE.

When the Communist-hunting House Un-American Activities Committee (HUAC) was formed in 1937, Chairman Martin Dies received this supportive telegram from the Ku Klux Klan:

EVERY TRUE AMERICAN, AND THAT INCLUDES EVERY KLANSMAN, IS
BEHIND YOU AND YOUR COMMITTEE IN ITS EFFORT TO TURN THE
COUNTRY BACK TO THE HONEST, FREEDOM-LOVING, GOD-FEARING
AMERICAN TO WHOM IT BELONGS.

By early 1946, less than a year after the end of World War II, the relationship between the United States and the Soviet Union was rapidly deteriorating. One of the key documents signaling the approach of the Cold War was the long, analytical telegram sent to Washington on February 22, 1946, by George Kennan, American chargé d'affaires in Moscow, which read in part:

USSR STILL LIVES IN ANTAGONISTIC "CAPITALIST ENCIRCLEMENT"
WITH WHICH IN THE LONG RUN THERE CAN BE NO PERMANENT
PEACEFUL COEXISTENCE. . . . WE HAVE HERE A POLITICAL FORCE
COMMITTED FANATICALLY TO THE BELIEF THAT WITH US THERE CAN
BE NO PERMANENT MODUS VIVENDI, THAT IT IS DESIRABLE AND
NECESSARY THAT THE INTERNAL HARMONY OF OUR SOCIETY BE
DISRUPTED, OUR TRADITIONAL WAY OF LIFE BE DESTROYED, THE
INTERNATIONAL AUTHORITY OF OUR STATE BE BROKEN, IF SOVIET
POWER IS TO BE SECURE. . . .

In July of 1947, Charlie Chaplin heard rumors that he would be among the first witnesses to be called up before HUAC, and he immediately fired off an open telegram to committee chairman J. Parnell Thomas, which ended:

WHILE YOU ARE PREPARING YOUR ENGRAVED SUBPOENA I WILL GIVE
YOU A HINT OF WHERE I STAND. I AM NOT A COMMUNIST. I AM A
PEACEMONGER.

In February of 1950, Senator Joseph McCarthy, looking for a big issue to fuel his run for a second term, gave a speech during which he held up a paper claiming to have proof that more than 200 State Department employees were card-carrying Communists. He followed this up with a long telegram to President Truman, part of which read:

> . . . THE STATE DEPARTMENT HARBORS A NEST OF COMMUNISTS AND COMMUNIST SYMPATHIZERS WHO ARE HELPING TO SHAPE OUR FOREIGN POLICY. . . . I HAVE IN MY POSSESSION THE NAMES OF 57 COMMUNISTS WHO ARE IN THE STATE DEPARTMENT AT PRESENT. . . . YOU WILL RECALL THAT YOU PERSONALLY APPOINTED A BOARD TO SCREEN STATE DEPARTMENT EMPLOYEES. . . . YOUR BOARD DID A PAIN-STAKING JOB AND NAMED HUNDREDS WHICH IT LISTED AS "DANGEROUS TO THE SECURITY OF THE NATION. . . ." I WOULD SUGGEST, THEREFORE, MR. PRESIDENT, THAT YOU SIMPLY PICK UP YOUR PHONE AND ASK MR. ACHESON HOW MANY OF THOSE WHOM YOUR BOARD HAD LABELED AS DANGEROUS HE FAILED TO DISCHARGE. . . . FAILURE ON YOUR PART WILL LABEL THE DEMOCRATIC PARTY OF BEING THE BED-FELLOW OF INTERNATIONAL COMMUNISM. . . .

President Truman's incensed reaction is reflected in the draft of a reply that he never sent:

> YOUR TELEGRAM IS NOT ONLY NOT TRUE AND AN INSOLENT APPROACH TO A SITUATION THAT SHOULD HAVE BEEN WORKED OUT BETWEEN MAN AND MAN BUT IT SHOWS CONCLUSIVELY THAT YOU ARE NOT EVEN FIT TO HAVE A HAND IN THE OPERATION OF THE GOVERNMENT OF THE UNITED STATES. I AM VERY SURE THAT THE PEOPLE OF WISCONSIN ARE EXTREMELY SORRY THAT THEY ARE REPRESENTED BY A PERSON WHO HAS AS LITTLE SENSE OF RESPONSIBILITY AS YOU HAVE.

The term "Iron Curtain" is often thought to have first been heard in a speech given by Winston Churchill at Fulton, Missouri. But an earlier appearance of the phrase was made in this May 5, 1945, telegram sent by the prime minister to new U.S. President Truman, voicing Churchill's fears about the possibility of future conflict with Soviet Russia:

A Western Union
advertisement aimed at
early air travelers
⚛⚛

I HAVE ALWAYS WORKED FOR FRIENDSHIP WITH RUSSIA BUT, LIKE
YOU, I FEEL DEEP ANXIETY BECAUSE OF THEIR MISINTERPRETATION
OF THE YALTA DECISIONS, THEIR ATTITUDE TOWARDS POLAND,
THEIR OVERWHELMING INFLUENCE IN THE BALKANS. . . . THE
COMBINATION OF RUSSIAN POWER AND THE TERRITORIES UNDER
THEIR CONTROL OR OCCUPIED COUPLED WITH THE COMMUNIST

TECHNIQUE IN SO MANY OTHER COUNTRIES, AND ABOVE ALL THEIR
POWER TO MAINTAIN VERY LARGE ARMIES IN THE FIELD FOR A LONG
TIME . . . AN IRON CURTAIN IS DRAWN DOWN UPON THEIR FRONT. I
DO NOT KNOW WHAT IS GOING ON BEHIND . . .

In October of 1949, Communists led by Mao Tse-tung established the People's Republic of China, and in December he embarked on a two-month visit to the Soviet Union to establish an alliance with Stalin, with whom tensions were high. As negotiations proceeded, Mao sent telegrams back to fellow officials in China, one of which read in part:

. . . MET WITH STALIN FOR TWO HOURS . . . HIS ATTITUDE WAS
REALLY SINCERE. . . . STALIN SAID THAT THE AMERICANS ARE
AFRAID OF WAR. THE AMERICANS ASK OTHER COUNTRIES TO FIGHT
THE WAR, BUT OTHER COUNTRIES ARE ALSO AFRAID TO FIGHT A
WAR. ACCORDING TO HIM, IT IS UNLIKELY THAT A WAR WILL BREAK
OUT, AND WE AGREE WITH HIS OPINIONS. . . .

In the Stalin era, no post office in the Soviet Union would accept a telegram to Stalin if it didn't open with: Radiant light of the people, eminent flower of communism . . .

And a month later:

COMRADE STALIN HAS FINALLY AGREED TO INVITE COMRADE CHOU
EN-LAI TO MOSCOW AND SIGN THE NEW SINO-SOVIET TREATY OF
FRIENDSHIP. . . . BY TAKING THIS ACTION, WE WILL GAIN
ENORMOUS ADVANTAGES. SINO-SOVIET RELATIONS WILL BE
SOLIDIFIED. . . . IN CHINA, WORKERS, PEASANTS, INTELLECTUALS,
AND THE LEFT WING OF THE NATIONAL BOURGEOISIE WILL BE
GREATLY INSPIRED, WHILE THE RIGHT WING OF THE NATIONAL

BOURGEOISIE WILL BE ISOLATED; AND INTERNATIONALLY, WE MAY
ACQUIRE MORE POLITICAL CAPITAL TO DEAL WITH THE IMPERIALIST
COUNTRIES. . . .

ISRAEL

THE ROOTS of the establishment of the Jewish state of Israel go back to
1917, when Zionist Chaim Weizmann persuaded the British government
to issue a statement—known as the Balfour Declaration—favoring the
establishment of a Jewish national home in Palestine. Large-scale immi-
gration of Jews from many countries sparked Arab fears in the 1930s that
Palestine would become a Jewish homeland, and by 1936, guerrilla fighting had broken out between the two factions. When Harry S. Truman
became president, he made it clear that his sympathies were with the
Jews, and on May 14, 1948, he recognized the new state of Israel. The
next day, the first day of Israeli independence, Arab armies invaded Israel
and the first Arab-Israeli war began. This undated telegram from Truman
to Prime Minister David Ben-Gurion, one of the founders of the state of
Israel, concerns the question of Palestinian refugees:

> . . . THE GOVT OF THE US IS SERIOUSLY DISTURBED BY THE
> ATTITUDE OF ISRAEL WITH RESPECT TO A TERRITORIAL SETTLEMENT
> IN PALESTINE AND TO THE QUESTION OF PALESTINIAN REFUGEES,
> AS SET FORTH BY THE REPRESENTATIVES OF ISRAEL AT
> LAUSANNE. . . . THE POSITION TAKEN BY DR. EYTAN APPARENTLY
> CONTEMPLATES NOT ONLY THE RETENTION OF ALL TERRITORY NOW
> HELD UNDER MILITARY OCCUPATION BY ISRAEL, WHICH IS CLEARLY
> IN EXCESS OF THE PARTITION BOUNDARIES . . . THE US GOVT AND
> PEOPLE HAVE GIVEN GENEROUS SUPPORT TO THE CREATION OF

WORDS COST ONLY A FEW CENTS. USE ENOUGH TO MAKE YOUR MESSAGE CLEAR.

Advice from the 1948 Western Union Telegrammar style guide.

ISRAEL BECAUSE THEY HAVE BEEN CONVINCED OF THE JUSTICE OF
THIS ASPIRATION. . . . THE US GOVT IS GRAVELY CONCERNED LEST
ISRAEL NOW ENDANGER THE POSSIBILITY OF ARRIVING AT A
SOLUTION OF THE PALESTINE PROBLEM IN SUCH A WAY AS TO
CONTRIBUTE TO THE ESTABLISHMENT OF SOUND AND FRIENDLY
RELATIONS BETWEEN ISRAEL AND ITS NEIGHBORS. . . . IF . . .
ISRAEL CONTINUES TO REJECT THE BASIC PRINCIPLES SET FORTH
BY . . . THE GENERAL ASSEMBLY . . . THE US GOVT WILL
REGRETFULLY BE FORCED TO THE CONCLUSION THAT A REVISION OF
ITS ATTITUDE TOWARD ISRAEL HAS BECOME UNAVOIDABLE.

THE NATION was divided on the question of whether to participate in the Korean War, and President Truman was besieged by adamant telegrams, mostly against involvement. A few examples:

—WE DEMAND THAT YOU STOP MURDERING AMERICAN BOYS AND KOREAN PEOPLE. . . .

—LET THEM HAVE THE ATOM BOMB NOW. . . .

—YOU DID IT ONCE BEFORE STOP DROP ONE OVER THE KREMLIN

On February 21, 1952, Mao telegraphed I. V. (not Joseph) Stalin, alleging the use by Americans of bacteriological weapons in North Korea, this excerpt of which has particular resonance today:

IN THE PERIOD FROM 28 JANUARY TO 17 FEBRUARY 1952 THE AMERICANS USED BACTERIOLOGICAL WEAPONS 8 TIMES, FROM PLANES AND THROUGH ARTILLERY SHELLS. . . . THE AMERICANS ARE EQUAL TO JAPANESE CRIMINALS. . . .

After being commander of U.S. forces in the Pacific during World War II, General Douglas MacArthur led the United Nations forces in Korea. It wasn't long, however, before there was a clash of positions between the general and President Truman, when MacArthur threatened to bomb China, a move seen as likely to start a third world war. Excerpts from this telegraphic exchange between the Joint Chiefs of Staff and MacArthur in late 1950 show their opposing viewpoints, which led to MacArthur's removal.

Joint Chiefs to MacArthur:

CHINESE COMMUNISTS NOW APPEAR . . . CAPABLE OF FORCING EVACUATION BY FORCES OF UN. . . . IN THE FACE OF INCREASED THREAT OF GENERAL WAR, THE JOINT CHIEFS OF STAFF BELIEVE COMMITMENTS OF ADDITIONAL UNITED STATES GROUND FORCES IN KOREA SHOULD NOT BE MADE, SINCE OUR VIEW IS THAT MAJOR WAR SHOULD NOT BE FOUGHT IN KOREA.

And MacArthur's response, in part:

> . . . EVACUATION OF OUR FORCES IN KOREA . . . WOULD AT ONCE
> RELEASE THE BULK OF THE CHINESE FORCES NOW ABSORBED BY THAT
> CAMPAIGN FOR ACTION ELSEWHERE—QUITE PROBABLY IN AREAS OF
> FAR GREATER IMPORTANCE THAN KOREA ITSELF. . . . I UNDERSTAND
> THOROUGHLY THE DEMAND FOR EUROPEAN SECURITY AND FULLY
> CONCUR IN DOING EVERYTHING POSSIBLE IN THAT SECTOR, BUT NOT
> TO THE POINT OF ACCEPTING DEFEAT ANYWHERE ELSE.

THE CUBAN MISSILE CRISIS

ON OCTOBER 22, 1962, President Kennedy, alarmed that Fidel Castro was establishing missile bases with the help of the Soviet Union, ordered U.S. air and naval forces to establish a "quarantine" of Cuba. An exchange of telegrams between Kennedy and Soviet Premiere Nikita Khrushchev followed.

On October 24, from Khrushchev to Kennedy:

> . . . YOU, MR. PRESIDENT, ARE NOT DECLARING A QUARANTINE,
> BUT RATHER ARE SETTING FORTH AN ULTIMATUM AND THREATENING
> THAT IF WE DO NOT GIVE IN TO YOUR DEMANDS YOU WILL USE
> FORCE. CONSIDER WHAT YOU ARE SAYING! . . . YOU ARE NO LONGER
> APPEALING TO REASON, BUT WISH TO INTIMIDATE US. . . . THE
> SOVIET UNION CONSIDERS THAT THE VIOLATION OF THE FREEDOM TO
> USE INTERNATIONAL WATERS AND INTERNATIONAL AIR SPACE IS AN
> ACT OF AGGRESSION WHICH PUSHES MANKIND TOWARD THE ABYSS OF
> NUCLEAR-MISSILE WAR. . . .

The next day, Kennedy reiterated the American position and pointed out that the Soviet leader had been less than straightforward:

... IN EARLY SEPTEMBER ... THIS GOVERNMENT RECEIVED THE
MOST EXPLICIT ASSURANCE FROM YOUR GOVERNMENT ... THAT NO
OFFENSIVE WEAPONS WERE BEING SENT TO CUBA. ... IN RELIANCE
ON THESE SOLEMN ASSURANCES I URGED RESTRAINT UPON THOSE IN
THIS COUNTRY WHO WERE URGING ACTION ... AND THEN I LEARNED
WITHOUT DOUBT WHAT YOU HAVE NOT DENIED ... THAT ALL THESE
PUBLIC ASSURANCES WERE FALSE AND THAT YOUR MILITARY PEOPLE
HAD SET OUT RECENTLY TO ESTABLISH A SET OF MISSILE BASES IN
CUBA.

On October 26, from Khrushchev to Kennedy:

... EVERYONE NEEDS PEACE: BOTH CAPITALISTS, IF THEY HAVE
NOT LOST THEIR REASON, AND, STILL MORE, COMMUNISTS ... WHO
KNOW HOW TO VALUE ... THE LIVES OF THE PEOPLES. WE,
COMMUNISTS, ARE AGAINST ALL WARS ... AND HAVE BEEN
DEFENDING THE CAUSE OF PEACE SINCE WE CAME INTO THE
WORLD. ... WAR IS OUR ENEMY AND A CALAMITY FOR ALL THE
PEOPLES. ... YOU ARE THREATENING US WITH WAR. ... WE MUST
NOT SUCCUMB TO INTOXICATION AND PETTY PASSIONS ... BUT IF
INDEED WAR SHOULD BREAK OUT THEN IT WOULD NOT BE IN OUR
POWER TO CONTAIN OR STOP IT, FOR SUCH IS THE LOGIC OF
WAR. ... WAR ENDS WHEN IT HAS ROLLED THROUGH CITIES AND
VILLAGES, EVERYWHERE SOWING DEATH AND DESTRUCTION. ... I
ASSURE YOU THAT YOUR ARGUMENTS REGARDING OFFENSIVE WEAPONS
ON CUBA ARE GROUNDLESS. ... ALL THE MEANS LOCATED THERE
HAVE A DEFENSIVE CHARACTER ... AND WE HAVE SENT THEM ... AT

Of all the jobs playwright Edward Albee ever had, from phonograph
record salesman to lunch counter server, he claimed that his favorite was
that of Western Union messenger, because it gave him the opportunity
to "walk-write."

THE REQUEST OF THE CUBAN GOVERNMENT. . . . DO YOU REALLY
SERIOUSLY THINK THAT CUBA CAN ATTACK THE UNITED STATES AND
THAT EVEN WE TOGETHER WITH CUBA CAN ADVANCE ON YOU FROM THE
TERRITORY OF CUBA? CAN YOU REALLY THINK THAT WAY?

There was an almost audible sigh of relief in this telegram of the twenty-eighth from President Kennedy:

. . . PERHAPS NOW, AS WE STEP BACK FROM DANGER, WE CAN
TOGETHER MAKE REAL PROGRESS. . . . I THINK WE SHOULD GIVE
PRIORITY TO QUESTIONS RELATING TO THE PROLIFERATION OF
NUCLEAR WEAPONS, ON EARTH AND IN OUTER SPACE, AND TO THE
GREAT EFFORT TO A NUCLEAR TEST BAN. . . . THE UNITED STATES
GOVERNMENT WILL BE PREPARED TO DISCUSS THESE QUESTIONS
URGENTLY, AND IN A CONSTRUCTIVE SPIRIT, AT GENEVA OR
ANYWHERE.

PRIDE AND PREJUDICE

RACIAL, ETHNIC, and religious biases have plagued this country persistently, but there has also been a concurrent stream of positive action, and both have been documented in telegrams.

The hanging of abolitionist John Brown after his raid to liberate slaves through armed intervention exacerbated the hysteria and rumors about slaves' hiding in the mountains around Harper's Ferry, preparing for a new attack on the town. This atmosphere is palpable in the following telegram sent from A. W. Barbour, superintendent of the arsenal at Harper's Ferry, to the secretary of war, on October 19, 1859:

I FIND A PERFECT PANIC HERE. YOU MUST BY ALL MEANS DETAIL A
TROOP TO MY RELIEF IMMEDIATELY. THE MARINES WILL LEAVE.

On December 17, 1862, Ulysses S. Grant, then military governor of the
Union-held Southern territory, signed General Order 11, mandating the
expulsion of "the Jews, as a class" from an area corresponding to what is
today northern Mississippi, Kentucky, and western Tennessee, "within 24
hours," as traitors to the Union for trading with the Confederate enemy.
Outraged, Cesar Kaskel and a group of other Paducah, Kentucky, merchants sent a telegram to President Lincoln on December 29:

> . . . THE UNDERSIGNED, GOOD AND LOYAL CITIZENS OF THE UNITED
> STATES AND RESIDENTS OF THIS TOWN FOR MANY YEARS, ENGAGED
> IN LEGITIMATE BUSINESSES AS MERCHANTS, FEEL GREATLY
> INSULTED AND OUTRAGED BY THIS INHUMAN ORDER, THE CARRYING
> OUT OF WHICH WOULD BE THE GROSSEST VIOLATION OF THE
> CONSTITUTION . . . AND WOULD PLACE US, BESIDES A LARGE NUMBER
> OF OTHER JEWISH FAMILIES OF THIS TOWN, AS OUTLAWS BEFORE
> THE WHOLE WORLD. WE RESPECTFULLY ASK FOR YOUR IMMEDIATE
> ATTENTION TO THIS ENORMOUS OUTRAGE ON ALL HUMANITY AND PRAY
> FOR YOUR EFFECTUAL AND IMMEDIATE INTERPOSITION. . . .

On January 3, 1863, two days after the Emancipation Proclamation went
into effect, Kaskel made a follow-up trip to Washington, where he was
granted a meeting with Lincoln, who had been unaware of the edict.
The president promptly ordered Army Chief of Staff Henry Halleck to
countermand the order to help "the children of Israel," which he did by
telegraphing Grant:

> A PAPER PURPORTING TO BE GENERAL ORDERS, NO. 11, ISSUED BY
> YOU DECEMBER 17, HAS BEEN PRESENTED HERE. BY ITS TERMS, IT
> EXPELLS ALL JEWS FROM YOUR DEPARTMENT. IF SUCH AN ORDER HAS
> BEEN ISSUED, IT WILL BE IMMEDIATELY REVOKED.

Grant revoked the order three days later.

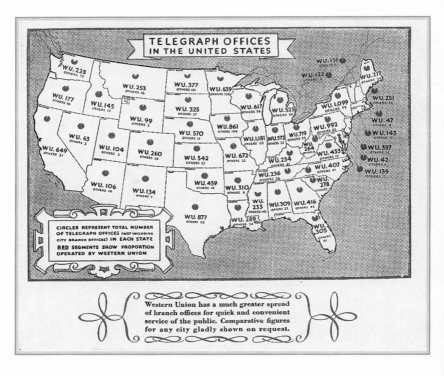

A map illustrating Western Union's regional market share numerically and graphically.

An undated missive expresses Lincoln's feelings about the use of black troops in the Civil War:

> I KNOW AS FULLY AS ONE CAN KNOW THE OPINIONS OF OTHERS,
> THAT SOME OF THE COMMANDERS OF OUR ARMIES IN THE FIELD, WHO
> HAVE GIVEN US OUR MOST IMPORTANT SUCCESSES, BELIEVE THE
> EMANCIPATION POLICY, AND THE USE OF COLORED TROOPS,
> CONSTITUTE THE HEAVIEST BLOW YET DEALT TO THE REBELLION,
> AND THAT AT LEAST ONE OF THOSE IMPORTANT SUCCESSES, COULD
> NOT HAVE BEEN ACHIEVED WHEN IT WAS, BUT FOR THE AID OF
> BLACK SOLDIERS. . . . I SUBMIT THESE OPINIONS AS BEING

ENTITLED TO SOME WEIGHT AGAINST THE OBJECTIONS, OFTEN
URGED, THAT EMANCIPATION, AND ARMING THE BLACKS, ARE UNWISE
AS MILITARY MEASURES, AND WERE NOT ADOPTED AS SUCH IN GOOD
FAITH.

In response to a telegram from President Theodore Roosevelt instructing relief leaders not to ignore the Chinese victims of the San Francisco
earthquake, this reply came from a group led by the city's mayor, E. E.
Schmitz, on April 24, 1906:

ALL REPORTS THAT THE PEOPLE OF THE ADMINISTRATION, OR THE
RELIEF COMMITTEE OF SAN FRANCISCO ARE MAKING ANY
DISTINCTION BETWEEN RELIEVING, SUCCORING OR PROTECTING THE
CHINESE, AND ANY OTHER PEOPLE DIFFERING IN RACE OR COLOR,
ARE TOTALLY UNFOUNDED. THE COMMITTEES AND EVEN THE HOMELESS
PEOPLE THEMSELVES ARE TREATING THE CHINESE AND ALL OTHER
UNFORTUNATES WITH THE CONSIDERATION AND KINDNESS WORTHY OF
OUR CIVILIZATION AND OUR COUNTRY. . . .

On August 16, 1906, President Theodore Roosevelt received a telegram
from the mayor of Brownsville, Texas, stating that members of a black
battalion of the U.S. Infantry—who had been harassed and beaten for
weeks—had begun firing on townspeople, killing one person. The wire
concluded:

. . . OUR WOMEN AND CHILDREN ARE TERRORIZED AND OUR MEN ARE
PRACTICALLY UNDER CONSTANT ALARM AND WATCHFULNESS. NO
COMMUNITY CAN STAND THIS STRAIN FOR MORE THAN A FEW
DAYS. . . . WE ASK YOU TO HAVE THE TROOPS AT ONCE REMOVED
FROM FORT BROWN AND REPLACED BY WHITE SOLDIERS.

Roosevelt ordered a thorough investigation by the War Department and
received a cautionary wire from one officer, Brigadier General William
S. McCaskey:

CITIZENS OF BROWNSVILLE ENTERTAIN RACE HATRED TO AN EXTREME
DEGREE. . . . PROVOCATION GIVEN THE SOLDIERS NOT TAKEN INTO
ACCOUNT.

Within a few days, Roosevelt had most of the battalion reassigned to Oklahoma.

Comedian Fred Allen had one of the most popular radio shows of the 1930s and 1940s. However, when black boxing champion Joe Louis made a guest appearance on his show in 1942, a Houston, Texas, couple dispatched this telegram in protest:

> AS LISTENERS AND ADMIRERS OF YOUR PROGRAM TONIGHT HEARD JOE LEWIS A NEGRO ADDRESS YOU AS FRED. WE BEYOND THE MASON & DIXON LINE DON'T TOLERATE OR LIKE IT AND WE OF THE SOUTH WILL APPRECIATE IT IF YOU WILL REFRAIN FROM ALLOWING NEGROES TO CALL YOU FRED OVER THE RADIO.

In cartoons, the name Western Union was avoided for legal reasons, and instead such substitutes as Eastern Union, Western Onion, and Western Bunions would be used.

A lifelong southerner, novelist William Faulkner, in the divisive times of the civil rights struggles of the 1950s, strongly condemned segregation but pleaded for moderation to avoid violence and bloodshed. In April of 1956, when civil rights legend W. E. B. Du Bois challenged Faulkner to a debate on integration on the steps of the courthouse in Sumner, Mississippi, where those accused in the Emmett Till murder trial had been acquitted by an all-white jury, the author declined in a telegram:

> I DO NOT BELIEVE THERE IS A DEBATABLE POINT BETWEEN US. WE BOTH AGREE IN ADVANCE THAT THE POSITION YOU WILL TAKE IS RIGHT MORALLY, LEGALLY AND ETHICALLY. IF IT IS NOT EVIDENT TO YOU THAT THE POSITION I TAKE IN ASKING FOR MODERATION AND PATIENCE IS RIGHT PRACTICALLY THEN WE WILL BOTH WASTE OUR BREATH IN DEBATE.

In 1957, when President Eisenhower sent federal troops to Arkansas to enforce integration, jazz great Louis Armstrong cheered him on with this telegram:

DADDY IF AND WHEN YOU DECIDE TO TAKE THOSE LITTLE NEGRO
CHILDREN PERSONALLY INTO CENTRAL HIGH SCHOOL ALONG WITH
YOUR MARVELOUS TROOPS PLEASE TAKE ME ALONG O GOD IT WOULD
BE SUCH A GREAT PLEASURE I ASSURE YOU. . . . MAY GOD BLESS
YOU PRESIDENT YOU HAVE A GOOD HEART. . . . AM SWISS KRISSLY
YOURS LOUIS SATCHMO ARMSTRONG

On October 20, 1958, the police of Birmingham, Alabama, arrested thirteen African-Americans for disobeying the segregated seating ordinance on buses. The next day, Reverend F. L. Shuttlesworth was arrested for conspiracy, and on the twenty-third, all fourteen protesters were held without bail and convicted. Four days later, three Montgomery ministers were arrested for vagrancy at the Shuttlesworth home, prompting Reverend Martin Luther King Jr. to send this telegram to former First Lady Eleanor Roosevelt, urging her to press officials for an investigation:

A VIRTUAL REIGN OF TERROR GRIPS BIRMINGHAM ALA. REV F L
SHUTTLESWORTH AND OTHER NEGRO LEADERS ARRESTED, DENIED
BAIL, HELD INCOMMUNICADO FOR 5 DAYS, DENIED COUNSEL,
DECLARED GUILTY AND NOW FACE UP TO 3 MONTHS AS RESULT OF
NON-VIOLENT EFFORT TO ERADICATE SEGREGATION. THREE
MONTGOMERY CLERGYMEN OFFERING SPIRITUAL COMFORT TO MRS
SHUTTLESWORTH WERE ARRESTED IN HER HOME. . . . THIS IS PART
OF A LAWLESS PATTERN WHICH RESULTS IN BOMBING THE CHURCHES,
SYNAGOGUES, SCHOOLS AND HOMES. . . . THE JAILING OF THESE

The telegram became a piece of conceptual art when Robert Rauschenberg composed one that read:

THIS IS A PORTRAIT OF IRIS CLERT IF I SAY SO

LEADERS IS AN ACT OF TERROR. . . . WE URGE YOU TO SEND
MESSAGES TO UNITED STATES ATTORNEY GENERAL, GOVERNOR OF
ALABAMA, MAYOR OF BIRMINGHAM AND NEWSPAPER PUBLISHERS AND
CIVIC LEADERS PROTESTING THIS NATIONAL SCANDAL. YOUR ACTION
CAN SAVE LIVES.

On December 10, 1961, this wire was sent by King and other civil rights
leaders to President John F. Kennedy:

WE URGE YOU ISSUE AT ONCE BY EXECUTIVE ORDER A SECOND
EMANCIPATION PROCLAMATION TO FREE ALL NEGROES FROM SECOND
CLASS CITIZENSHIP. FOR UNTIL THE GOVERNMENT OF THIS NATION
STANDS AS FORTHRIGHTLY IN DEFENSE OF DEMOCRATIC PRINCIPLES
AND PRACTICES HERE AT HOME AND PRESSES AS INCREASINGLY
FOR EQUAL RIGHTS OF ALL AMERICANS AS IT DOES IN AIDING
FOREIGN NATIONS WITH ARMS, AMMUNITION AND THE MATERIALS
OF WAR FOR ESTABLISHMENT DEFENSE OF HUMAN RIGHTS BEYOND
OUR SHORES . . .

Baseball great Jackie Robinson was a major player in the battle for civil
rights—in addition to his role in desegregating major league baseball. On
June 15, 1963, he sent a three-page telegram to President John F.
Kennedy, in response to the death of Medgar Evers, reading in part:

IT MIGHT SEEM FANTASTIC TO IMAGINE THAT EVEN IN THE STATE
OF MISSISSIPPI ANYONE WOULD SEEK TO DO INJURY TO A NON-
VIOLENT LEADER LIKE DR MARTIN LUTHER KING AS HE GOES THERE
THIS MORNING ON A MISSION OF SORROW. YET IT WAS FANTASTIC
BUT TRUE THAT SOME DEPRAVED ASSASSIN GUNNED DOWN ANOTHER
MAN OF NON-VIOLENCE THE LATE MEDGAR EVERS WHOSE FUNERAL DR
KING AND HIS ASSOCIATES WILL BE ATTENDING TODAY IN JACKSON.
SHOULD HARM COME TO DR KING TO ADD TO THE MISERY WHICH
DECENT AMERICANS OF BOTH RACES EXPERIENCED WITH THE MURDER
OF MR EVERS THE RESTRAINT OF MANY PEOPLE ALL OVER THIS
NATION MIGHT BURST ITS BONDS AND BRING ABOUT A BRUTAL
BLOODY HOLOCAUST THE LIKE OF WHICH THIS COUNTRY HAS NOT

SEEN. . . . FOR TO MILLIONS MARTIN KING SYMBOLIZES THE
BEARING FORWARD OF THE TORCH FOR FREEDOM SO SAVAGELY
WRESTED FROM THE DYING GRIP OF MEDGAR EVERS. AMERICA NEEDS
AND THE WORLD CANNOT AFFORD TO LOSE HIM TO THE WHIMS OF
MURDEROUS MANIACS.

Robinson continued his civil rights activism under the next administration, as seen in this March 9, 1965, telegram to President Lyndon Johnson, in reference to events in Selma:

IMPORTANT YOU TAKE IMMEDIATE ACTION IN ALABAMA ONE MORE DAY
OF SAVAGE TREATMENT BY LEGALIZED HATCHET MEN COULD LEAD TO
OPEN WARFARE BY AROUSED NEGROES AMERICA CANNOT AFFORD THIS
IN 1965

In 1964, when Reverend Martin Luther King Jr. was facing mob violence in Saint Augustine, Florida, the more openly confrontational Malcolm X sent King a telegram offering his services:

IF THE FEDERAL GOVERNMENT WILL NOT SEND TROOPS TO YOUR AID,
JUST SAY THE WORD AND WE WILL IMMEDIATELY DISPATCH SOME OF
OUR BROTHERS THERE TO ORGANIZE SELF DEFENSE UNITS AMONG OUR
PEOPLE AND THE [KU KLUX KLAN] WILL THEN RECEIVE A TASTE OF
ITS OWN MEDICINE. THE DAY OF TURNING THE OTHER CHEEK TO
THOSE BRUTE BEASTS IS OVER.

The following year, Malcolm X fired off another telegram, this time to
George Lincoln Rockwell, leader of the American Nazi party:

THIS IS TO WARN YOU THAT I AM NO LONGER HELD IN CHECK FROM
FIGHTING WHITE SUPREMACISTS BY ELIJAH MUHAMMAD'S SEPARATIST
BLACK MUSLIM MOVEMENT, AND THAT IF YOUR PRESENT RACIST
AGITATION AGAINST OUR PEOPLE THERE IN ALABAMA CAUSES
PHYSICAL HARM TO REVEREND KING OR ANY OTHER BLACK AMERICANS
WHO ARE ONLY ATTEMPTING TO ENJOY THEIR RIGHTS AS FREE HUMAN
BEINGS, THAT YOU AND YOUR KU KLUX KLAN FRIENDS WILL BE MET
WITH MAXIMUM PHYSICAL RETALIATION FROM THOSE OF US WHO ARE

NOT HAND-CUFFED BY THE DISARMING PHILOSOPHY OF NONVIOLENCE
AND WHO BELIEVE IN ASSERTING OUR RIGHT OF SELF-DEFENSE—BY
ANY MEANS NECESSARY.

On September 4, 1967, Martin Luther King Jr. sent a wire stretching the definition of nonviolence to a Milwaukee colleague, Reverend James E. Groppi:

. . . WE IN THE CIVIL RIGHTS STRUGGLE MUST FIND A MIDDLE
GROUND BETWEEN RIOTS AND TIMID SUPPLICATIONS FOR JUSTICE
THIS MEANS ESCALATING NONVIOLENCE EVEN TO THE SCALE OF
CIVIL DISOBEDIENCE IF NECESSARY. . . .

On June 13, 1962, less than two months before her death, Marilyn Monroe sent this tongue-in-cheek telegram, equating her problems with the Twentieth Century Fox studio with the ongoing civil rights struggle, to Robert and Ethel Kennedy:

ATTY GENERAL AND MRS ROBERT KENNEDY: I WOULD HAVE ACCEPTED
YOUR INVITATION HONORING PAT AND PETER LAWFORD.
UNFORTUNATELY I AM INVOLVED IN A FREEDOM RIDE PROTESTING
THE LOSS OF THE MINORITY RIGHTS BELONGING TO THE FEW
REMAINING EARTHBOUND STARS. AFTER ALL, ALL WE DEMANDED WAS
OUR RIGHT TO TWINKLE.

VIETNAM

HO CHI MINH, the Vietnamese nationalist leader who would become North Vietnam's president and prime minister in 1954, sent this telegram to President Harry Truman in February of 1946, during the Indochinese war against the French:

. . . FRENCH POPULATION AND TROOPS ARE MAKING ACTIVE
PREPARATIONS FOR A COUP DE MAIN IN HANOI AND FOR MILITARY
AGGRESSION STOP I THEREFORE MOST EARNESTLY APPEAL TO YOU
PERSONALLY AND TO THE AMERICAN PEOPLE TO INTERFERE URGENTLY
IN SUPPORT OF OUR INDEPENDENCE. . . . .

In November of 1973, individual Americans demanded Richard
Nixon's resignation or impeachment in 275,000 telegrams that over-
loaded Western Union circuits in Washington.

On November 28, 1961, Secretary of Defense Robert McNamara sent
a telegram to two military leaders, Admiral Henry D. Felt and General
Lionel McGarr, which read in part:

SITUATION IN VIETNAM OBVIOUSLY CAUSING GREAT CONCERN
HERE. . . . POLITICAL UNCERTAINTY OF DIEM'S POSITION AND
DOUBTS AS TO HIS WILLINGNESS TO TAKE STEPS TO MAKE HIS GOVT
MORE EFFECTIVE MUST NOT PREVENT US FROM GOING AHEAD FULL
BLAST (WITHOUT PUBLICITY, UNTIL POLITICAL DISCUSSIONS ARE
COMPLETED) ON ALL POSSIBLE ACTIONS SHORT OF LARGE SCALE
INTRODUCTION OF US COMBAT FORCES. . . . RECENT ADVERSE
PUBLICITY MAKING JOB MUCH MORE DIFFICULT. . . .

On August 29, 1963, U.S. Ambassador to South Vietnam Henry Cabot
Lodge sent this cable to Secretary of State Dean Rusk, making it clear
that the United States was in favor of a coup in Vietnam:

WE ARE LAUNCHED ON A COURSE FROM WHICH THERE IS NO
RESPECTABLE TURNING BACK: THE OVERTHROW OF THE DIEM
GOVERNMENT. THERE IS NO TURNING BACK IN PART BECAUSE U.S.
PRESTIGE IS ALREADY PUBLICLY COMMITTED TO THIS END . . . AND

WILL BECOME MORE SO AS THE FACTS LEAK OUT. IN A MORE
FUNDAMENTAL SENSE THERE IS NO TURNING BACK BECAUSE THERE IS
NO POSSIBILITY, IN MY VIEW, THAT THE WAR CAN BE WON UNDER A
DIEM ADMINISTRATION. . . .

On August 31, Rusk sent a wire (read and approved by President
Kennedy) to Lodge, instructing him on how to bring pressure to bear on
South Korean President Ngo Dinh Diem. It read in part:

US CANNOT ABANDON VIET-NAM AND WHILE IT WILL SUPPORT
VIETNAMESE EFFORT TO CHANGE GOVERNMENT THAT HAS GOOD
PROSPECTS SUCCESS US SHOULD NOT AND WOULD NOT MOUNT AND
OPERATE ONE. TO USE YOUR METAPHOR, WHEN THE SPAGHETTI WAS
PUSHED, IT CURLED; NOW WE MUST TRY PULLING. . . . OUR PRIMARY
OBJECTIVE REMAINS WINNING THE WAR AND WE CONCUR YOUR
SUGGESTION THAT WE SHOULD NOW REOPEN COMMUNICATIONS WITH DIEM

This was followed almost immediately by a second "Eyes Only" missive
from Rusk to Lodge, saying:

. . . WE MUST KEEP OUR EYES FIXED ON THE MAIN PURPOSE OF OUR
PRESENCE IN SOUTH VIET-NAM . . . : WHY WE ARE THERE, WHY WE
ARE ASKING OUR FELLOWS TO BE KILLED AND WHAT IS GETTING IN
THE WAY OF ACCOMPLISHING OUR PURPOSE. . . . [DIEM] MUST
MAKE . . . A DEMONSTRATION TO THE AMERICAN PEOPLE THAT WE ARE
NOT ASKING AMERICANS TO BE KILLED TO SUPPORT MADAME NHU'S
DESIRE TO BARBECUE BONZES.

In protest of the Vietnam War, playwright Arthur Miller sent the following telegram to President Johnson in 1965:

WHEN THE GUNS ROAR, THE ARTS DIE.

WHEN GEORGE HERBERT WALKER BUSH was special envoy to China under President Gerald Ford, he did whatever he could to improve relations between the two countries, as shown in this 1975 telegram to Oscar Armstrong at the State Department:

```
SUBJ: GIFT OF MUSK OX TO CHINESE
THE MORE I THINK ON IT THE MORE I LIKE THE IDEA OF HAVING
THE CHINESE RECEIVE ANOTHER OX FROM THE US. MILTY IS DEAD
BUT A YOUNG AND VIRILE BULLWINKLE COULD DO A LOT OF GOOD
FOR RELATIONS (DIPLOMATIC RELATIONS, THAT IS).
```

> "We are in great haste to construct a magnetic telegraph from Maine to Texas; but Maine and Texas, it may be, have nothing important to communicate."
> —Henry David Thoreau

And while he was living in China in June of 1975, Bush Sr. determined to have a real American Fourth of July, sent the following telegram to the Department of State, headlined THE GREAT HOTDOG ROLL CRISIS:

```
1. THERE IS NOT A HOTDOG ROLL TO BE FOUND IN CHINA. IS
THERE ANY WAY YOU COULD SHIP US 700 HOTDOG ROLLS FOR
GUARANTEED DELIVERY PRIOR TO JULY 4?
2. WE ALSO NEED 100 LARGE BAGS OF POTATO CHIPS IN SAME
SHIPMENT.
3. PLEASE ADVISE SOONEST.
```

DISASTERS

THROUGHOUT WIRELESS HISTORY, major natural and other disasters have been marked by telegraphic cries for help, blow-by-blow descriptions, and after-the-fact reports. Here are a few examples:

On October 8, 1871, the great Chicago fire broke out after a cow owned by a Mrs. O'Leary kicked over a lantern in her barn. One of the most destructive conflagrations in American history, it swept over 2,100 acres, burned more than 17,000 buildings, killed several hundred people, and left 98,000 homeless. The next day, General Philip Sheridan wired his report of the conflagration to Secretary of War W. W. Belnap:

THE CITY OF CHICAGO IS ALMOST UTTERLY DESTROYED BY FIRE.
THERE IS NO REASONABLE HOPE OF ARRESTING IT IF THE WIND,
WHICH IS YET BLOWING A GALE, DOES NOT CHANGE. I ORDERED, ON
YOUR AUTHORITY, RATIONS FROM ST. LOUIS, TENTS FROM
JEFFERSONVILLE, AND TWO COMPANIES OF INFANTRY FROM OMAHA.
THERE WILL BE MANY HOUSELESS PEOPLE, MUCH DISTRESS

Sheridan followed this up with another on the same day:

THE FIRE HERE LAST NIGHT AND TO-DAY HAS DESTROYED ALMOST
ALL THAT WAS VERY VALUABLE IN THIS CITY. THERE IS NOT A
BUSINESS, HOUSE, BANK, OR HOTEL LEFT. MOST OF THE BEST PART
OF THE CITY IS GONE. WITHOUT EXAGGERATING, ALL THE VALUABLE
PORTION OF THE CITY IS IN RUINS. I THINK NOT LESS THAN
100,000 PEOPLE ARE HOUSELESS, AND THOSE WHO HAD THE MOST
WEALTH ARE NOW POOR. IT SEEMS TO BE SUCH A TERRIBLE
MISFORTUNE THAT IT MAY WITH PROPRIETY BE CONSIDERED A
NATIONAL CALAMITY.

On September 8, 1900, a hurricane of incredible force smashed into the Texas coast at Galveston, with winds reaching as high as 120 miles an hour. Water inundated the city to a depth of fifteen feet and two-thirds of the buildings of the city were destroyed, leaving an estimated ten to twelve thousand people dead along the coast, making it the worst national disaster in U.S. history. Three days later, the following desperate telegram was sent from J. H. W. Stele to Governor Joseph D. Sayers:

> SEND MILITARY SUPPLIES FIRE ARMS ANIMAL AND HUMAN FOOD STUFF DANGER FOOD RIOTS ANY MOMENT. SITUATION HORRIBLE CANT DISCRIBE FOR GOD SAKE HELP US.

Another disaster of cataclysmic proportions was the earthquake that struck San Francisco at five in the morning on April 18, 1906—the worst ever to hit this country. After the tremors subsided, fires raged for three days, decimating half the city and leaving 500 dead, 1,500 injured, and more than a quarter of a million homeless. On the nineteenth, Secretary of War William Howard Taft informed William Randolph Hearst that the consequent confusion was too great for individuals to be located for the delivery of telegrams. Three days later, the president of the San Francisco Chamber of Commerce sent the following dispatch, via the Telegraph Company, to chambers of commerce throughout the East:

> A SEVERE SHOCK OF EARTHQUAKE EXPERIENCED HERE. . . . CONSIDERABLE ALARM FELT AT TIME OF OCCURRENCE. A GOOD MANY BUILDINGS ON MAN-MADE GROUND INJURED. CUSTOM HOUSE AND CITY HALL, BOTH POORLY CONSTRUCTED . . . HAVE FALLEN IN. . . . TOTAL LOSS ON PROPERTY WILL NOT EXCEED $300,000.

That same evening, a meeting of the California Club was held at the Waldorf-Astoria in New York, attended by the likes of Mrs. Cornelius Vanderbilt and Mrs. E. H. Harriman, and presided over by Mark Twain, with the express purpose of providing aid to the people of San Francisco. They sent the following telegram:

> SAN FRANCISCO SHALL RISE MORE BEAUTIFUL THAN EVER. WE GLORY IN THE BRAVERY OF HER CITIZENS AND HAVE UNBOUNDED BELIEF IN THEIR ABILITY AND DETERMINATION TO SUSTAIN THIS GREAT CATASTROPHE. . . .

The alphabet code used to send messages over wires, with dots representing a short tap, dashes a more sustained one.

✂︎✂︎✂︎

Twain suggested that they add a tribute to the doctors, firemen, and soldiers involved.

On the fateful night of April 14, 1912, when the *Titanic* struck an iceberg and began to sink, her two radio officers, John George (Jack)

Phillips and Harold Bride, stayed at their radio until the last moment, sending out SOS messages to other ships and receiving replies. Unfortunately, an important one was missed by the *Titanic* because its telegraph had been shut down to cool. Some of these messages were:

```
SAW MUCH HEAVY PACK ICE AND GREAT NUMBER OF LARGE ICEBERGS
SAY, OLD MAN, WE ARE STOPPED AND SURROUNDED BY ICE.
REQUIRE IMMEDIATE ASSISTANCE. COME AT ONCE. WE STRUCK AN
ICEBERG. SINKING
```

A barrage of other increasingly frantic cables went out from the *Titanic's* telegraph room, known as the "Silent Room," which employed the most powerful equipment in use at the time. Most were general calls to all vessels within hearing range:

```
WE HAVE STRUCK ICEBERG SINKING FAST COME TO OUR ASSISTANCE.
WE ARE SINKING FAST PASSENGERS BEING PUT INTO BOATS
WOMEN AND CHILDREN IN BOATS, CANNOT LAST MUCH LONGER
COME AS QUICKLY AS POSSIBLE OLD MAN: THE ENGINE-ROOM IS
FILLING UP TO THE BOILERS
```

Thanks to another of these messages, the liner *Carpathia* arrived on the scene an hour and twenty minutes after the *Titanic* sank and rescued some 700 survivors. Details did not immediately reach the mainland. On April 15, 1912, J. P. Morgan responded to a rumor he had heard in a telegram to his son Jack:

```
HAVE JUST HEARD FEARFUL RUMOR ABOUT TITANIC WITH ICEBERG
WITHOUT ANY PARTICULARS. HOPE FOR GOD SAKE NOT TRUE . . .
```

Guglielmo Marconi, inventor of the wireless telegraph that was used on the *Titanic,* narrowly escaped being on the fateful voyage of the *Lusitania,* which was sunk by German submarines on May 7, 1915, causing the deaths of nearly 1,200 passengers, 234 of them Americans. A passenger on the ship's final westbound voyage, Marconi had intended to catch the return passage east until pressing business matters caused him to alter his plans. When news of the ship's destruction reached his wife, Beatrice, she wired him:

DEEPLY THANKFUL YOUR ESCAPE LUSITANIA MY MOST LOVING
THOUGHTS PLEASE BE CAREFUL ABOUT RETURNING. . . . STOP VERY
WORRIED.

9/11

ALTHOUGH THE TELEGRAM HAS by now lost most of its power and popularity, it is still sometimes called upon to relay urgent public messages. One of the more recent examples: as soon as Russian Federation President Vladimir Putin was informed of the fateful September 11, 2001, terrorist attack on New York, he sent this telegram to U.S. President George W. Bush:

DEAR GEORGE, I AM DEEPLY SHOCKED BY REPORTS OF THE TRAGIC
EVENTS THAT HAVE OCCURRED TODAY ON THE TERRITORY OF THE
USA. THE SERIES OF BARBARIC TERRORIST ACTS, DIRECTED
AGAINST INNOCENT PEOPLE, HAS EVOKED OUR ANGER AND
INDIGNATION. PLEASE CONVEY OUR MOST SINCERE CONDOLENCES TO
THE RELATIVES OF THE VICTIMS OF THIS TRAGEDY, AS WELL AS TO
ALL THOSE INJURED, THE WHOLE AMERICAN PEOPLE. WE WELL
UNDERSTAND YOUR GRIEF AND PAIN. THE RUSSIANS HAVE
THEMSELVES EXPERIENCED THE HORROR OF TERROR. THERE IS NO
DOUBT THAT SUCH INHUMAN ACTIONS CANNOT BE LEFT UNPUNISHED.
THE WHOLE INTERNATIONAL COMMUNITY MUST RALLY IN THE FIGHT
AGAINST TERRORISM.

And on the same day came a telegram from Pope John Paul II:

SHOCKED BY THE UNSPEAKABLE HORROR OF TODAY'S INHUMAN
TERRORIST ATTACKS AGAINST INNOCENT PEOPLE IN DIFFERENT
PARTS OF THE UNITED STATES I HURRY TO EXPRESS TO YOU AND
YOUR FELLOW CITIZENS MY PROFOUND SORROW AND MY CLOSENESS IN
PRAYER FOR THE NATION AT THIS DARK AND TRAGIC MOMENT.
COMMENDING THE VICTIMS TO ALMIGHTY GOD'S ETERNAL MERCY, I
IMPLORE HIS STRENGTH UPON ALL INVOLVED IN RESCUE EFFORTS
AND IN CARING FOR THE SURVIVORS. I BEG GOD TO SUSTAIN YOU
AND THE AMERICAN PEOPLE IN THIS HOUR OF SUFFERING AND
TRIAL.

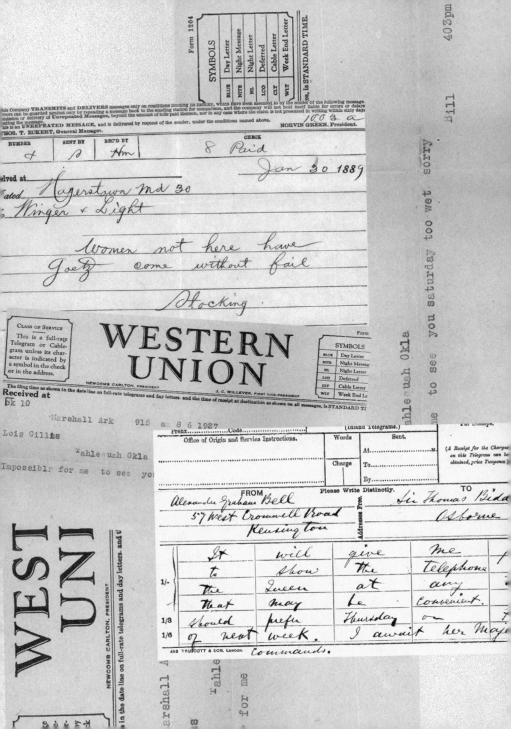

Form 1204

SYMBOLS
BLUE	Day Letter
NITE	Night Message
NL	Night Letter
LCO	Deferred
CLT	Cable Letter
WLT	Week End Letter

is STANDARD TIME.

This Company TRANSMITS and DELIVERS messages only on conditions limiting its liability, which have been assented to by the sender of the following message.
Errors can be guarded against only by repeating a message back to the sending station for comparison, and the company will not hold itself liable for errors or delays
in transmission or delivery of Unrepeated Messages, beyond the amount of tolls paid thereon, nor in any case where the claim is not presented in writing within sixty days
after sending the message.
This is an UNREPEATED MESSAGE, and is delivered by request of the sender, under the conditions named above.

THOS. T. ECKERT, General Manager.   NORVIN GREEN, President.

| NUMBER | SENT BY | REC'D BY | CHECK |
| 4 | B | Hm | 8 Paid |

Jan 30 1889

Received at Hagerstown Md 30

To Winger + Light

Women not here have
Goetz come without fail

Stocking

CLASS OF SERVICE
This is a full-rate
Telegram or Cable-
gram unless its char-
acter is indicated by
a symbol in the check
or in the address.

NEWCOMB CARLTON, PRESIDENT

WESTERN UNION

J. C. WILLEVER, FIRST VICE-PRESIDENT

Form

SYMBOLS
BLUE	Day Letter
NITE	Night Message
NL	Night Letter
LCO	Deferred
CLT	Cable Letter
WLT	Week End Le

The filing time as shown in the date line on full-rate telegrams and day letters, and the time of receipt at destination as shown on all messages, is STANDARD TI

Received at
bk 10

Marshall Ark   915 a 8 6 1927

Lois Gillis

Tahlequah Okla

Impossible for me to see yo

403pm

Bill   sorry   too wet   saturday   you   see   to   me   Okla   Tahlequah

WEST
UNI

NEWCOMB CARLTON, PRESIDENT

in the date line on full-rate telegrams and day letters, and t

Marshall A   Tahle   for me

(Inland Telegrams.)

Office of Origin and Service Instructions.   Prefix.   Code.   Words   Sent.   For Stamps.

Charge   At.......................M.
To.......................
By.......................

(A Receipt for the Charges
on this Telegram can be
obtained, price Twopence.)

Please Write Distinctly.

FROM   Alexander Graham Bell   TO   Sir Thomas Bidd
57 West Cromwell Road   Osborne
Kensington

It	will	give	me
to	show	the	telephone
1/-	the	Queen	at	any
that	may	be	convenient.
1/3	should	prefer	Thursday	on
1/6	of	next	week.	I await	her Maje
	Commands.			

JAS TRUSCOTT & SON, LONDON.

TELEGRAPH TIME LINE

SINCE THE BEGINNING of time, man has experimented with ways of sending information over great distances. Smoke signals, fire towers, flags, and talking drums were all used as early systems of communication. But it was the development of electricity that enabled the modern telegraph to come into being.

1727. In London, Stephen Gray transmits electricity 700 feet through a wire suspended in the air by silk threads.

1745. The Leyden jar—forerunner of the electrical condenser—is accidentally discovered by a Dutchman named Musschenbroek, who finds that the charge from such a device can be conveyed over a distance via a wire conductor.

1747. An English cleric named Dr. Watson transmits an electric impulse through 16,000 feet of wire suspended between poles. Benjamin Franklin performs a similar experiment transmitting electricity across the Schuylkill River in Philadelphia.

1753. The first practical suggestion for an electrical telegraph is made in Scotland by an anonymous contributor, known only by the initials C. M., to the *Scots Magazine*.

1774. The first functioning telegraph is demonstrated in Geneva, Switzerland, by George Louis Lesage. It utilizes a device that depends upon twenty-four wires—each representing a different letter of the alphabet—separated from one another by insulators. At the end of each wire is a pith ball, which is repelled when a current passes through that particular wire, so that when a ball moves, it signifies a letter.

1791. On March 2, in France, Claude Chappe and his three brothers, using a crude version of semaphore code, succeed in sending a message over a distance of ten miles.

1793. On July 2, the word *"telegramme"* is used with reference to sending and receiving messages by means of the optical communication system devised by the Chappe brothers. This is believed to be the first use of the word.

1794. Based upon the Chappe semaphore system, the first segment of the French State Telegraph network begins operation. Since this system is purely optical—coded messages are read with the aid of a telescope—it cannot be used at night. Even so, it is very successful. Aware of its military value, Napoléon Bonaparte will order the network extended, and similar systems will spring up in many parts of Europe and America, remaining in use until the rise of the electrical telegraph.

1800. Italian physicist Alessandro Volta invents the voltaic pile, or battery, the first means of storing electricity.

1825. The electromagnet is invented in England by William Sturgeon, laying the foundations for large-scale electrical communications.

1830. Princeton physics professor Joseph Henry demonstrates the potential of Sturgeon's device for long-distance communications by sending an electronic current over a mile-long wire to activate an electromagnet, which causes a bell hammer to strike.

1831. In January, Henry publishes an article relating to the possibility of an electric telegraph. He increases the electromagnet's power and builds a primitive device, which he does not patent on the grounds that it would "not be compatible with the dignity of science."

1832. Following a dinner-party conversation about the scientific advances of the day, including the electrical magnet, aboard the sailing packet *Sully,* Samuel Finley Breese Morse—unaware that the idea of instantaneous communication is not his original concept—propounds the theory that information can be transmitted by opening and closing an electrical circuit. He suggests that digits could be used for a code more easily than letters because there are fewer of them, and in combinations, they could be employed to represent words. Shortly after, he makes his first notes describing a "Recording Electric Magnetic Telegraph" that would utilize a dot-dash code.

1835. On September 2, Morse, then a teacher of art at New York University, stretches 1,700 feet of wire from one classroom to another and succeeds in transmitting signals, impressing a student named Alfred Vail who will figure in the development of the telegraph. Morse uses pulses of current to deflect an electromagnet, which moves a marker to produce written strokes on a strip of paper.

1836. Morse builds his first functional telegraph instrument using a frame constructed from the wooden stretcher bars normally employed to support artists' canvases (Morse is also a successful portrait painter). The mechanical action of an electromagnet attached to this frame operates a lever to which a pencil has been attached, and the wheels of a pendulum clock carry a thin strip of paper forward. Electricity provided by a version of Joseph Henry's 1831 "intensity batteries" is used to activate the electromagnet. The flow of electricity is interrupted for shorter or longer periods by holding down a key. The resulting dots and dashes can be recorded on a printer or interpreted orally. Morse shares his experiments with Professor Leonard D. Gale, a chemistry professor at the university, who suggests an improved electromagnet. Soon Morse is able to send messages through reels on which are wound ten miles of wire.

Morse is unaware that a German named Steinheil has devised a similar dot-dash alphabet for his own version of the telegraph, built two years earlier.

1837. September 2, Morse demonstrates his improved telegraph to a group of professors and others including Alfred Vail, now a graduate student, whose father is the proprietor of a prosperous New Jersey iron works. Vail convinces his father and brother to back the invention.

Meanwhile, a rival British telegraph system—which depends on the swinging of five needles actuated through five lines of wire—is built by William Fothergill Cooke and Charles Wheatstone and operates over a distance of thirteen miles.

1838. Morse enters into an agreement with Dr. Gale, who assists him with technical advice, and Alfred Vail, who supplies the money. On January 6, Morse and Vail demonstrate their telegraph publicly for the first time in a factory room of the Speedwell Iron Works (owned by Vail's father) in Morristown, New Jersey. The encoded message, PATIENT WAITER IS NO LOSER, is transmitted across three miles of wire and successfully deciphered. Probably at Vail's suggestion, a dots-and-dashes code is by now used to represent letters of the alphabet, rather than digits corresponding to a list of words.

January 24. Morse demonstrates the telegraph over a ten-mile circuit, at a speed of ten words per minute.

February 21. Morse demonstrates the telegraph to President Martin Van Buren and his cabinet, creating a sensation.

1840. Morse patents his "Recording Electric Telegraph" and "Telegraph Symbol."

1842. October 18. Morse installs a submarine cable in New York harbor, stretching between the Battery and Governors Island.

1843. Congress grants Morse $30,000 to build the first telegraph line between Washington and Baltimore. The first telegraphic news dispatch announces the nominations of Henry Clay and Peter Frelinghuysen at the May 1 Whig convention in Baltimore.

1844. May 24. Sitting in the U.S. Supreme Court room in the capital, with such dignitaries as Dolley Madison and Henry Clay looking on, Morse sends the first public telegraph message over an experimental line to Alfred Vail, situated more than forty miles away in the Baltimore & Ohio railway station in Baltimore. The message is

What

This sentence was written from Washington by me at the Baltimore Terminus at 8ʰ 45 min. A.M. on Friday May 24ᵗʰ 1844, being the first ever transmitted from Washington to Baltimore, by Telegraph and was indited by my much loved friend Annie G. Ellsworth.

Saml. F. B. Morse. Superintendent of Elec. Mag. Telegraphs.

Part of a notarized copy of Samuel Morse's first telegram.

the biblical phrase "What Hath God Wrought!," the suggestion of Annie Ellsworth, the young daughter of the commissioner of patents.

May 25. A Washington correspondent for the *Baltimore Patriot* becomes the first journalist to send a news dispatch by telegraph.

Train dispatching by telegraph is adopted in England, using the rival Cooke and Wheatstone system.

1845. April 1. The Washington–Baltimore telegraph line is commercialized. The tariff is one cent per four characters. During the first four days, the total receipts amount to one cent.

May 15. The Magnetic Telegraph Company, the first in the United States, comes into being, formed by Morse and two partners. The best customer of the early telegraph is the press.

1848. The Associated Press is founded in New York by representatives of six newspapers to pool the costs of transmitting news by telegraph.

The first marriage is performed via telegraph, with the bride in Boston and the groom in New York.

1849. Engineer Royal E. House's teleprinter (which resembled a small piano), the first instrument to print actual letters, numbers, and punctuation marks rather than code symbols, is used for communications between New York and Philadelphia.

1850. Sound reading replaces tape registers for receiving wires. A Morse operator can transmit forty to fifty words per minute.

1851. There are now over fifty separate telegraph companies operating in the United States, and rates can be as high as twenty dollars for a telegram.

September 22. The Erie Railroad introduces use of the telegraph to regulate train movements.

1852. April 6. The word "telegram" is first used in the *Albany Evening Journal*.

1853. A newly published book states: "Telegraphing, in this country, has reached that point, by its great stretch of wires and great facilities for transmission of communications, as to almost rival the mail in the quantity of matter sent over it."

1854. Military telegraph is used for the first time at Varna during the Crimean War.

Morse is granted the patent for the telegraph by the U.S. Supreme Court.

1856. April 8. The New York and Mississippi Valley Printing Company, incorporated in Rochester, New York, in 1851, is renamed the Western Union Telegraph Company, reflecting its union of thirteen different companies. Within two decades, it will become the largest and most powerful corporation in the United States.

1858. August 5. The telegraph systems of Europe and North America are connected. The first official transatlantic cables are exchanged between Queen Victoria and President James Buchanan. News of the linkup is celebrated across America with tolling bells and bonfires (one of which nearly burns down New York's City Hall). Preachers intone telegraphic-sounding biblical passages, and poets extol the brotherhood of man. Tiffany's sells spare pieces of cable as mementos, but despite all this, the cable fails three months after its inauguration.

1859. Western Union sets up a code of numbered phrases: for instance, #73 denotes "My love to you" and #30 means "The end."

1860. June 16. Congress passes the historic Pacific Telegraph Bill, calling for competitive bids for constructing a telegraph line from the Missouri River to San Francisco. Western Union is awarded the contract.

1861. June 17. The world's first telegraphic transmission from the air is relayed from the hydrogen gas balloon *Enterprise* at a height of 500 feet, in a demonstration conducted by Thaddeus Lowe for President Lincoln. As a result aerial balloon reconnaissance is used in the Civil War.

The transcontinental telegraph is completed. For the first time, on October 24, telegrams are sent across the United States, as Stephen J. Field, chief justice of California, sends a message to President Abraham Lincoln in Washington. At the same time, the mayor of San Francisco sends one to the mayor of New York City. The transcontinental line immediately proves highly profitable.

The telegraph will play a key role in the Civil War, keeping President Lincoln informed via daily dispatches received in the military telegraph office near the White House. Soon after the outbreak of the war, the general manager of Western Union becomes chief of all the military lines of the United States as well. By the end of the war, the company will have outdistanced all its rivals, possessing 44,000 miles of wire and 1,014 telegraph offices, its westward expansion bringing an abrupt end to the brief existence of the Pony Express— which took ten days to transmit a letter from Missouri to California.

1862. Lincoln establishes governmental control of the U. S. telegraph system.

1863. A separate entity known as the U.S. Telegraph Service is formed.

1866. Western Union introduces stock tickers to speed New York Stock Exchange quotes to brokerage firms.

April 1. With capital of about forty million dollars, Western Union absorbs the U.S. Telegraph Company, making it America's first complete monopoly, serving all parts of the country with uniform rates.

July 27. The laying of the first fully successful cable between America and Europe is completed.

1867. 5,879,282 messages are transmitted via Western Union this year.

Western Union's interest in laying a transcontinental cable across the Bering Strait leads to the United States's purchase of Alaska for two cents an acre.

A United States
military telegraph
wagon.

❀

1869. May 10. A transcontinental rail link is established when the Union Pacific and the Central Pacific railroads meet at Promontory, Utah, news of which is flashed by telegraph to a waiting nation. A cannon in New York fires a 100-gun salute. Soon, much of the telegraph line is relocated to run along the railroad.

1873. Alexander Graham Bell develops the basic idea of the telephone while working on a version of a multiple telegraph.

1874. Thomas Edison—onetime telegraph operator—invents the "quadruplex" method for the simultaneous transmission of four messages.

1880s. Walter P. Phillips of the Associated Press invents a code of about 3,000 symbols for the most common English words and phrases, e.g., V=of which, X=in which, 7=that is.

1881. The Postal Telegraph Company is organized.

1884. Western Union is one of the original eleven stocks tracked in the first Dow Jones average.

1890. Sixteen-year-old Guglielmo Marconi successfully transmits wireless telegraph signals between tin plates mounted on posts in his mother's garden.

1891. A patent for wireless telegraphy is issued to Thomas Edison.

1893. At the Chicago World's Fair, a machine for transmitting actual handwriting causes a sensation. Two years later an improved machine sends handwriting 431 miles from Cleveland to Chicago.

1895. Western Union is now transmitting 58 million messages annually. Average price of a telegram has dropped from $1.04 in 1868 to 30 cents.

1899. The Associated Press uses Marconi's wireless to cover the America's Cup yacht race, the first such test of the new telegraph.

1902. Marconi transmits the first radio (wireless telegraph) signal across the Atlantic.

1903. January 18. The first wireless telegram is transmitted between America and Europe when President Theodore Roosevelt sends a message to King Edward VII via Morse code.

1904. Western Union begins using radio telegraph to reach passengers aboard ships at sea.

Arthur Korn sends the first telegraphic transmission of photographs from Munich to Nuremberg.

1908. AT&T gains control of Western Union, making it possible to order telegrams by phone.

1917. During World War I, the sight of an approaching Western Union messenger fills the public with dread, since it often signals news of a combat fatality.

1920s. Western Union begins to station telegraphers at ringside at boxing matches and in the press box at baseball games, flashing inning-by-inning reports to newspapers and radio stations.

1929. Western Union employs 8,000 messenger boys.

1930s. A complete wardrobe department is now needed to outfit Western Union's 14,000 uniformed messengers.

Introduction of tape printing machines, which print the message on a narrow, preglued paper tape that is then pasted on a telegraph blank for delivery to the addressee.

1930. The last Associated Press Morse wire is closed.

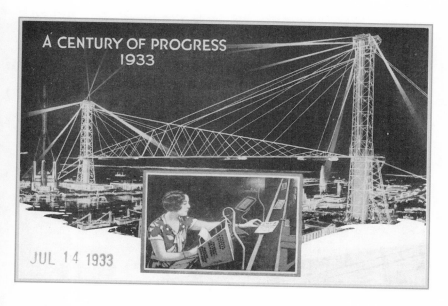

A postcard from the 1933 Chicago World's Fair.

1933. The singing telegram is introduced on July 28, the first delivered to crooner Rudy Vallee on his thirty-second birthday and sung by a Western Union operator named Lucille Lipps. Western Union public relations officer George P. Oslin came up with the idea to give telegrams a more positive image. The public goes wild for them after Walter Winchell reports on Vallee's telegram in his newspaper column.

1935. Western Union begins to offer standardized text holiday messages—illustrated by such artists as Norman Rockwell and N. C. Wyeth—for twenty-five cents. These are followed by Santagrams, Bunnygrams, Storkgrams, Kiddiegrams, Dollygrams, and Melodygrams.

1940s. Telegram messengers patrolled the bombed-out streets of London during World War II, taking down messages from people whose homes had been destroyed.

1943. Postal Telegraph and Western Union merge, eliminating the possibility of any competition in domestic telegraph service.

1949. Western Union terminates its agreements with U.S. railroads, relinquishing its ownership of equipment, marking the beginning of the end of the telegraph as a means of communication.

1960. Western Union sends its last Morse code telegram.

1989. Western Union Telegraph Company is reorganized as Western Union Corporation, primarily to handle money transfers.

PERMISSIONS

Anonymous to Fred Allen: From Robert Taylor, *Fred Allen, His Life and Wit*, Boston: Little, Brown and Company, 1989.

Louis Armstrong: Louis Armstrong–Dwight D. Eisenhower, September 24, 1957, Official File 124-A-1-School-Arkansas-Initial (2), Box 920, White House Central Files, the Dwight D. Eisenhower Library; permission of the Louis Armstrong Educational Fund.

John Barrymore, Ethel Barrymore, and Diana Barrymore: From Margot Peters, *The House of Barrymore*, New York: Alfred A. Knopf, 1990.

Bernard Baruch: Previously printed in James Grant, *Bernard Baruch: The Adventures of a Wall Street Legend*, New York: Simon & Schuster, 1983.

Alexander Graham Bell: Alexander Graham Bell Family Papers, Library of Congress.

Robert Benchley: Permission of Nathaniel R. Benchley.

Irving Berlin: Reprinted by permission of the Estate of Irving Berlin.

Burton Bernstein: Permission of Burton Bernstein.

Sam and Jennie Bernstein: Permission of Burton Bernstein; the Leonard Bernstein Collection, American Memory, Library of Congress.

Yogi Berra: Used with permission of LTD Enterprises.

Humphrey Bogart: Permission of Stephen Humphrey Bogart.

George Burns: Permission granted by the George Burns Estate; Bob Hope Collection, Motion Picture, Broadcasting and Sound Division, Library of Congress.

Frank Capra: Permission of Frank Capra Jr. and Wesleyan University Cinema Archives.

Charlie Chaplin: Property of the Chaplin Archives, Roy Export Company Establishment; permission of Josephine Chaplin.

Clementine Churchill: Reproduced from *Speaking for Themselves*, ed. Mary Soames, with permission of Curtis Brown Ltd., London, on behalf of Lady Soames, DBE.

Winston Churchill: (to Harry S. Truman) Churchill College, the Churchill Archives Centre, Churchill Papers, CHAR 20/218/110, 12 May 1945, permission of Her Majesty's Stationery Office; (to Clementine Churchill) reproduced from *Speaking for Themselves*, ed. by Mary Soames, with permission of Curtis Brown Ltd., London, on behalf of Winston S. Churchill © Winston S. Churchill, the Baroness Spencer-Churchill Papers and the Chartwell Papers, the Churchill Archives Centre, Churchill College, Cambridge; (to Franklin D. Roosevelt) Churchill College, Churchill Archives

Centre, Churchill Papers, November 6, 1940, c-37x PREM 3/468/63 Reports, WSC, II, 553–54 R&C, November 30, 1941, c-60x PSF: GB: WSC.FRUS,1941, v.79–80, WSC, III,178–79 T&C, permission of Her Majesty's Stationery Office.

Gary Cooper, John Wayne, Bill Boyd, Roy Rogers and Harry Carey: From Christopher Finch and Linda Rosenkrantz, *Gone Hollywood: The Movie Colony in the Golden Age*, Garden City, N.Y.: Doubleday and Company, 1979.

Veronica (Mrs. Gary) Cooper: From Jeffrey Meyers, *Gary Cooper, American Hero*, New York: HarperCollins Publishers Inc., 1998.

Noël Coward: Noël Coward Telegrams by kind permission of the Estate of Noël Coward, copyright agent: Alan Brodie Representation Ltd., 211 Piccadilly, London W1J 9HF, info@alanbrodie.com.

Bette Davis: Bette Davis under license by CMG Worldwide Inc., CMG Worldwide.com.

Marlene Dietrich: Permission of Die Marlene Dietrich Collection GmbH.

Walt Disney: Used by permission of Disney Enterprises, Inc.

Roy Disney: Permission of Roy E. Disney.

Dwight D. Eisenhower: (to Mamie Eisenhower) Cable No. W-9650, Dwight D. Eisenhower to Mamie Eisenhower, Mamie Doud (Mrs. D.D.), *The Papers of Dwight D. Eisenhower*, family file 1478, Cable 9650, confidential, Box 173, Principal Series, Dwight D. Eisenhower Pre-Presidential Papers, 1916–1952, Dwight D. Eisenhower Library; (to General George C. Marshall) *The Papers of Dwight D. Eisenhower*, 1396, Cable W6017, secret; 1657 Cable S50908, secret; 1660, Cable S50965, secret, Dwight D. Eisenhower Library; (to Badoglio) *The Papers of Dwight D. Eisenhower*, 1247 Cable 443, secret, Dwight D. Eisenhower Library.

William Faulkner: Ober-Faulkner Collection (#8969), the Albert and Shirley Small Special Collections Library, University of Virginia Library.

W. C. Fields: Courtesy of the W. C. Fields Foundation.

F. Scott Fitzgerald: (to Gerald Murphy, Zelda Sayre, and Maxwell Perkins), the Papers of F. Scott Fitzgerald, Manuscripts Division, Department of Rare Books and Special Collections, Princeton University Library, published with permission of the Princeton University Library; (to H. L. Mencken), © 1980 by Frances Scott Fitzgerald Smith, reprinted by permission of Harold Ober Associates Incorporated, H. L. Mencken Papers, Manuscripts and Archives Division, the New York Public Library, Astor, Lenox and Tilden Foundations; (to Harold Ober) courtesy Lilly Library, Indiana University, Bloomington, from *As Ever, Scott Fitz—*, reprinted by permission of Harold Ober Associates Incorporated, copyright © 1972 by S. J. Lanahan; (to Maxwell Perkins, [3/19/25, 10/6/1936], to Gerald Murphy [9/21/39]), reprinted by permission of Scribner, an imprint of Simon & Schuster Adult Publishing Group, from *F. Scott Fitzgerald: A Life in Letters*, ed. Matthew J. Bruccoli, copyright © 1994 by the Trustees under agreement dated July 3, 1975, created by Frances Scott Fitzgerald Smith; (to Maxwell Perkins [1/28/34, 7/3/38]), reprinted by permission of Harold Ober Associates Incorporated, copyright © 1980 by Frances Scott Fitzgerald Smith.

Sigmund Freud: Library of Congress.

Robert Frost: Permission of the Estate of Robert Frost.

Greta Garbo: Permission of the Estate of Greta Garbo and Harriet Brown and Company, Inc., and Department of Special Collections, Margaret Herrick Library, Motion Picture Academy of Arts and Sciences.

Martha Gellhorn: By kind permission of the Literary Executor.

George Gershwin: Permission of the George Gershwin Family Trust.

Ulysses S. Grant: The Abraham Lincoln Papers, the Library of Congress.

Graham Greene: Permission of David Higham Associates—Greene/29.11.02, and Georgetown University Library.

Dashiell Hammett: Copyright © 2001 by Josephine Hammett Marshall and Richard Layman, reprinted by permission of Counterpoint Press, a member of Perseus Books, LLC, and Harry Ransom Humanities Research Center, University of Texas in Austin.

Moss Hart: Permission of Kitty Carlisle Hart.

William Randolph Hearst: Than Vanneman Ranck Papers, Manuscripts and Archives, Yale University Library.

Ben Hecht: Copyright © Newberry Library, for the Ben Hecht Papers, c/o William Morris Agency, Inc., Permissions, 1325 Avenue of the Americas, New York, NY 10019.

Joseph Heller: From Joseph Heller, *Now and Then: From Coney Island to Here*, New York: Alfred A. Knopf, 1998.

Mark Hellinger: Mark Hellinger Collection, USC Cinema–Television Library.

Ernest Hemingway: Copyright © 2003, printed with the permission of the Ernest Hemingway Foundation.

Al Jolson: Courtesy of the Estate of Al Jolson.

Frida Kahlo: Frida Kahlo papers, Archives of American Art, Smithsonian Institution.

George S. Kaufman: Printed with the permission of Anne Kaufman Schneider.

Elia Kazan: Permission of Elia Kazan; Steve Trilling File, the Jack L. Warner Collection, USC Cinema–Television Library.

John F. Kennedy: Courtesy of the John F. Kennedy Library Foundation; John F. Kennedy Library; (to Cam Newberry), previously printed in Nigel Hamilton, *JFK: Reckless Youth*, New York: Random House, 1992.

Joseph Kennedy: Courtesy of the John F. Kennedy Library Foundation; (to Franklin D. Roosevelt) Franklin Delano Roosevelt Library; (to Rose Kennedy) Rose Fitzgerald Kennedy and Joseph P. Kennedy Papers, John F. Kennedy Library.

Martin Luther King: Copyright by Dr. Martin Luther King Jr., copyright renewed by Coretta Scott King. Reprinted by arrangement with the Estate of Martin Luther King Jr., c/o Writers House as agent for the proprietor, New York, NY; (to James Groppi) Groppi, James, 1930–, Papers, 1964–1978, Milwaukee Manuscript Collection EX and Milwaukee Tape 5, Wisconsin Historical Society, Milwaukee Area Research Center, Golda Meir Library, University of Wisconsin-Milwaukee.

Serge Koussevitsky: Reprinted by permission of the Koussevitzky Music Foundation, Inc., copyright owner, the Leonard Bernstein Collection, American Memory, Library of Congress.

T. E. Lawrence: Quoted by permission of the Trustees of the Seven Pillars of Wisdom Trust.

Louis Leakey: Permission of Richard E. Leakey.

John Lennon: Permission of Yoko Ono Lennon.

Lotte Lenya: Permission of the Kurt Weill Foundation for Music.

Huey Long: Records of Ross S. Sterling, Texas Office of the Governor, Archives and Information Services Division, Texas State Library and Archives Commission.

Douglas MacArthur: The General Douglas MacArthur Foundation, Norfolk, Virginia.

Malcolm X: Malcolm X under license by CMG Worldwide Inc., CMGWorldwide.com.

Herman Mankiewicz: Permission of Frank Mankiewicz.

Joseph Mankiewicz: Permission of Thomas F. Mankiewicz.

Groucho Marx: Courtesy Groucho Marx Productions.

Harpo Marx: Printed by permission of Bill Marx, trustee for the Estate of Harpo Marx; U.S. National Archives and Records Administration, John F. Kennedy Library.

Joseph McCarthy: National Archives and Records Administration, Harry S. Truman Library.

H. L. Mencken: Printed by permission of the Enoch Pratt Free Library, in accordance with the terms of the will of H. L. Mencken.

Arthur Miller: Permission of Arthur Miller.

Margaret Mitchell: With permission of G.W.T.W. Literary Rights.

Marilyn Monroe: Marilyn Monroe under license by CMG Worldwide, Inc., MarilynMonroe.com, CMGWorldwide.com.

Tennessee Williams: Copyright © 1998 by the University of the South, reprinted by permission of the University of the South, Sewanee, Tennessee. William Wyler: Permission of the William Wyler Estate.

ILLUSTRATION PERMISSIONS

Page 4, Sigmund Freud: Library of Congress
Page 15, Abraham Lincoln: Abraham Lincoln Papers, Records of the Office of the Secretary of War, U.S. National Archives and Records Administration, Library of Congress
Page 19, W. C. Fields: Permission of W. C. Fields Productions
Page 22, Jennie and Sam Bernstein: Leonard Bernstein Collection, Music Division, Library of Congress
Page 44, Western Union messenger: Archives Center, National Museum of American History, Smithsonian Institution
Page 46, Orville Wright: Wright Brothers Papers, Library of Congress
Page 53, Harpo Marx: John F. Kennedy Library, U.S. National Archives and Records Administration
Page 54, Humphrey Bogart: Leonard Bernstein Collection, Music Division, Library of Congress
Page 56, Alexander Graham Bell: Alexander Graham Bell Family Papers, Library of Congress
Page 62, F. Scott Fitzgerald: Princeton University Library
Page 64, Walt Disney: Walt Disney Productions
Page 66, Frida Kahlo: Archives of American Art, Smithsonian Institution
Page 81, Greta Garbo: Department of Special Collections, Margaret Herrick Library, Motion Picture Academy
Page 97, Joe DiMaggio: © Bettman/CORBIS
Page 111, Field telegraph station: Abraham Lincoln Papers, Library of Congress
Page 125, Richard Nixon: John F. Kennedy Library, U.S. National Archives and Records Administration
Page 141, Pasting up a telegram: Esther Bubley, photographer, Collection of Farm Security Administration, Office of War Information Photograph Collection, Library of Congress
Page 145, Franklin D. Roosevelt: Franklin D. Roosevelt Library, U.S. National Archives and Records Administration

First of all, I would like to thank the descendants, siblings, and surviving spouses of telegramistes represented in the book, who have been without exception extremely gracious and generous, namely Nathaniel R. Benchley, Burton Bernstein, Dale Berra, Stephen Humphrey Bogart, Ronnie Burns, Frank Capra Jr., Josephine Chaplin, Roy E. Disney, Ronald J. Fields, Todd Gershwin, Kitty Carlisle Hart, Gray Horan, Nancy Roosevelt Ireland, Richard E. Leakey, Yoko Ono Lennon, Frank Mankiewicz, Tom Mankiewicz, Bill Marx, Peter Riva, Anne Kaufman Schneider, Daniel Selznick, Katherine Thalberg, Walfredo Toscanini, Audrey L. Wilder, and Catherine Wyler, as were Arthur Miller and Elia Kazan.

Curators and archivists at various institutions who have been especially accommodating include Natalie Adams at Churchill College, Cambridge, Jean Ashton at Columbia University, Kelly D. Barton at the Ronald Reagan Library, David Clark at the Harry S. Truman Library and Museum, Robert Clark at the Franklin Delano Roosevelt Library, Ned Comstock at University of Southern California Cinema-Television Library, Colonel William J. Davis at the General Douglas MacArthur Foundation, Margaret Ferre at Her Majesty's Stationery Office, Elizabeth E. Fuller at the Rosenbach Museum and Library, Wayne Furman at the New York Public Library, Barbara Hall at the Margaret Herrick Library, Academy of Motion Picture Arts and Sciences, Diana Haskell at the Newberry Library, Leigh G. Johnson at Wesleyan University Cinema Archives, Averil J. Kadis at Enoch Pratt Free Library Mencken Collection, Professor J. Gerald Kennedy of the Ernest Hemingway Foundation, Nancy Kuhl at the Beinecke Rare Book and Manuscript Library at Yale University, Cristel Maas at the University of Wisconsin-Milwaukee, Laura Mankin at the Koussevitzky Foundation, Richard W. Oram at the Harry Ransom Humanities Research Center, University of Texas at Austin, Herbert L. Pankratz at the Dwight D. Eisenhower Library, Kay Peterson at the Smithsonian Institution, Michael Plunkett at the University of Virginia Library, Margaret Rich at the Princeton University Library,

Jennifer J. Quan at the John F. Kennedy Library Foundation, Margaret Sherry Rich at the Princeton University Library, David Smith at the Walt Disney Archives, Dave Stein at the Kurt Weill Foundation for Music, Dwight E. Strandberg at the Dwight D. Eisenhower Library, Saundra Taylor at the Lilly Library, Indiana University, J. Rigbie Turner at the Morgan Library, and Barbara Woolf at Albert Einstein Archives, Jewish National and University Library.

Others who have contributed above and beyond their professional obligations include Margaret Adamic, Paul H. Anderson, Caryn Burtt, Emanuela Di Castelbarco, John C. Donnelly, Lisa Dowdeswell, Tom Erhardt, Anita Fore, Peter A. Gilbert, Kate Guyonvarch, Kelly C. Hill, Ali Howarth, James S. Kaplan, Mark Lawless, Colleen McDonough, Beatrice McMillan, Linda Patterson Miller, Leigh Montville, Anthea Morton-Saner, Margot Peters, Michele Rubin, Harvey Sachs, Lynne Slawson, Craig Tenney, Robin Walton, Jeremy Williams, Alice Wilson, Lydia Zelaya, and Wesley Zirkle.

Especially warm thanks, too, to my supportive agent, Judith Riven, and my meticulous editor, Deborah Brody, both of whom have made extraordinary efforts on my behalf, to the indefatigable Daniel Reid, a staunch companion through the maze of illustration and permissions pursuit, and to Liz Stein for her initial input.

To the many friends and acquaintances who made a variety of valuable connective, supportive, and technological contributions to the work and to my welfare, especially Jennifer Abbott, Samoan Barish, Nancy Hardin, Barnaby Harris, Kate Hirson, Anne Nielsen, Sam and Martha Peterson, Joan Rosenbaum, Pamela Satran, Owen Scott, Karen Shapiro, Marilyn Shapiro, and Suzanne Weil—my heartfelt appreciation.

And finally, to my husband, Christopher Finch, who contributed to this book in every conceivable way—and then some—my infinite gratitude.

INDEX

Page numbers in **bold** refer to illustrations

LINDA ROSENKRANTZ is the author of the novel *Talk,* the memoir *My Life as a List,* and numerous other nonfiction books, including the bestselling baby-naming guide *Beyond Jennifer and Jason* (with Pamela Redmond Satran), and is also a nationally syndicated columnist. She lives in Los Angeles with her husband and daughter.

9/05